Managerial Paper P5

INTEGRATED MANAGEMENT
For exams in 2006

Practice & Revision Kit

In this January 2006 new edition

- New guidance on how to obtain easy marks

- More help, including tips on approaching questions, answer plans and questions annotated with BPP's analysis

- Targeted at CIMA's syllabus

- Question formats reflect exam question styles

- Guidance on study planning and techniques

- Guidance on sitting exam including use of reading time

- Includes November 2005 exam to attempt as a mock under exam conditions

BPP's **i-Pass** product also supports this paper.

BPP
PROFESSIONAL EDUCATION

First edition 2005
Second edition January 2006

ISBN 0 7517 2521 8 (previous edition 0 7517 1979 X)

British Library Cataloguing-in-Publication Data
A catalogue record for this book
is available from the British Library

Published by

BPP Professional Education
Aldine House, Aldine Place
London W12 8AW

www.bpp.com

Printed in Great Britain by
W M Print
45-47 Frederick Street
Walsall
WS2 9NE

We are grateful to the Chartered Institute of
Management Accountants for permission to reproduce
past examination questions. The answers to past
examination questions have been prepared by BPP
Professional Education.

Contents

Review form & free prize draw

After you've qualified

Go to page (xxv) to see the training BPP provides for other qualifications and professional development.

Question and Answer checklist/index

The headings in this checklist/index indicate the main topics of questions, but questions often cover several different topics.

Preparation questions, listed in italics, provide you with a firm foundation for attempts at standard questions.

Mock exam 1

Mock exam 2 (November 2005)

Topic index

Listed below are the key Paper P5 syllabus topics and the numbers of the questions in this Kit covering those topics.

If you need to concentrate your practice and revision on certain topics or if you want to attempt all available questions that refer to a particular subject, you will find this index useful.

Note that Section A questions are not included in this index.

Effective revision

What you must remember

Effective use of time as you approach the exam is very important. You must remember:

> **Believe in yourself**
>
> **Use time sensibly**

Believe in yourself

Are you cultivating the right attitude of mind? There is absolutely no reason why you should not pass this **exam** if you adopt the correct approach.

- **Be confident** – you've passed exams before, you can pass them again
- **Be calm** – plenty of adrenaline but no panicking
- **Be focused** – commit yourself to passing the exam

Use time sensibly

1   **How much study time do you have?** Remember that you must **eat**, **sleep**, and of course, **relax**.

2   **How will you split that available time between each subject?** A **revision timetable**, covering **what** and **how** you will revise, will help you organise your revision thoroughly.

3   **What is your learning style?** AM/PM? Little and often/long sessions? Evenings/ weekends?

4   **Do you have quality study time?** Unplug the phone. Let everybody know that you're studying and shouldn't be disturbed.

5   **Are you taking regular breaks?** Most people absorb more if they do not attempt to study for long uninterrupted periods of time. A five minute break every hour (to make coffee, watch the news headlines) can make all the difference.

6   **Are you rewarding yourself for your hard work?** Are you leading a **healthy lifestyle?**

What to revise

Key topics

You need to spend most time on, and practise full questions on, **key topics.**

> Key topics
>
> - Recur regularly
> - Underpin whole paper
> - Appear often in compulsory questions
> - Discussed currently in press
> - Covered in recent articles by examiner
> - Shown as high priority in study material
> - Tipped by lecturer

Difficult areas

You may also still find certain areas of the syllabus difficult.

Difficult areas

- Areas you find dull or pointless
- Subjects you highlighted as difficult when taking notes
- Topics that gave you problems when you answered questions or reviewed the material

DON'T become depressed about these areas; instead do something about them.

- Build up your knowledge by **quick tests** such as the quick quizzes in your BPP Study Text.

- Work carefully through **numerical examples** and **questions** in the Text, and refer back to the Text if you struggle with computations in the Kit.

- **Note down weaknesses** that your answers to questions contained; you are less likely to make the same mistakes if you highlight where you went wrong.

Breadth of revision

Make sure your revision has sufficient **breadth**. You need to be able to answer all the compulsory questions and enough optional questions on the paper. On certain papers all major topics in the syllabus will be tested, through short answer questions or longer questions. On some papers it will be impossible to predict which topics will be examined in compulsory questions, which topics in optional questions.

How to revise

There are four main ways that you can revise a topic area.

Write it!

The Course Notes and the Study Text are too bulky for revision. You need a slimmed down set of notes that summarise the key points. Writing important points down will help you recall them, particularly if your notes are presented in a way that makes it easy for you to remember them.

Read it!

You should read your notes or BPP Passcards actively, testing yourself by doing quick quizzes or Kit questions while you are reading.

Teach it!

Exams require you to show your understanding. Teaching what you are revising to another person helps you practise explaining topics. Teaching someone who will challenge your understanding, someone for example who will be taking the same exam as you, can help both of you.

Do it!

Remember that you are revising in order to be able to answer questions in the exam. Answering questions will help you practise **technique** and **discipline**, which examiners emphasise over and over again can be crucial in passing or failing exams.

1   The more exam-standard questions you do, the more likely you are to pass the exam. At the very least, you should attempt the **key questions** that are highlighted from page (x) onwards.

2   You should produce **full answers** under **timed conditions,** and don't cheat by looking at the answer! If you are struggling, look back at your notes or the BPP Study Text; also read the guidance attached to certain questions and the questions with analysis. Produce answer plans if you are running short of time.

3   Always read the **guidance** in the answers. It's there to help you, and will show you which points in the answer are the most important.

4   **Don't get despondent** if you didn't do very well. Refer to the **topic index** and try another question that covers the same subject. In particular, see how you could have gained **easy marks** on the question. Also study carefully the guidance accompanying the answers to the questions with analysis.

5   When you think you can successfully answer questions on the whole syllabus, attempt the **two mock exams** at the end of the Kit. You will get the most benefit by sitting them under strict exam conditions, so that you gain experience of the four vital exam processes.

- Selecting questions
- Deciding on the order in which to attempt them
- Managing your time
- Producing answers

BPP's Learning to Learn Accountancy gives further valuable advice on how to approach revision.
BPP has also produced other vital revision aids.

- **Passcards** – Provide you with clear topic summaries and exam tips

- **Success CDs** – Help you revise on the move

- **i-Pass CDs** – Offer you tests of knowledge to be completed against the clock

You can purchase these products by visiting www.bpp.com/mybpp

---

Learn Online

Learn Online uses BPP's wealth of teaching experience to produce a fully **interactive** e-learning resource **delivered via the Internet**. The site offers comprehensive **tutor support** and features areas such as **study**, **practice**, **email service**, **revision** and **useful resources**.

Visit our website www.bpp.com/cima/learnonline to sample aspects of Learn Online free of charge.

Detailed revision plan

The table below gives you one possible approach to your revision for *Integrated Management.* There are of course many ways in which you can tackle the final stages of your study for this paper and this is just a suggestion: simply following it is no guarantee of success. You or your college may prefer an alternative but equally valid approach.

The BPP plan below requires you to devote a **minimum of 18 hours** to revision of Paper P5. Any time you can spend over and above this should only increase your chances of success.

Suggested approach

1   For each section of the syllabus, **review** your **notes** and the relevant chapter summaries in the Paper P5 **Passcards**.

2   Then do the **key questions** for that section. These questions have boxes round the question number in the table below. Even if you are short of time you must attempt these questions if you want to pass the exam. Try to complete your answers without referring to our solutions.

3   For some questions we have suggested that you prepare **answer plans** rather than full solutions. This means that you should spend about 40% of the time allowance for the question brainstorming the question and drawing up a list of points to be included in the answer.

4   Once you have worked through all of the syllabus sections attempt **mock exam 1** under strict exam conditions. Then have a go at **mock exam 2**, again under strict exam conditions.

Syllabus section	2006 Passcards chapters	Questions in this Kit	Comments	Done ☑
Management of relationships	1–6	1–4	Answer all of these objective test questions.	☐
Management	1	18	You need a good understanding of what general management is about and this basic question is good test of that.	☐
		15	This is a good question for getting to grips with the reality of managing people. Prepare a full answer.	☐
		7	Do an answer plan only. This is an important topic.	☐
		13	Group and teams are related topics and of significant interest to the manager. Prepare note form answers for both these questions.	☐
		14		☐
Organisational design	2	29(a)	Prepare full answer to part(a)

Organisation structure is fundamental to the management of organisations. This is a basic question, which you should be able to answer with ease. | ☐ |
| | | 22 | This much longer question will probe your knowledge of the very important matrix form. Do a full answer. | ☐ |
| | | 9 | You must be aware of modern trends. Do an answer in note form for this question. | ☐ |

Syllabus section	2006 Passcards chapters	Questions in this Kit	Comments	Done ☑
Control	3	25	Control as a separate management topic has a place in the new syllabus it did not have in the syllabus for the old Paper 11 This question is representative of how we expect this topic to be examined.	☐
Managing people	4	30	This question is likely to become a classic. It is from the May 2005 exam and deals with an important syllabus topic.	☐
		16	Discipline is important in any organisation. It is also one of the functions that in the real world is hedged about legal provisions. You cannot make it up as you go along, either in the exam or at work.	☐
		17	Appraisal is another HRM activity that all managers must be familiar with. Prepare an answer plan this question.	☐
Corporate governance and ethics		11, 39	Ethics and, perhaps to a slightly lesser extent, corporate governance, are likely to feature regularly in the exam as a matter of policy. Governments and professional bodies all over the west are very concerned about recent ethical failures and are doing everything they can to promote higher standards. This includes setting questions about ethics and corporate governance in your exam. Answer these questions in full.	☐
		5	Prepare an answer plan for this question.	☐
		6	Prepare an answer plan for this question.	☐
		28	Answer this question in full. The work you did for question 6 will help you with part (b).	☐
Management skills	6	21	The topics that fall under this heading are essentially practical ones and question about them should be answered in a practical fashion. Note, however, that this does not mean that 'common sense' is all you need to do so! You will also need background knowledge. Answer this question in full.	☐
		8	Prepare an answer plan for this question.	☐
		20	Prepare an answer plan for this question.	☐
Strategic management	7–9	31, 32	Answer all these objective test questions.	☐
Strategic theory	7	36	Theories about how business strategy is prepared are fairly unlikely topics for questions: they are essential background knowledge, however. On the other hand, you must be prepared to think about the practical interaction of theory and business problems. This question is a good example of that interaction. Prepare a note form answer.	☐

Syllabus section	2006 Passcards chapters	Questions in this Kit	Comments	Done ☑
Mission and culture	4		Culture, whether it be national, organisational or managerial, is a popular topic with examiners. You should ensure that you both understand and can apply the basic ideas and models.	
		33	Prepare a full answer to this question.	☐
		33	Prepare a full answer to this question.	☐
		33	Prepare a full answer to this question.	☐
			These three questions should give you a good workout on the basics of culture.	
Strategic tools	9	46	This is a gentle introduction to the use of strategic ideas. Most examination questions built around strategic models are likely to require you to decide which model to use. Prepare a full answer to this question.	☐
Project management	10, 11	48,49	Answer all of these objective test questions.	
Project management	10	55	This is a good rapid cover for both project management ideas and the specific techniques used to manage projects. You will not time to go into great detail but you should be able to deal with all the important points. Prepare a full answer to this question.	☐
		57	This question gives good general coverage of the nature of project management and is of a type that we should expect to recur in the future.	
Project management techniques		56	You need to be able to draw a basic network quickly and accurately. The logic of dependencies and interactions must be carefully analysed and the critical path arithmetic completed. Prepare a full answer.	☐
		58	This is a comprehensive question that you should attempt in full. Pay attention to your time management and do not overlook part (c)!	
		53	This is an interesting question with slightly different slant.	
Various		61 62 63 64 65 66	These six questions formed Part B of the Pilot Paper. They differ from the May 2005 exam questions in that they form two sets of linked case study questions. We do not know if the examiner will use this technique again, but you should attempt full answers to these questions so as to be prepared if he does. They are also good, wide-ranging questions in their own right.	☐

The exam paper

Format of the paper

		Number of marks
Section A:	Up to 10 multiple choice and other objective test questions, 2-4 marks each	20
Section B:	3 compulsory questions, 10 marks each	30
Section C:	2 out of 3 questions, 25 marks each	50
		100

Time allowed: 3 hours

Question weighting will reflect syllabus weighting.

Section A will always contain some multiple choice questions but will not consist solely of multiple choice questions. Section A may contain types of objective test questions that are different from those included in the pilot paper.

Further guidance on objective test questions and multiple choice questions is included on pages (xvii) to (xviii).

Section B may include a short scenario that could relate to several of the questions.

Section C questions are likely to be scenario-based and include sub questions. Their style will be similar to old syllabus Paper 11 *Organisational Management* questions.

November 2005

Section A

1.1 Stakeholders
1.2 *Hofstede*
1.3 Transaction cost theory
1.4 Project life cycle
1.5 Mentoring
1.6 Rational model of strategy
1.7 Project life cycle
1.8 Project stakeholders

Section B

2 Mission and objectives
3 Project management methodology
4 Disciplinary procedure

Section C

5 Leadership style and project management skills
6 Approaches to strategy
7 Meetings; project closure

This paper is Mock exam 2 in this Kit.

May 2005

> **Examiner's comments.** Common errors included failure to read the question with sufficient care and failure to answer all parts of the question. Most candidates did quite well on Section A, less well on Section B and least well of all on Section C.
>
> A common weakness was a liking for repeating elements of the scenario as an answer. A further problem was a lack of ability in summarisation of key points.

Pilot paper

Approaching the exam

General comments

Bear in mind that any syllabus areas can be tested in any section of the paper. It is not yet possible to comment on the examiner's apparent intentions and habits as we have only the pilot paper and the May 2005 exam to work with. The most noticeable feature of the latter was a 10 mark question on stress management: the very tenuous nature of the link between this topic and the syllabus may indicate a willingness to stretch the syllabus boundaries to a considerable extent.

Many Section C questions require you to apply a theoretical idea or model to a practical situation. Sometimes a question will simply ask for an explanation for a piece of theory. In the latter case, fairly obviously, all the marks are available for theory. However, in the former case, it is unlikely that it will be possible to obtain a pass mark simply by expounding the underlying theory or model: think in terms of a maximum of one third of the total marks being available for such explanation. Where there is a practical situation to deal with, a pass mark demands the application of theory to it.

Reading time/Order of tackling paper

During the 20 minutes reading time you are allowed to write on the exam paper but not in your exam answer book. This gives you a great chance to tackle a lot of the objective questions. (See below for guidance on multiple choice and other objective test questions). Once the exam starts, we recommend you try to finish off the Section A questions first, then tackle as many of the Section B questions as possible.

Easy marks

Easy marks generally arise from knowledge of theory; the more difficult marks are awarded for applying knowledge to a given scenario; for analysis; and for reaching reasoned conclusions.

General discussion questions that are not applied to specific scenarios are normally the easiest marks on this paper.

10 mark section A questions are primarily tests of knowledge and the easy marks are simply what you know.

Approach to questions

Most Section B and Section C questions will involve a scenario. Many students find these difficult to deal with. If you have this problem, try the approach outlined below.

Step 1   Read the requirements first to identify the knowledge areas being tested and see if there are links between them. This helps with focusing on what's important in the scenario. Ensure you can define technical terms used so that you know what the question is about (e.g. demerger, control risk, objectivity, proprietary estoppal).

Step 2   Identify the action verbs in the requirement because this conveys the level of skill you need to exhibit (e.g. define, illustrate, evaluate require quite different skills see what the examiner means list on page (xxiii).

Step 3   Identify the parts to the question. For example a requirement with 'and' implies two parts to the question that may be linked.

Step 4   Check mark allocation of each section. This shows you the depth anticipated and helps allocate time

Step 5   Read scenario/preamble and put key points under headings related to requirements (e.g. by marginal notes, highlighting or jotting down on page).

Step 6   Scribble a plan answer (just a few words jotted untidily under the key requirements not a summary that someone else could write the answer from. Perhaps a brainstorm or spider diagram/mindmap).

Step 7   Write answer.

Tackling multiple choice questions

The MCQs in your exam will contain four possible answers. You have to **choose the option that best answers the question**. The three incorrect options are called distracters. There is a skill in answering MCQs quickly and correctly. By practising MCQs you can develop this skill, giving yourself a better chance of passing the exam.

You may wish to follow the approach outlined below, or you may prefer to adapt it.

Step 1   Skim read all the MCQs and identify which appear to be the easier questions and which questions you will not need a calculator to answer.

Step 2   Remember that the examiner will not expect you to spend an equal amount of time on each MCQ; some can be answered instantly but others will take time to work out.

Step 3   Attempt each question **The questions** identified in Step 1 are questions which you should be able to answer during the 20 minutes reading time. Read the question thoroughly. You may prefer to work out the answer before looking at the options, or you may prefer to look at the options at the beginning. Adopt the method that works best for you.

You may find that you recognise a question when you sit the exam. Be aware that the detail and/or requirement may be different. If the question seems familiar, read the requirement and options carefully – do not assume that it is identical.

Step 4   Read the four options and see if one matches your own answer. Be careful with numerical questions, as the distracters are designed to match answers that incorporate **common errors**. Check that your calculation is correct. Have you followed the requirement exactly? Have you included every stage of the calculation?

Step 5   You may find that none of the options matches your answer.

- Re-read the question to ensure that you understand it and are answering the requirement

- Eliminate any obviously wrong answers

- Consider which of the remaining answers is the most likely to be correct and select that option

Step 6   If you are still unsure, make a note and continue to the next question. Likewise if you are nowhere near working out which option is correct, leave the question and come back to it later.

Step 7   Revisit unanswered questions. When you come back to a question after a break, you often find you can answer it correctly straightaway. If you are still unsure, have a guess. You are not penalised for incorrect answers, so **never leave a question unanswered!**

Step 8   **Rule off answers** to each MCQ in the answer booklet.

Tackling objective test questions

What is an objective test question?

An objective test (**OT**) question is made up of some form of **stimulus**, usually a question, and a **requirement** to do something.

- **MCQs.** Read through the information on page (xviii) about MCQs and how to tackle them.

- **True or false**. You will be asked if a statement is true or false.

- **Data entry**. This type of OT requires you to provide figures such as the answer to a calculation, words to fill in a blank, single word answers to questions, or to identify numbers and words to complete a format.

- **Word-limited answers**. You may be asked to state, define or explain things in no more than a certain number of words or within a single line in the answer booklet.

- **Hot spots**. This question format may ask you to identify specific points on a graph or diagram.

- **Interpretation.** You may be asked to interpret or analyse graphical data.

- **Multiple response.** These questions provide you with a number of options and you have to identify those that fulfil certain criteria.

- **Listing**. You may be asked to list items in rank order.

- **Matching.** This OT question format could ask you to classify particular costs into one of a range of cost classifications provided, to match descriptions of variances with one of a number of variances listed, and so on.

OT questions in your exam

Section A of your exam will contain different types of OT questions. It is not certain how many questions in your exam will be MCQs and how many will be other types of OT, nor what types of OT you will encounter in your exam. Practising all the different types of OTs that this Kit provides will prepare you well for whatever questions come up in your exam.

Dealing with OT questions

Again you may wish to follow the approach we suggest, or you may be prepared to adapt it.

Step 1 Work out **how long** you should allocate to each OT, taking into account the marks allocated to it. Remember that you will not be expected to spend an equal amount of time on each one; some can be answered instantly but others will take time to work out.

Step 2 **Jot down answers, workings or ideas** for as many OTs as possible on the question paper during the 20 minutes reading time.

Step 3 **Attempt each question**. Read the question thoroughly, and note in particular what the question says about the **format** of your answer and whether there are any **restrictions** placed on it (for example the number of words you can use).

You may find that you recognise a question when you sit the exam. Be aware that the detail and/or requirement may be different. If the question seems familiar read the requirement and options carefully – do not assume that it is identical.

Step 4   Read any options you are given and select which ones are appropriate. Check that your calculations are correct. Have you followed the requirement exactly? Have you included every stage of the calculation?

Step 5   You may find that you are unsure of the answer.

- Re-read the question to ensure that you understand it and are answering the requirement

- Eliminate any obviously wrong options if you are given a number of options from which to choose

Step 6   If you are still unsure, **continue to the next question**.

Step 7   Revisit questions you are uncertain about. When you come back to a question after a break you often find you are able to answer it correctly straightaway. If you are still unsure have a guess. You are not penalised for incorrect answers, so **never leave a question unanswered!**

Step 8   Make sure you show your **workings** clearly on calculation OTs, as you may gain some credit for workings even if your final answer is incorrect.

Step 9   Rule off answers to each OT in the answer booklet.

Exam technique

Passing professional examinations is half about having the knowledge, and half about doing yourself full justice in the examination. You must have the right approach at the following times.

> **Before the exam**
>
> **Your time in the exam hall**

Before the exam

1 Set at least one **alarm** (or get an alarm call) for a morning exam.

2 Have **something to eat** but beware of eating too much; you may feel sleepy if your system is digesting a large meal.

3 Allow plenty of **time to get to the exam hall**; have your route worked out in advance and listen to news bulletins to check for potential travel problems.

4 **Don't forget** pens, pencils, rulers, erasers, watch. Also make sure you remember **entrance documentation** and **evidence of identity**.

5 Put **new batteries** into your calculator and take a spare set (or a spare calculator).

6 **Avoid discussion** about the exam with other candidates outside the exam hall.

Your time in the exam hall

1 **Read the instructions (the 'rubric') on the front of the exam paper carefully**

   Check that the exam format hasn't changed. Examiners' reports often remark on the number of students who attempt too few – or too many – questions, or who attempt the wrong number of questions from different parts of the paper.

2 **Use reading time effectively**

   You will be allowed 20 minutes' reading time at the start of the exams. During the reading time you:

   - **CAN** open and read the exam paper
   - **CANNOT** open the answer booklet
   - **CAN** use pens or highlighters to annotate the question book
   - **CANNOT** use calculators

   Remember we recommend you spend the reading time:

   - answering as many as possible of the objective test questions
   - planning answers to longer Section B questions
   - selecting which Section C questions you'll do and jotting down ideas for answering these

3 **Select questions carefully**

   Select the optional questions that you feel you can answer best. Read through the paper once, underlining the key words in the question and jotting down the most important points. You should base your selection on:

- The **topics** covered

- The **requirements of the whole question** (see page (xxiv) for the guidance on what the examiner means)

- How easy it will be to **apply the requirements** to the details you are given

- The availability of **easy marks**

Make sure that you are planning to answer the **right number of questions,** all the compulsory questions plus the correct number of optional questions.

4   **Plan your attack carefully**

Consider the **order** in which you are going to tackle questions. It is a good idea to start with your best question to boost your morale and get some easy marks 'in the bag'.

5   **Check the time allocation for each question**

Each mark carries with it a **time allocation** of 1.8 minutes (including time for selecting and reading questions, and checking answers). A 25 mark question therefore should be selected, completed and checked in 45 minutes. When time is up, you **must** go on to the next question or part. Going even one minute over the time allowed brings you a lot closer to failure.

6   **Read the question carefully and plan your answer**

Read through the question again very carefully when you come to answer it. Remember what you've learnt about approaching questions in this paper. Plan your answer taking into account how the answer should be **structured**, what the **format** should be and **how long** it should take.

Confirm before you start writing that your plan makes **sense**, covers **all relevant points** and does not include **irrelevant material.** Two minutes of planning plus eight minutes of writing is virtually certain to earn you more marks than ten minutes of writing.

7   **Answer the question set**

Particularly with written answers, make sure you **answer the question set**, and not the question you would have preferred to have been set.

8   **Gain the easy marks**

Include the obvious if it answers the question and don't try to produce the perfect answer. Remember the guidance you've seen in this kit.

Don't get bogged down in small parts of questions. If you find a part of a question difficult, get on with the rest of the question. If you are having problems with something, the chances are that everyone else is too.

9   **Produce an answer in the correct format**

The examiner will **state in the requirements** the format in which the question should be answered, for example in a report or memorandum.

10   **Follow the examiner's instructions**

You will **annoy** the examiner if you ignore him or her.

11   **Lay out your numerical computations and use workings correctly**

Make sure the layout fits the **type of question** and is in a style the examiner likes. Show all your **workings** clearly and explain what they mean. **Cross reference** them to your solution. This will help the examiner to follow your method (this is of particular importance where there may be several possible answers).

12   **Present a tidy paper**

You are a professional, and it should show in the **presentation of your work**. Students are penalised for poor presentation and so you should make sure that you write legibly, label diagrams clearly and lay out your work neatly. Markers of scripts each have hundreds of papers to mark; a badly written scrawl is unlikely to receive the same attention as a neat and well laid out paper.

13   **Stay until the end of the exam**
Use any spare time **checking and rechecking** your script. This includes checking:

- You have **filled out** the **candidate details correctly.**
- Question parts and workings are **labelled clearly.**
- Aids to navigation such as **headers and underlining** are used effectively.
- **Spelling, grammar** and **arithmetic** are correct.

14   **Don't discuss an exam with other candidates afterwards**

There's nothing more you can do about it so why discuss it?

15   **Don't worry if you feel you have performed badly in the exam**

It is more than likely that the other candidates will have found the exam difficult too. Don't forget that there is a competitive element in these exams. As soon as you get up to leave the exam hall, **forget that exam** and think about the next – or, if it is the last one, celebrate!

> BPP's *Learning to Learn Accountancy* gives further valuable advice on how to approach the day of the exam.

What the examiner means

The table below has been prepared by CIMA to help you interpret exam questions.

Learning objective	Verbs used	Definition	Examples in the Kit
1 Knowledge What you are expected to know	• List • State • Define	• Make a list of • Express, fully or clearly, the details of/facts of • Give the exact meaning of	 9
2 Comprehension What you are expected to understand	• Describe • Distinguish • Explain • Identify • Illustrate	• Communicate the key features of • Highlight the differences between • Make clear or intelligible/state the meaning of • Recognise, establish or select after consideration • Use an example to describe or explain something	13 5 27
3 Application How you are expected to apply your knowledge	• Apply • Calculate/compute • Demonstrate • Prepare • Reconcile • Solve • Tabulate	• To put to practical use • To ascertain or reckon mathematically • To prove the certainty or to exhibit by practical means • To make or get ready for use • To make or prove consistent/compatible • Find an answer to • Arrange in a table	 58
4 Analysis How you are expected to analyse the detail of what you have learned	• Analyse • Categorise • Compare and contrast • Construct • Discuss • Interpret • Produce	• Examine in detail the structure of • Place into a defined class or division • Show the similarities and/or differences between • To build up or complete • To examine in detail by argument • To translate into intelligible or familiar terms • To create or bring into existence	8 29 50 11 20
5 Evaluation How you are expected to use your learning to evaluate, make decisions or recommendations	• Advise • Evaluate • Recommend	• To counsel, inform or notify • To appraise or assess the value of • To advise on a course of action	29 6

Useful websites

The websites below provide additional sources of information of relevance to your studies for *Management Accounting – Decision Management.*

- BPP   www.bpp.com

  For details of other BPP material for your CIMA studies

- CIMA   www.cimaglobal.com

  The official CIMA website

- *Financial Times*   www.ft.com

- *The Economist*   www.economist.com

- *Wall Street Journal*   www.wsj.com

CIMA professional development requirements

Soon, you will possess a professional qualification. You know its value by the effort you have put in. To uphold the prestige of the qualification, CIMA, with the other professional bodies that form the International Federation of Accountants (IFAC), requires its members to undertake continuous professional development (CPD). Happily, BPP Professional Education is here to support you in your professional development with materials, courses and qualifications.

> For further information, please see CIMA's website: www.cimaglobal.com

Professional development with BPP

You do not have to do exams for professional development (PD) – but you need relevant technical updating and you may also benefit from other work-related training. BPP can provide you with both. Visit our professional development website, www.bpp.com/pd for details of our PD courses in accounting, law, general business skills and other important areas. Offering defined hours of structured CPD, and delivered by top professionals throughout the year and in many locations, our courses are designed to fit around your busy work schedule. Our unique PD passport will give you access to these PD services at an attractive discount.

> For further information, please see BPP's website: www.bpp.com/pd

Oxford Institute of International Finance, (OXIIF) MBA

BPP supports the OXFII MBA. The MBA, accredited by AMBA (the Association of MBAs), lasts 30 months, and is taught by distance learning. Experts from Oxford Brookes University give online seminars to a global student base over the Internet. BPP provides the user-friendly materials. Flexibility, global reach and value for money underpin a high-quality learning experience.

The qualification features an introductory module (*Foundations of Management*). Other modules include *Global Business Strategy, Managing Self Development*, and *Organisational Change and Transformation*.

Research Methods are also taught, as they underpin the **research dissertation**.

> For further information, please see the Oxford Institutes's website: www.oxfordinstitute.org and BPP's website: www.bpp.com/mba

Diploma in International Financial Reporting

The Diploma in International Financial Reporting is designed for those whose country-specific accounting knowledge needs to be supplemented by knowledge of international accounting standards. BPP offers books and courses in this useful qualification.

> For further information, please see ACCA's website: www.accaglobal.com and BPP's website: www.bpp.com/dipifr

Tax and financial services

If you are interested in tax, BPP trains for CIMA's CPD module in Business Taxation. We also offer courses for the ATT (tax technician) and CTA (Chartered Tax Adviser, formerly ATII) qualifications. You can also buy our user-friendly CTA texts to keep up-to-date with tax practice.

> For further information, please see BPP's website: www.bpp.com/att and www.bpp.com/cta

If your role involves selling financial services products, such as pensions, or offering investment advice, BPP provides learning materials and training for relevant qualifications. BPP also offers training for specialist financial markets qualifications (eg CFA®) and insolvency.

> For further information, please see BPP's website: www.bpp.com/financialadvisers

Other business qualifications

BPP supports many business disciplines, such as market research, marketing, human resources management and law. We are the official provider of distance learning programmes for the Market Research Society. We train for the Chartered Institute of Personnel and Development qualification, with a number of other supporting qualifications in training and personnel management. BPP's law school is an industry leader.

> Visit www.bpp.com for further details of all that we can offer you. BPP's personalised online information service, My BPP, will help you keep track of the details you submit to BPP.

Questions

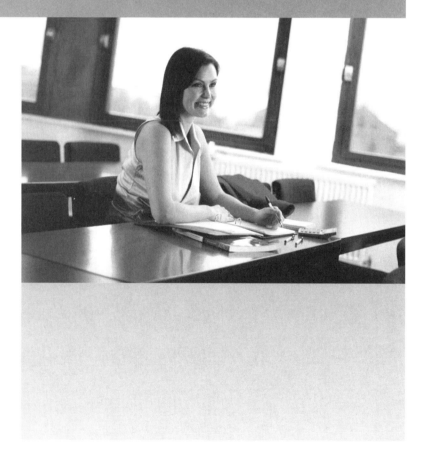

Section A questions: Management of relationships

1 Objective test questions   36 mins

1.1   *Handy* suggests that managers are frequently required to resolve managerial dilemmas. Which of the following is not one of the dilemmas he discussed?

    A   Trust – control dilemma
    B   Dilemma of time horizons
    C   Authority – accountability dilemma
    D   Dilemma of the cultures   **(2 marks)**

1.2   A chartered management accountant working as head of internal audit reports to the audit committee of the group board that the finance director of a certain SBU has falsified the end of year stock valuation. The report is an example of:

    A   Whistle blowing
    B   Compliance based ethics
    C   Social responsibility
    D   Professional ethics   **(2 marks)**

1.3   Which of the following is not a component of *Mintzberg's* model of the organisation?

    A   Technostructure
    B   Operating core
    C   Ideology
    D   Administration staff   **(2 marks)**

1.4   *William Ouchi* identified three types of control within organisations. Which of the following is not one of them?

    A   Clan
    B   Contingency
    C   Bureaucratic
    D   Market   **(2 marks)**

Handwritten annotation: "It was clan Bureaucratic + Market } ouchi."

1.5   Double loop control exist when there is:

    A   Comparison of results with plan and standards of performance
    B   Incorporation of feedback in the control system
    C   Ability to modify the plan and standards of performance in the light of achievement
    D   Comparison of extrapolated future results with original plan.   **(2 marks)**

1.6   *Burns and Stalker* identified two organisational types. What were they?

    A   Machine bureaucracy and professional bureaucracy
    B   Social and technical
    C   Mechanistic and organic
    D   Functional and matrix   **(2 marks)**

1.7 Which of the following would be a valid objective for an appraisal scheme?

    A   Provide the manager with an opportunity for friendly one-to-one interaction with staff

    B   Generate documentary evidence of positive management techniques for potential future use at employment tribunals.

    C   Strengthen the performance of organisational systems by identifying the weaknesses of those who operate them

    D   Establish the level of an individual's performance against standard for the purpose of adjusting bonuses   **(2 marks)**

1.8 Identify the term that completes this statement from the list below.

    'The ....Shaper...:........... is extrovert, dominant and passionate about the task.'

    (Finisher, plant, monitor-valuator, resource-investigator, shaper, implementer)   **(2 marks)**

1.9 Identify the terms that complete this table from the list below.

Configuration	Co-ordination mechanism	Key part
Machine bureaucracy		
Adhocracy		

    (Direct supervision, support staff, standardised outputs, standardised work processes, operating core, middle line, technostructure, standardised skills, mutual adjustment, strategic apex)   **(4 marks)**

(Total = 20 marks)

---

2 Objective test questions   36 mins

2.1 Which author(s) analysed the spectrum of management styles into (1) exploitative autocratic, (2) benevolent authoritative, (3) participative, (4) democratic?

    A   Rensis Linkert
    B   Frederick Herzberg
    C   Tannenbaum and Schmidt
    D   Huneryager and Heckman   **(2 marks)**

2.2 Which of the following is not one of the four management styles identified in the *Ashridge College* research?

    A   Sells
    B   Guides
    C   Tells
    D   Consults   **(2 marks)**

2.3 Which of the following is not one of the categories of needs identified by *John Adair* as crucial to the leadership process?

    A   Individual
    B   Group
    C   Task
    D   Control   **(2 marks)**

2.4   Which of the following is not a feature of a good disciplinary procedure as defined by the UK ACAS code?

   A   Disciplinary matters are dealt with without delay
   B   Except for a first offence, workers are dismissed for gross misconduct
   C   Disciplinary action is not taken until the case has been carefully investigated
   D   There is a right of appeal   **(2 marks)**

2.5   What were the stages in team development identified by *Tuckman*?

   A   Givens, processes, leadership, outcomes
   B   Forming, storming, norming, performing
   C   Argument, competition, conflict, consensus
   D   Forming, norming, storming, performing   **(2 marks)**

2.6   Which of the following is one of the team roles identified by *Belbin*?

   A   Resource – implementer
   B   Team – finisher
   C   Resource – co-ordinator
   D   Monitor – evaluator   **(2 marks)**

2.7   *Blake and Mouton's* management grid analyses managerial behaviour on which two factors?

   A   Concern for people and concern for production
   B   Task needs and group needs
   C   Task behaviour and relationship behaviour
   D   Task structure and leader-subordinate relations   **(2 marks)**

2.8   Under UK employment law, what is unfair dismissal?

   A   Resignation by the employee provoked by the employer's breaches of the terms of the contract of employment

   B   Dismissal within the terms of the contract of employment but for a legally unacceptable reason

   C   Dismissal that breaches the terms of the contract of employment

   D   Dismissal without notice   **(2 marks)**

2.9   What is indirect discrimination?

   A   A group of people is treated less favourably than other groups

   B   Conditions are imposed with which a substantial proportion of a particular group cannot comply

   C   Preference is given to a particular group of people

   D   Women are not allowed to return to part-time work after maternity leave, having previously worked full-time   **(2 marks)**

2.10 Which of the following is characteristic of a team but not of a group?

   A   Sense of identity
   B   Loyalty
   C   Leadership
   D   Work organisation   **(2 marks)**

                                                                            (Total = 20 marks)

3 Objective test questions

36 mins

3.1 Typically, vary large bureaucratic organisations will present problems of management that differ from those of small organisations. Which of the following is not a problem you would expect to find in a large bureaucratic organisation?

    A   Poor record of innovation
    B   Tendency towards slow collective decision-making
    C   Workforce alienation
    D   None of the above

(2 marks)

3.2 Mission is sometimes defined in terms of four elements: purpose; strategy; policies and standards of behaviour; and values. Which of the following would not constitute an example of 'policies and standards of behaviour, for an international parcels carrier?

    A   Staff at all levels are expected to behave in an ethical fashion
    B   When deliveries are delayed, the customer is to be informed promptly
    C   The company values its employees highly and will reward loyalty with loyalty
    D   Operations will not be subcontracted; the company will retain control over consignments at all times

(2 marks)

3.3 Responsibility for safety in the workplace is with:

    A   The employer
    B   The employee
    C   Both of the above
    D   Neither of the above

(2 marks)

3.4 The management theories known as the 'human relations' school is most closely associated with which author?

    A   Peter Drucker
    B   Henry Mintzberg
    C   Elton Mayo
    D   Rensis Likert

(2 marks)

3.5 An employee who exposes the ethical misconduct of others in an organisation is known as a(n):

    A   Ombudsman
    B   Whistleblower
    C   Stakeholder
    D   Monitor

(2 marks)

3.6 Which of the following organisational structures violate the 'unity of command' principle as stated by *Henry Fayol*?

    A   Functional
    B   Matrix
    C   Geographical
    D   Divisional

(2 marks)

3.7 If a manager justifies an instruction to a subordinate by saying, 'because I am your superior', she is relying on which one of the following power bases?

    A   Referent
    B   Reward
    C   Legitimate
    D   Expert

(2 marks)

3.8 Problems of managing complex work and providing a progressive career structure are associated with:

A   Wide span of control
B   Tall organisations
C   Decentralisation
D   All of the above   **(2 marks)**

3.9 Which of the following is not a characteristic of *Burns and Stalkers'* organic (or organismic) organisation?

A   Doing the job takes priority over serving the interests of the organisation.

B   Commitment to the concern's mission is more highly valued than loyalty as such.

C   Knowledge and experience of the way the organisation does things is less highly valued than general knowledge and expertise.

D   Job descriptions and responsibility are carefully defined.   **(2 marks)**

3.10 *Hofstede* identified four dimensions of difference in national managerial cultures. Which of the following is not one of them?

A   'Masculinity'
B   Uncertainty avoidance
C   Power distance
D   Independence – centralisation   **(2 marks)**

                                                   (Total = 20 marks)

4 Objective test questions   **36 mins**

4.1 In the analysis of power in organisations, what is the term that is used to describe the power exerted by mangers by virtue of the positions they hold?

A   Legitimate power
B   Expert power
C   Resource power
D   Personal power   **(2 marks)**

4.2 Hydra Ltd has three product managers each responsible for the development and marketing of one of the product groups manufactured in its single factory. The finance director has provided each product manager with a part-qualified management accountant for four mornings each week to assist with budgets and costs. Is this an example of:

A   Project management
B   Matrix structure
C   Functional departmentation
D   Complex organisational form   **(2 marks)**

4.3 John Adair's action centred model of leadership identified three sets of needs that require the leader's attention. Which of the following is not one of those sets of needs?

A   Group needs
B   Individual needs
C   Task needs
D   Functional needs   **(2 marks)**

4.4 In the typical hierarchical organisation, the requirement of a lower-level manager to answer to a higher-level manager in the chain of command is referred to as

    A   Authority
    B   Empowerment
    C   Accountability
    D   Super ordination   **(2 marks)**

4.5 The division of an organisation into various departments such as purchasing, manufacturing, marketing, finance, research and development results in what kind of organisational structure?

    A   Network
    B   Functional
    C   Product
    D   Matrix   **(2 marks)**

4.6 An effective appraisal system involves

    A   Assessing the personality of the appraisee.
    B   A one-sided process by the manager.
    C   Advising on the faults of the appraisee.
    D   A participative, problem-solving process between the manager and appraisee.   **(2 marks)**

4.7 Recent developments toward greater employee involvement, flexible working and flatter organisational structures have placed greater emphasis on which ONE of the following styles of management?

    A   Exploitative authoritative
    B   Autocratic
    C   Participative
    D   Benevolent authoritative   **(2 marks)**

4.8 Research on group effectiveness has concluded that the most consistently successful groups

    A   are those in which all members are innovative
    B   comprise a range of roles undertaken by various members
    C   are those in which all members are very intelligent
    D   comprise a range of roles all undertaken by a few members of the group   **(2 marks)**

4.9 Any claim that unethical behaviour is in an organisation's best interest is an attempt to

    A   follow the principle of procedural justice
    B   do the right thing for society
    C   rationalise the unethical conduct
    D   look after the interests of oneself   **(2 marks)**

4.10 According to *FW Taylor*, which ONE of the following is a characteristic of scientific management?

    A   Work specialisation
    B   Group working
    C   Socio-technical system
    D   The informal system   **(2 marks)**

(Total = 20 marks)

Section B questions: Management of relationships

5 Code of conduct
18 mins

Required

Explain why it is necessary for chartered management accountants to adhere to a professional code of conduct.

(10 marks)

6 Question with answer plan: Professional ethics
18 mins

Required

Recommend the steps that both professional accountancy bodies and organisations more generally can take to ensure that their members take seriously the ethical principles included in their organisations' codes of conduct.

(10 marks)

7 Preparation question: Scientific management

Telephone call centres have grown rapidly in recent years. In the USA, they employ 3% of the working population and already account for one in a hundred of the working population in the UK.

These call centres are often part of an after-sales service which provides customer support but many also operate to sell goods and services via the telephone. The operators, mainly young people, are carefully selected for their voice characteristics, telephone manner and computer keyboard skills. Training is provided in the carefully detailed procedures that have been found to be most efficient and effective in providing the service.

The use of modern technology in these centres provides the ultimate means for work measurement; almost every aspect of the telephone operators' work can be, and is, measured. Supervisors in these centres can monitor the calls of each operator for speed of response and the duration of each call. Time away from the workstation is easily tracked and recorded. The quality of the operators' performance can be, and is, constantly monitored by weekly customer 'call backs'. The means for controlling the workforce is thus complete.

Performance-related payment is common in these centres and provides the main means of maintaining employee performance. The rapid and continuing growth of these centres is testimony to the fact that they provide a profitable business opportunity for investors but the working conditions in these centres raise questions about whether they are also such a great opportunity for workers.

The design of the work in telephone call centres appears to owe much to scientific management.

Required

(a)   What is scientific management and why does the design of jobs in telephone call centres appear to owe so much to this approach to management?

(b)   Scientific management has been much criticised. What are these criticisms and to what extent do they apply to the design of jobs in telephone call centres?

8 Dr Strong

18 mins

The C Pharmaceutical Company is in a state of crisis. The development of new drugs and treatments on which the vary survival of the organisation depends has slowed dramatically in recent years. An investigation into the operation of the organisation's research and development (R&D) unit has revealed that the slow rate of innovation has much to do with the way the department has been managed.

The head of the unit, Dr Strong, regards it as his duty not to exceed the unit's budget allocation and has introduced strict controls to avoid this happening. Members of the R&D unit are set clear targets with time limits and expected to be working in the laboratory or office on a 9-5 basis every working day. This system of control is not to the liking of research staff and several of the most innovative members have left. The morale of the remaining staff is very low and further resignations are expected.

Required

Analyse why the problems in the R&D unit of the C Pharmaceutical Company might have developed. Recommend what actions could be taken to encourage creativity and innovation.

(10 marks)

Helping hand

First of all, ensure that you understand exactly what the question is asking you to do. 'Analyse' means 'examine in detail the structure of'. To do this, you must ask yourself some questions:

- Exactly what are the problems that have arisen
- Who is encountering them
- Where have they come from or who has cause them?
- How have they arisen?

The second thing you have to do is to ask yourself if you have any theoretical knowledge that might be relevant. Here, we may say that whenever innovation is a problem, the ideas explained by *Burns and Stalker* are likely to be relevant. If you are not confident about these, go to your BPP Study Text now and read about them.

The question asks you to make recommendations. Your analysis should indicate what has gone wrong: base your recommendations firmly upon it and don't hesitate to be bold in what you suggest (though impractical ideas should be avoided).

---

9 Virtual organisation

18 mins

Define the nature of a 'virtual organisation', and account for the emergence of this organisational form. **(10 marks)**

---

10 Leadership style

18 mins

It has been observed that different styles of leadership are required at different stages of an organisation's development.

Required

Explain why the style of leadership may need to change as an organisation passes through the various stages of birth, growth, maturity and decline.

(10 marks)

11 Sheila

18 mins

Until October 2002, Sheila was the Chief Executive Officer (CEO) of X Company, a manufacturer of washing machines and similar products. As Marketing Manager in the late 1990s, Sheila had been responsible for adding new products to the company range that boosted company profits, a success that had been largely responsible for Sheila's promotion to CEO.

In 2000, however, the company suffered a number of setbacks, and Sheila, in order to boost sales by bringing products to the market sooner, ordered that all testing of new products should stop. The consequences were disastrous; X Company was overwhelmed with returned merchandise.

In an effort to keep the share price high, Sheila ordered the Finance Director, Bob, to omit the recording of returned products. Bob initially protested that this would be unethical accounting but eventually complied with Sheila's order. Under further pressure, Bob was also persuaded by Sheila to show an increase in sales and respectable earnings per share figures. Bob managed to do this by adjusting the way the company reported sales, by understating expenses and by generating several hundred false invoices.

A year-end audit exposed the misconduct of the two executives. Sheila was sent to prison for two years. Bob was imprisoned for one year and was struck off from membership of his professional body. *✳ Big disadvantages of unethical behaviour.*

Required

Discuss the measures the board of Directors of X Company might take to ensure that the abuse of power and authority that occurred in X Company does not occur again. **(10 marks)**

12 Icebergs

18 mins

Organisations have been compared to icebergs, with the formal aspects being the visible part and the informal and cultural aspects being the much larger hidden part.

Required

Explain the nature of informal organisation and detail its disadvantages and advantages for a business. **(10 marks)**

The following data are given for questions 13 and 14 below

The T Aerospace Company is in the early stages of planning the development of its latest commercial jet, the 007. The aircraft industry is a fiercely competitive one, dominated by a few large global players who operate at the forefront of technology. In this industry, competitors quickly copy any advance in technology or new management technique that might provide them with a competitive edge. Some of the T Aerospace Company's competitors have adopted team working as a means of speeding up their development and production processes.

The T Aerospace Company is thus considering the adoption of team working in its operations, but some of the traditionalists in the company are doubtful. They are concerned that the benefits of work specialisation will be lost. Some of the managers have had negative experiences with team working and so have strong reservations about the proposed changes.

13 Question with tutor's answer: Aerospace team 1 — 18 mins

Required

Describe briefly the essential features of a team. **(4 marks)**

Identify the benefits that the T Aerospace Company can expect to gain from the adoption of team working.

(6 marks)

(Total = 10 marks)

14 Question with tutor's answer: Aerospace team 2 — 18 mins

Required

Describe the difficulties that the company is likely to encounter in the management of its teams and recommend how it might overcome these. **(10 marks)**

15 Joan Timmins — 18 mins

Before taking up her position as head of the finance department of the SOFT Corporation, Joan Timmins had enjoyed a career in the army where she had attained the rank of major. The military style of command had suited Joan's personality. She is by nature an assertive kind of individual, so giving orders is something that comes naturally to her.

The start of her new post of head of finance has not been easy. She has found that her previous style of management has not been well received by her new staff. Her enthusiasm for improving the way things are done in the department is not matched by that of her staff. In fact, if anything, an air of resentment seems to exist in the department. More generally, she is finding it difficult to adjust to the whole way of operating in the SOFT Corporation. In her view, so much time seems to be spent in meetings and in consultation generally that she wonders how the organisation manages to compete the in the market place as successfully as it does.

Required

Using any appropriate theory of management style, explain why Joan Timmins is experiencing the difficulties described in her new post, and recommend the kind of management style which might be more appropriate.

(10 marks)

16 Disciplinary procedure — 18 mins

NYO.com was established in February 2000. Since then, the company, which provides on-line financial advice, has experienced rapid growth and the management has not really had the time to get all management systems and procedures into place.

The company has asked you to look at the way in which the company deals with its disciplinary problems and procedures. The chief executive officer has asked you to do two things.

Required

Explain why NYO.com should have a formal disciplinary procedure. **(10 marks)**

17 Preparation question: Performance appraisal

The performance appraisal process is now well established in large organisations.

Required

(a)   Describe briefly the most common objectives of a performance appraisal system.

(b)   Explain why appraisal systems are often less effective in practice than they might be, and advise what management can do to try and ensure their effectiveness.

18 Functions   18 mins

Drury has argued that the primary objective of management accounting is to provide management with information for decision-making. In order to be aware of the information needs of management, we must first understand the management functions that accounting serves. *Drucker*, following *Fayol,* has suggested that management consists of the functions of planning, controlling, organising, communicating and motivating.

Required

Describe *any two* of the functions of management, using appropriate examples from an organisation with which you are familiar.   **(10 marks)**

19 Question with analysis: Stress management (5/05)   18 mins

Theory Y | Functional role | Common practices

T, the **HR manager** of X Investment Bank is keen to develop and introduce **policies** that will **enhance the relationship between managers and their subordinates** . Having recently attended a conference on | The vital bit

workplace stress, T has recommended that the Bank should introduce a **stress management** programme. He feels that the introduction of such a programme would not only minimise the harmful impact that stress can have on **organisational performance** , but could also improve **working relationships** .

Two aspects

Required

Discuss the measures that T could introduce as part of the proposed stress management programme to minimise stress related problems.   **(10 marks)**

20 PB Company   18 mins

Background and Introduction

The PB company sells an Internet security product called OneR. This product guarantees the security of electronic transmissions over the Internet by providing an easy-to-use encryption system.

PB has been in business for 6 years, and now has an annual turnover of $45 million. The company's clients include many government departments as well as 11 of the top 100 companies in the country in which it operates.

Sales systems

Sales are generated by potential customers visiting the company's website and reading about the product, or by referral from existing customers. An initial enquiry to PB results in a sales representative booking an appointment with the potential customer to demonstrate the OneR product. The demonstration normally lasts a whole day due to the complexity in setting up OneR to run on different computer configurations. However, most demonstrations result in sales.

A significant minority of demonstrations fail because the hardware configuration at the potential customer cannot run the OneR product, or where the OneR system cannot be configured to run on the operating system on the computer.

The effectiveness of sales representatives is monitored on whether on not they have achieved their sales targets for each month. Under-achieving the target results in representatives being encouraged to do better next month, although the sales target remains the same. Selling more than the target results in a small bonus for that representative, with the target being increased to encourage the representative to sell even more of the product.

Amendments to sales system

The Board of PB are investigating the possibility of amending the method of selling the OneR product. Most companies already have an Internet connection, so it is possible to download a version of the OneR product from the Internet. Rather than visit the client's premises, sales representatives can then provide e-mail and telephone support to help the customers install and try out the product for themselves. The main benefits to PB are a decrease in travelling time and expenses of sales representatives, and representatives being able to complete two demonstrations each day rather than one.

Sales representatives have reacted poorly to this suggestion with fear of job losses, decreased commission and loss of other benefits such as company cars all being given as reasons not to change the existing system. Although

PROFESSIONAL EDUCATION

all representatives appear to share these views, the representatives who joined the company only 4 months ago appear to be the most vocal opponents of the move. Other representatives appear to want to know more about the proposals and so are reserving their judgement.

To try and resolve this issue, the Managing Director of PB has organised a meeting with the sales representatives for next Saturday morning to discuss the situation and try and resolve the problems. Saturday was chosen for the meeting because it is a non-working day and so it will minimise the disruption to clients and loss of commission to the sales representatives.

The MD has recognised that holding a meeting may produce additional conflict between the sales representatives and the senior management of the company; however, he is keen to go ahead. He has asked you, as a recently qualified Management Accountant, to use your extensive study skills to assist him in preparing for the meeting.

Required

Produce briefing notes for the Managing Director which provide an outline agenda for the meeting with reasons for the different subjects on the agenda. **(10 marks)**

Section C questions: Management of relationships

21 Question with answer plan: Workload   45 mins

Laura Lee switched off the light and prepared to lock up the accounts office. This was the third time this week she had worked after seven o'clock in the evening and the eighth occasion this month. She had thought that her workload would drop after the busy first few weeks following her appointment as financial accountant at ZX Systems Limited but if anything the workload was increasing.

As financial accountant she was responsible for nine staff in the sales, purchase and nominal ledger sections, two staff from the cashiers office and three payroll administration staff. All 14 staff were classified as accounts assistants under the company's job description scheme. In addition Laura carried specific responsibility for the monthly financial reports, VAT operations and the preparation to first draft stage of the company's annual accounts. Laura reported directly to the chief accountant who, from time to time, gave her special projects.

As she saw the situation, her work pressure problems fell into three distinct groups.

- The constant stream of queries and questions from the accounts assistants who seemed unable or unwilling to use any initiative in problem solving

- The need to meet the tight timetables on monthly, quarterly and annual reporting

- The special jobs and projects received from the chief accountant, always with an 'urgent sticker' attached

Eventually one aspect of her work would suffer. She could not keep up her present rate of work for much longer without some sign that the workload would reduce to a more reasonable level.

Required

(a)   Discuss ways in which Laura Lee can manage better the job pressures she is experiencing.   **(15 marks)**

(b)   Delegation can assist in such situations but needs to be effectively managed. Explain how Laura Lee might achieve this.   **(10 marks)**

(Total = 25 marks)

22 ICC   *Sales & Marketing + Sales engineering support*   45 mins

The International Computing Corporation is incorporated in the USA and is a major world-wide manufacturer of mainframe processors, associated disk access storage devices, network communications hardware and its own proprietary operating system software. ICC has two major world-wide customer functions. The sales and marketing (S&M) function which sells the product and the sales engineering support (SES) function which installs the product and provides customer technical support and maintenance. Within each country functional management (S&M, SES and other functions such as Finance) report to the country Vice President (Operations) and also to the functional Vice President located at the Head Office in the USA. For example, the ICC country Finance manager for Germany reports and provides support to the German Vice President (Operations) but also has a line responsibility to the Vice President (Finance) located at head office in the USA.

Within this country however S&M and SES are organised as independent divisions. The S&M division organises its sales teams on the basis of product groups, for example, printers or network hardware. S&M product specialisation is seen as essential if sales staff are to develop the level of product technical expertise deemed necessary to sell advanced technologies to computing professionals. The SES division, on the other hand, organises on the basis of customers not products. The intention is that the customer has only one SES contact for any hardware or software problem and the SES teams are equipped to deal with any aspect of technical support. SES activity is seen as a means of assisting product sales, as potential sales leads are picked up by SES staff and passed on to the S&M sales teams.

PROFESSIONAL EDUCATION

Recently there have been a growing number of country based problems in co-ordination between S&M and SES. One result has been a number of instances of sales leads not being passed by SES to S&M. Another has been instances of hardware being sold by S&M which later proved unsuitable in performance terms. This created significant workload problems for SES engineers in reconfiguring to a specification which met the customers performance criteria.

Required

(a) The 'international to country' functional management at ICC provides an example of the matrix form of organisational structure. Briefly explain why you feel that ICC has chosen to manage its international operations in this way. **(7 marks)**

(b) Discuss how the adoption of a country based matrix structure combining S&M and SES could assist in resolving the apparent co-ordination problems between the two divisions. **(9 marks)**

(c) The matrix organisational form has been described as 'no place for a middle manager seeking security and stability'. Discuss the issues which organisation design must address if the matrix form is to function effectively. **(9 marks)**

(Total = 25 marks)

23 Work performance 45 mins

Jane has recently taken charge of the accounts office of a medium-sized organisation. The office comprises ten clerical and administrative staff. Her role includes overall responsibility for accounting operations and the management of the associated office staff. She reports to the Finance Director of the organisation. The organisation has a system of staff appraisal based on annual interviews conducted by line managers. The system is administered by the personnel department who have informed Jane that she will be responsible for conducting the appraisal interviews for the staff in her office. The next series of annual appraisals is not due to commence for another three months.

Jane has recently become aware of an apparent problem with one of her staff. This has taken a number of forms: occasional lateness and absence during working hours, small but nevertheless frequent mistakes in paperwork, lateness in meeting deadlines, and a general impression of fatigue and lack of motivation. This is a long-standing member of staff and there is no apparent prior history of such problems. It is clear that the other staff in the office are also aware of the situation and are watching to see how Jane, as their new manager, deals with the problem.

Required

(a) Jane has decided to take early action and has asked the staff member to come to see her for a general discussion about work performance. Advise Jane on how she should prepare for and plan to conduct the meeting. **(14 marks)**

(b) In conversation with a manager fro another department, Jane has mentioned the approach which she plans to take. The manager has advised her against an early meeting and suggests that she waits and deals with the matter through the forthcoming staff appraisal interview. Consider the merits of this suggestion.
(5 marks)

(c) Explain why Jane, in her approach to the review of the work performance, must be clear as to the distinctions between a review meeting and a disciplinary meeting. **(6 marks)**

(Total = 25 marks)

24 PSTV 45 mins

PSTV is a public service television company regulated by the government of the country in which it operates. It has been the major producer and broadcaster of television programmes since its creation in 1930. PSTV is not allowed to broadcast commercial advertising and its main source of revenue is a licence fee payable by any household with a television.

When it was originally conceived, the mission of PSTV was to provide a public service with definite standards. This meant that it must instruct and inform as well as entertain its audience. In the seven decades since the first broadcast, this mission has become somewhat diluted as PSTV has come to recognise the need to be responsive to customer demands.

Until 1960, PSTV enjoyed a monopoly position as the only television company in the country in which it operates. This comfortable position helped to foster the development of a bureaucratic type of organisation with a tall hierarchical structure and a process of centralised decision-making that relied heavily on rules and procedures laid down by its Board of Governors and enforced by a Director General.

The change of legislation in 1960 allowed the introduction of competitors and with it the development of a market in TV programme production and broadcasting. The new TV companies could not depend on a state licence but had to earn their revenues and profits by charging for advertising. This dependence on advertising revenue put enormous pressure on the new commercial TV companies to obtain a substantial percentage, and preferably a majority, of the TV viewing audience. Any loss of viewers was, and is, translated into a loss of revenue. For PSTV, this battle for audience share had the effect of threatening its ability to fulfil its stated objectives.

Developments in technology, including the transmission of programmes by cable and satellite, the use of video cassette recorders that allow recording of programmes, and the advent of digital TV all provide opportunities for new entrants to the market. The potential of digital TV is enormous, providing the potential for interactive TV, access to the internet and through this to home shopping and banking and other services.

These processes also provided opportunities for the development of a new kind of company known as 'integrated multi-media corporations' that combine television with motion pictures, book and magazine publishing etc. These integrated multi-media corporations seek to derive synergy from the combination of a range of related businesses.

It is in this kind of competitive arena that PSTV has to try to survive in the 21st century.

Required

(a)   Describe the common features of a bureaucratic structure as adopted by PSTV and explain why this organisational form may have difficulty coping with the rapid changes now taking place in the media industry.
(7 marks)

(b)   Explain why an 'organic' form of organisational structure may be better suited to the kind of rapid changes now facing PSTV.
(8 marks)

(c)   Explain why effective co-ordination and control may become more difficult to achieve in an integrated multi-media corporation than in an organisation like PSTV.
(10 marks)

(Total = 25 marks)

25 S Company
45 mins

S Company develops accountancy software for small to medium-sized businesses. S Company was established 15 years ago by a graduate in accounting. Despite an increasingly competitive environment, it has grown and diversified to become a global provider of specialised accountancy software. In order to cope with the increasing size and diversity of the business, additional levels of management and control systems have been introduced, including additional policies, rules and procedures. Unfortunately, the increase in bureaucracy is having the effect of slowing down decision-making processes and limiting ideas for new software development. The Chief Executive Officer is aware of the conflict between the structural changes and the need for continuous creativity and innovation that are critical to new software development and the future success of the business, but is not sure how to overcome the problem.

PROFESSIONAL EDUCATION

Required

(a)   Explain

    (i)   why formal control systems are increasingly necessary as an organisation grows and diversifies; and

    (ii)   why the use of bureaucratic forms of control in S Company might limit creativity and innovation.

(14 marks)

(b)   Discuss how S Company could balance control with autonomy to assist continuous creativity and innovation.

(11 marks)

(Total = 25 marks)

26 Group roles

45 mins

Research into group behaviour suggests that the effectiveness of any work group/team depends on it having the right balance of group roles.

Required

(a)   Explain why an understanding of group roles is important when forming an effective work group. Use any accepted classification of group roles to illustrate your answer.

(12 marks)

(b)   Discuss factors other than group roles that contribute towards the development of an effective group.

(13 marks)

(Total = 25 marks)

27 Configurations

45 mins

X is a small, owner-managed, family restaurant business which employs 10 people. Y is a university with 800 academic, 200 administrative and 100 ancillary staff. The academic staff teach a wide range of courses and conduct research. The administrative staff ensure that university policies and procedures are observed and provide administrative support for teaching and research functions. The ancillary staff provide other necessary services such as security, maintenance, catering and cleaning. Z is a large manufacturing company which produces a wide range of products and employs 30,000 people in its various business divisions. Each of its eight divisions produces a different product and serves a different market. The business divisions enjoy a fair degree of autonomy but are expected to operate within the overall umbrella of the company's corporate strategy.

Required

drawa diagram off.

- Professional bureaucracy. etc.

(a)   Using Mintzberg's typology of organisational configurations, identify the most appropriate configuration for the X business, Y University, and Z Company. Justify your choice in each case.   **(15 marks)**

simple business structure.

(b)   Discuss the implications of increased environmental uncertainty for the design of organisational structures.

(10 marks)

(Total = 25 marks)

Helping hand. There is a small problem of organizing your answer to part (a): do not be tempted to structure your answer around Mintzberg's five types. If you do this, you will provide unnecessary detail. Instead, divide your answer into three parts relating respectively to X, Y and Z. Each part can then discuss the characteristics of the form you recommend and why each characteristic is (or, possibly, is not) appropriate. The fact that there are fifteen marks available for this part of the question supports this approach, since we might reasonably expect five marks to be available for each organization. Note that it would be unlikely that three marks would be available for discussing each of Mintzberg's five types (the approach we have already rejected) since two of them could not really be related to the scenario.

28 Key influences   45 mins

The discovery of heavily overstated profits in some of the largest US corporations in 2002 undermined investor confidence in company accounts and called into question the integrity of senior managers, their professional staff and the presumed independence of external auditors.

Required

(a)   Describe the *key influences* on the ethical conduct of senior management of business corporations, their professional staff and those involved with auditing their accounts   **(12 marks)**

(b)   Explain what both businesses and professional bodies can do to influence the ethical behaviour of their organisational members.   **(13 marks)**

(Total = 25 marks)

29 Question with analysis and helping hand: Structure and innovation (5/05)

45 mins

A is the **Chief Executive Officer** (CE) [In a position to make things happen] [Manufacturing work] **manufactures and sells** electrical appliances such as vacuum cleaners, washing machines and dish-washers. She founded the company fifteen years ago, [Eye not kept on the ball] along with W who provided the financial backing for the business. Whilst A is the CEO, her **main interest is inventing new product designs**. The company's competitive advantage has, in the past, been achieved through **innovative technological and design features** that have been difficult for other companies to copy. This has allowed the company to charge **premium prices** for its products. [Advantage of differentiations] [Large] [Innovation and design are core competences]

Over the years the company has grown significantly, and it now employs over **1,000 staff**. It has diversified into **producing televisions** and **media equipment** and has more recently moved into the **PC market**. The company has manufacturing plants around the world, but the headquarters remains in country G. [More complex technology] [Mintzberg, Harrison]

When the company was first established it was very much based on an **entrepreneurial structure** with no formal control systems in place. Staff joined the company because it provided an exciting and creative environment in which to work. **Teamworking and lateral communications** to solve problems were encouraged. **Everyone was on first name terms** and the company invested in the development of staff. [Burns and Stalker] [Why?]

However, over time the company has changed to a **functional structure and bureaucratic and rigid** control mechanisms have been put in place. In **recent months sales have slowed down**. A is concerned that the company may have lost its ability to be creative and innovative, as well as its entrepreneurial spirit. This could mean disaster in the future. [Important]

Required

(a)   (i)   Compare and contrast an entrepreneurial structure and a functional structure.   **(7 marks)**

(ii)   Advise A why a functional structure may no longer be appropriate for L Company   **(6 marks)**

(b)   Discuss the different approaches that could be used to encouraged creativity and innovation in L Company.   **(12 marks)**

(Total = 25 marks)

30 Question with analysis: Departmental conflict (5/05)

45 mins

Power

V is the **Chief Executive** of M Company, a manufacturer of prepared frozen foods. The company is facing difficult business conditions with **strong competition from supermarket own brand products and consumer demand for variety and new products** as their tastes change.

Important background

However, V is aware of the problems the company has encountered when undertaking new product development (NPD) in the past. Whilst collaboration is essential, instead there have been **disagreements and arguments** between the various departments.

Fundamental problem

5 depts each with its own concerns: is there any co-ordinating vision?

The **marketers** complain that the Research and Development **(R&D)** department is very slow in responding to their proposals for new recipes and the whole process of R&D takes too long. The **production** department has protested that R&D does not consider the implications for the production process when coming up with new recipes and product packaging. The **sales team** is frustrated by the length of time the whole NPD process takes. The lack of new products puts it at a disadvantage when negotiating with retailers to sell M Company products.

The **Finance** department is concerned that the investment in NPD does not provide adequate returns, and both the marketing and R&D departments are always over budget. However, other departments see Finance as controlling and sanctioning spend rather than supporting new product development.

V knows that to remain competitive, changes need to be made to the NPD process in the company. He has decided to establish a **cross-functional team** to work on a new range of ready prepared frozen foods to appeal to the luxury end of the market.

Sounds like a good start

Required

(a)   Analyse the nature and sources of conflict between the different departments in M Company.

(10 marks)

(b)   Describe the factors that V should consider in building a successful cross-functional project team.

(15 marks)

(Total = 25 marks)

STRATEGIC MANAGEMENT

Questions 31 to 47 cover strategic management, the subject of Part B of the BPP Study Text for Paper P5.

Section A questions: Strategic management
36 mins

31 Objective test questions

31.1 Which of the following is least likely to be characteristic of a strategic decision?

    A   Matches the organisation's activities to its environment
    B   Sets the organisation's overall long term direction
    C   Determines the organisation's choice of accounting software
    D   Has important implications for organisational change   **(2 marks)**

31.2 Which of the following is an aspect of an organisation's environment?

    A   A history of labour disputes

    B   A declining share price, which limits the organisation's ability to raise new capital

    C   Pressure from the production director to adopt a demanding trade association-approved testing system

    D   Acceptance of a government-promoted commitment to reduce atmospheric pollution   **(2 marks)**

31.3 What is business strategy concerned with?

    A   What business the organisation should be in
    B   How the organisation approaches a particular market
    C   Decisions of strategic importance at operational level
    D   Decision of strategic scope   **(2 marks)**

31.4 What is the difference between (a) a deliberate strategy and (b) a realised strategy?

    A   (b) is one type of (a)
    B   (a) is the result of detailed planning while (b) emerges from a pattern of behaviour
    C   (a) is one type of (b)
    D   (a) is the result of detailed planning while (b) derives from logical incrementalism   **(2 marks)**

31.5 With which of the phrases below, associated with assessing the processes the organisation must excel at, are the names *Kaplan and Norton* associated?

    A   Goal congruence
    B   Internal business perspective
    C   Critical success factors
    D   System goals   **(2 marks)**

31.6 Bargaining, satisficing and sequential attention are all methods of dealing with what?

    A   Goal conflict
    B   Stakeholders
    C   Ideological goals
    D   Goal congruence   **(2 marks)**

31.7 Which of the following are connected stakeholders, as opposed to internal or external stakeholders?

    A   A company's work force
    B   A company's local municipal authority
    C   A company's management
    D   A company's suppliers   **(2 marks)**

31.8 Which of the following does not feature in the McKinsey 7S model?

    A   Style
    B   Shared objectives
    C   Skills
    D   Staff   **(2 marks)**

31.9 In a multi-divisional organisation producing a range of products for different markets, business strategy is primarily concerned with:

    A   Setting the direction for the organisation.
    B   The competitiveness of a particular division.
    C   The efficiency of production, marketing and other functions.
    D   Alignment of strategy with other organisations.   **(2 marks)**

31.10 The external stakeholders of an organisation include

    A   Pressure groups, government, community.
    B   Employees, Board of Directors, middle management.
    C   Government, Board of Directors, suppliers.
    D   Community, management, government.   **(2 marks)**

(Total = 20 marks)

32 Objective test questions

36 mins

32.1 The concept of asset specificity generally supports a strategy of:

    A   Horizontal integration
    B   Vertical integration
    C   Cost leadership
    D   Market development   **(2 marks)**

32.2 The logical incrementalist approach to strategy resembles the rational model in that it

    A   Is similarly dependent on detailed medium-term forecasting
    B   Depends on managerial activity
    C   Emphasises the possession of core comptences
    D   Can deal with a wide range of strategic possibilities   **(2 marks)**

32.3 *Mintzberg* suggests that systems goals can subvert mission. Which of the following is likely to be a system goal rather than an element of mission?

    A   Performance standards
    B   Purpose
    C   Values
    D   Growth   **(2 marks)**

32.4 Say whether the statement below is true or false.

'Conflict between goals will inevitably lead to a policy of accepting merely adequate performance in a number of areas.'   **(1 mark)**

32.5 Say whether the statement below is true or false.

'The organismic (or organic) organisation described by *Burns and Stalker* appears to have much in common with the task-oriented organisation described by *Harrison*.   **(1 mark)**

32.6 The Boston Consulting Group matrix classifies companies in terms of two business variables. What are they?   **(2 marks)**

32.7 In *Porter's* value chain model, is procurement:

A   a primary function
B   a support activity
C   a primary activity
D   none of the above   **(2 marks)**

32.8 *Michael Porter* identifies five competitive forces in the task environment. State four of them *other than current competitor rivalry*.   **(4 marks)**

32.9 Identify the terms that complete this statement from the list below.

'*Mendelow* proposed classifying stakeholders in terms of their level of .... and

....

(shareholding, authority, interest, turnover, power influence, profitability)   **(2 marks)**

32.10 Which of the following is described as a primary activity in *Porter's* value chain?

A   Procurement
B   Human resource management
C   Service
D   Technology development   **(2 marks)**

                                                                                                          (Total = 20 marks)

Section B questions: Strategic management

The following data are given for questions 33 and 34 below

A very successful multinational fast food company (FFC) from country S has just opened a small group of restaurants in country C, but a range of problems has affected the new venture. Customers have complained about the menus, the seating arrangements and the music that is played. Local residents have protested about the architecture of restaurant buildings, and the restaurant employees have complained about the style and practices of the managers from country S who run the business.

33 Fast food culture 1   18 mins

Required

Using your knowledge of national and corporate cultures, explain why FFC is experiencing the problems noted in the scenario.   **(10 marks)**

34 Fast food culture 2   18 mins

Required

Based on your analysis in answer to question 35, recommend ways the board of FFC might resolve its problems.

(10 marks)

35 Sam and Frank   18 mins

Sam is the Chief Executive Officer (CEO) of T Inc, a tobacco company. He has traditional views about the purpose of business in general and his own organisation in particular. Though he is frequently pressured by a variety of groups and organisations that think he should run his organisation differently, he sticks firmly to the view that the overriding purpose of business is to make money for the shareholders. His son, Frank, who is being coached to take over the CEO role, takes a very different perspective. In his view, T Inc has a responsibility to a wide range of stakeholders.

Required

Explain how

(a)   Sam would justify his view that the overriding purpose of the business is to make money for the shareholders

(b)   Frank would justify his view that T Inc has a responsibility to a wide range of stakeholders.   **(10 marks)**

The following data are given for questions 36 and 37 below

The E Company consists of automobile engine, marine engine and aerospace engine businesses. It has built its global reputation for engine design and quality on its engineering capability. Though the marine engine business has not been performing well for some time, the E Company has dominated the supply of engines for the luxury end of the automobile market for years. Unfortunately for the E Company, however, the market in luxury automobiles is changing. Exchange rate movements and increased production costs have made the E Company less competitive and its rivals are rapidly catching up in terms of engine quality and design. As a result, the latest annual report shows turnover down, margins reduced and the company barely breaking even.

You have just attended a strategy meeting at the E Company in which:

- Manager A argued that the automobile engine business strategy was wrong;

- Manager B claimed that the major problem had been the failure to properly implement functional strategies;

- Manager C said that more attention should be paid to the threats and opportunities of the external environment so that the E Company could position itself more realistically; and

- Manager D claimed that the company should really be seeking to develop further its core engineering competence if it was going to re-gain its competitiveness in the market place

After the meeting, a junior manager who had been in attendance asks you to explain what his senior colleagues had been talking about.

36 Engines 1   18 mins

Required

Explain the differences between corporate level strategy, business level strategy and functional level strategy in the E Company.   **(10 marks)**

37 Engines 2   18 mins

Required

For the benefit of the junior manager, explain the theoretical perspective on strategy formation adopted by manager C and manager D.   **(10 marks)**

38 Question with helping hand: Screen   18 mins

Screen was established in 1960 as a charitable trust to promote and increase public awareness of the cinema as an entertainment and cultural medium. Screen is managed through a part-time board of governors drawn from the film industry, from government nominees and from the membership of the Screen Institute. Screen has five major activity areas or operational divisions each of which has its own manager. These are as follows.

- The multi-screen Film Theatre (FT) which provides performances for the general public of new releases, classic films and minority interest films.

- The Museum of the Cinema (MoC) which provides a permanent exhibition of the history and development of the film industry.

- The Globe restaurant, bars and cafeteria, which are open to cinema goers and to the general public.

- The Film Archive Unit (FAU), which is concerned with the transfer of old film archive material to video as a means of long-term preservation.

- The Screen Institute (SFI), membership of which is open to members of the public by annual subscription. Members receive preferential bookings to events, seat discounts and a free copy of CiniCentre's monthly magazine, 'Film Fan'. The magazine and associated publishing activities also form part of the responsibilities of the film institute.

Screen is partly funded by government grant and partly funded from its own commercial activities. However, as a part of government policy to reduce the contribution to the arts, the grant to Screen will, over the next three years, be reduced by 20%.

The board of governors were directed by the government to bring in an external CEO as a result of a series of management problems, which have attracted considerable adverse publicity.

- A failure to stay within government financial guidelines of not operating an annual financial deficit.

- Press criticism about the loss of archive film due to the failure to speed up the transfer to video tape.

- Further press criticism on the recent imposition of an admission charge to the Museum of the Cinema.

- Reports of poor quality service and expensive food in the Globe restaurants.

- Persistent labour relations problems with the public sector staff trade union, which represents almost all the non-managerial museum, film theatre, clerical and catering staff.

- Complaints from the CFI membership that the film season has concentrated too much on popular income earning mainstream films with a subsequent fall in the number of showings of classic and non-English language films.

Required

Identify four different Screen stakeholder groups, indicating for each, its potential power and influence and its likely expectations. **(10 marks)**

Helping hand. Avoid the obvious mistake of discussing more than four stakeholder groups!

The first step in dealing with this question is to identify your stakeholders. This is going to be a little more complex than taking the first ones you think of, because for each one you choose you have to talk about influence and expectations. While it would be satisfactory to choose a group that had little influence and limited expectations, it would be silly to choose one with none at all, since you would be denying yourself the opportunity to produce sensible discussion points. Choose groups you can talk about.

The requirement to discuss power and influence depends to a great extent on your knowledge of how organisations work. We give you some ideas in the BPP Study Text but you will have to apply wider reading and experience in questions like this. In this question, you need not go into much detail, since there can only be two and a half marks available for each group.

---

39 Question with answer plan: Social responsibility (5/05)

18 mins

Many organisations now include explicit reference to their commitment to act in a socially responsible manner in their mission statement. This then forms an integral part of organisational strategies and policies. However, some shareholders see social responsibility as conflicting with their main interest in the company which is that of creating maximum shareholder wealth.

Required

Explain the main arguments for and against the view that socially responsible business decisions can achieve sustainable competitive performance and improve shareholder value. **(10 marks)**

The following data are given for questions 40 and 41 below

In order to avoid payment of the tariffs imposed on imports by a Western country, W, a Japanese automobile company, J, has decided to produce its cars within W. Company J intends to staff the car plant initially with its own Japanese managers and supervisors and to use Japanese working practices. Production-line and other employees will be recruited from the country in which it is located.

40 Company J 1   18 mins

Required

Explain the factors that can influence the culture of an organisation. Discuss why Company J's new plant may develop a different culture to other Western plants.   **(10 marks)**

41 Company J 2   18 mins

Required

Describe the differences in expectations and resulting problems that might arise in Company J due to the cultural differences between Japanese managers and the company's Western employees. Recommend the actions that Company J could takes to minimise the problems.   **(10 marks)**

Section C questions: Strategic management

42 Supreme football 45 mins

The Supreme Football Club (SFC), a profit-making company with directors and shareholders, has received a take-over bid from one of the satellite-broadcasting corporations. The club is currently assessing whether to accept the bid.

SFC is a multi-million dollar business. Its income consists of gate receipts, fees for TV rights, merchandising, sponsorship, conferencing and catering. The club is very successful; the team's performance on the pitch has made it a very popular club and this success has been reflected in growth in turnover and profits in recent years. The advent of satellite TV has made football a worldwide spectator sport and the club has fans throughout the world.

The success of the club has not, however, prevented it from receiving some criticism. One of the issues causing continuing concern has been the constantly-changing replica shirts as worn by the club's football team. Parents of young fans have felt pressurised into spending large sums of money every year or so because the club has changed its shirt style six times in as many years.

Another issue has been the increase in ticket prices over the past few years. These have risen far faster than inflation, and the fan club has made several representations to the board of SFC in protest at these increases.

The income from TV rights is much welcomed by the club, but matches have been rescheduled at short notice to suit satellite stations and their exclusive audiences. It is perhaps not surprising therefore that the bid to take over the club by the satellite-broadcasting corporation has been met with hostility by the fans and others who see the club they have supported and the game they love as being treated like any other profit-making organisation.

Required

(a)   Identify the stakeholder groups of the SFC. Describe the particular interest of each stakeholder group in the club. **(15 marks)**

(b)   Explain which stakeholder groups are likely to exert the most influence on the decision to accept/reject the takeover bid, indicating their power and influence. **(10 marks)**

(Total = 25 marks)

43 Bureaucracy 45 mins

S Company Limited assembles mountain bikes and related products, and retails them by mail order. The company was started by Sunil (a cycling enthusiast) and grew rapidly in the 1990s as mountain biking became popular as a leisure activity and competitive sport. Like many entrepreneurs, Sunil employed relatives and friends in the early days of the business and, even today, still prefers to employ people recommended by his own employees rather than go through any formal recruitment process. In fact, this is typical of the way the business is ruin. There is an absence of formal rules, systems and procedures. The organisation structure is flat, with Sunil making most of the decisions. Sunil's style of management means that relationships with employees are generally friendly and informal.

But everything is not going well. The company is experiencing a number of problems that are minor in themselves, but taken together are proving damaging to the company's performance. The most serious of these is the increasing number of returns from customers who are dissatisfied with bike assembly, missing parts or product quality. But there are other problems such as late deliveries, lost invoices, slow response to customer requests and complaints that, taken together, are having a negative impact on the company's profitability.

In the face of all these problems, Sunil has reluctantly hired a management consultant to conduct an investigation into the running of the business. The consultant's report has now been completed and the main recommendation involves the implementation of bureaucratic procedures. Sunil read the report with disbelief. He had always been led to believe that bureaucracy was something that produced inefficiency!

Required

(a)   Explain why the adoption of the features of bureaucracy (such as those advocated by Max Weber) would assist S Company Limited to overcome its problems and improve its efficiency.   **(15 marks)**

(b)   Explain why Sunil may be right to be suspicious of bureaucratic procedures as a solution to his company's problems.   **(10 marks)**

(Total = 25 marks)

44 Question with analysis: GIC insurance

45 mins

Old-fashioned?

GIC was an **old-established** insurance company, offering life insurance, pensions, mortgages and related products. It **turned itself into a plc six months** ago having previously been a mutual company, owned by those taking out insurance policies.

Big change

Top management consisted of a Chief Executive Officer, Sales, Investment and Finance Directors. The Chief Executive and the Directors were appointed by the policy holders. In practice, policy holders never attended the annual meetings, and the **Directors reappointed themselves**.

Corporate governance?

The performance of the company was judged by the bonuses provided on insurance policies maturing after ten years or longer. It depended on the investment and actuarial abilities of the company, rather than on its **efficiency**.

Important

What does this motivate towards?
Sales at any price?

In the past, all sales have been through company salespersons, paid by **commission only**. They were chosen for their initiative and interpersonal skills, left to manage on their own, and were able to achieve unusually high earnings. They were based in branch offices, each with a manager. Nominally, reporting lines were upwards to the Sales Director, but little information was passed in practice.

Competition – more
response needed – change

In recent years, banks and other financial institutions have **entered the insurance market**, often with novel tax-saving financial products and innovative sales strategies such as direct telephone selling.

Changes in senior management

When the plc was formed, the Chief Executive Officer became Chairman of the new board of directors, and recruited a **new Chief Executive** from outside the organisation. He in turn recruited a Marketing Director to whom the former Sales Director reports.

Disturbing for the old guard

Because many customers were sold policies which were not appropriate to their circumstances, the regulations regarding insurance policies and other financial products have been tightened up and revised several times. All policies sold over the last few years will have to be re-examined to meet regulators' requirements. For this purpose a **compliance department** has been set up.

Aha!

How popular will this be?

One of the first proposals of the new Marketing Director was to focus sales on new clients, whose attitude to the organisation was untainted by **past errors**, rather than on existing clients. The branch managers disagreed with this because of the close relations the salespersons have with the existing clients. The branch managers' attitude was supported by the Finance Director, **who feared a loss of revenue**.

Conflict

Bureaucracy

Salespersons now are carefully trained to complete several pages of questionnaires, and to follow **standard procedures** in dealing with clients. To reduce costs, they have been switched to a **salaried reward system**, and it is hoped that this will also prevent the sale of policies not suitable for the client.

better

The company is also introducing direct selling by telephone, as a method of reducing costs. The Marketing Director has **created two separate divisions** – one for personal selling, and one for telephone selling.

Another big change.

Required

Organisational culture is the set of values, guiding beliefs, and ways of thinking that are shared by members of an organisation.

(a)   Identify the cultural features within GIC.   **(15 marks)**

(b)   Discuss what changes in culture may be required to correspond to the changes made in GIC.

(10 marks)

(Total = 25 marks)

45 J & T   **45 mins**

J & T is a partnership. It is a successful merchanting business which has been selling packaging materials to industry since the 1950s. The senior partners, Jones and Thompson, were joined in the early years by other merchants with detailed commercial knowledge relating to particular areas of the United Kingdom. As a result, a network of eight offices was established in major towns in the UK. Each was managed by one of these merchants, who became junior partners in J & T.

These new junior partners had been chosen partly because of their knowledge of local conditions, partly because of their contacts in their areas, and partly because they shared the same values as their seniors. They were all family men, active, well-known, and respected for their community voluntary work. Their business life was conducted to the highest ethical standards, which took precedence over opportunities to make easy money.

The overall aim of the business was to establish itself with its customers as the customer's main supplier. With many major firms it became the sole supplier, because it was known that it would always choose the best source of supply, even if it were not profitable for J & T.

Although supplies were sourced from all over the world, the business had a special relationship with a few UK suppliers, to whose products it gave preference, effectively becoming their sole agents.

J & T's suppliers were all private limited companies. They produced paper, cartonboard, plastic sheets, bags and bottles – all using continuous processes with a relatively small number of production workers, most of whom were unskilled. Maintenance, purchasing, quality control, and research and redevelopment were important functions with skilled and professional staff. These functions were managed by directors who were not themselves shareholders. The main raw materials were wood pulp, raw chemicals, water and electric power.

Each branch of J & T is run as an investment centre. 35% of the profits are shared among the local partner and staff in proportion to their salaries, the rest among the partners as a whole. The branches each employ between 25 and 40 people, including salesmen. The latter are paid a good basic salary, but they also earn commission on their own sales.

During the takeover boom in the 1970s and 1980s, many of the local customers were absorbed by national and multinational organisations. There were also amalgamations among the UK suppliers. Other trends during the last ten years have been the increased number of overseas sources of supply, the much wider choice of packaging materials, and the increased sophistication of their specifications.

Following the recent death of Jones, Thompson has decided to retire. A further merger between the suppliers means that all the former UK suppliers of J & T have become a horizontally integrated group of companies employing nearly 2,000 people. Because the group has relied for all its UK sales on J & T, it has proposed a takeover of the business and buying out the partners.

The funds for the takeover would be raised by 'going public'. The public flotation would be arranged by placing the shares with a small number of large investing institutions. This would leave the remaining partners and the former owners of the supplier companies as major shareholders, with about half the shares between them, although none of them would hold more than 5% of the shares. The new company would be called IC plc.

Required

(a)   Recommend what actions IC plc could take to respond to the environmental influences at a global and local level.   **(15 marks)**

(b)   Using an appropriate framework, describe the organisational culture of J & T.   **(10 marks)**

(Total = 25 marks)

46 Imperial Traders plc   45 mins

Imperial Traders plc was established in 1785 and its head office has always been in London. Currently, most of its business takes place in and around the 'Pacific Rim', ie in Japan, Korea, Malaysia and Australia.

Required

(a)   Explain what a position audit is and describe the benefits to Imperial Traders plc of conducting such an audit in respect of a possible move of the head office from London to a Pacific Rim country.   **(10 marks)**

(b)   Discuss the effects of a relocation to a Pacific Rim country on the various aspects considered by the position audit.   **(10 marks)**

(c)   Describe briefly the cultural differences that Imperial Traders plc may encounter in its new domicile.

(5 marks)

(Total = 25 marks)

47 Bowland Carpets   45 mins

Bowland Carpets Ltd is a major producer of carpets within the UK. The company was taken over by its present parent company, Universal Carpet Inc, in 1993. Universal Carpet is a giant, vertically integrated carpet manufacturing and retailing business, based within the USA but with interests all over the world.

Bowland Carpets operates within the UK in various market segments, including the high value contract and industrial carpeting area – hotels and office blocks etc – and in the domestic (household) market. Within the latter the choice is reasonably wide ranging from luxury carpets down to the cheaper products. Industrial and contract carpets contribute 25% of Bowland Carpets' total annual turnover which is currently £80 million. During the late 1980s the turnover of the company was growing at 8% per annum, but since 1992 sales have dropped by 5% per annum in real terms.

Bowland Carpets has traditionally been known as a producer of high quality carpets, but at competitive prices. It has a powerful brand name, and it has been able to protect this by producing the cheaper, lower quality products under a secondary brand name. It has also maintained a good relationship with the many carpet distributors throughout the UK, particularly the mainstream retail organisations.

The recent decline in carpet sales, partly recession induced, has worried the US parent company. It has recognised that the increasing concentration within the European carpet manufacturing sector has led to aggressive competition within a low growth industry. It does not believe that overseas sales growth by Bowland Carpets is an attractive proposition as this would compete with other Universal Carpet companies. It does, however, consider that vertical integration into retailing (as already practised within the USA) is a serious option. This would give the UK company increased control over its sales and reduce its exposure to competition. The president of the parent company has asked Jeremy Smiles, managing director of Bowland Carpets, to address this issue and provide guidance to the US board of directors. Funding does not appear to be a major issue at this time as the parent company has large cash reserves on its balance sheet.

Required

Acting in the capacity of Jeremy Smiles, you are required to outline the various issues which might be of significance for the management of the parent company. Your answer should cover the following.

(a)   Discuss the extent to which the distinctive competences of Bowland Carpets conform with the key success factors required for the proposed strategy change?   **(10 marks)**

(b)   Identify the main entry barriers prevalent in the carpet retailing sector.

(7 marks)

(c)   In an external environmental analysis concerning the proposed strategy shift, what are likely to be the key external influences which could impact upon the Bowland Carpets decision?   **(8 marks)**

(Total = 25 marks)

Helping hand. This is a difficult question simply because competences and key success factors can be difficult to identify. Do not, therefore, look too deeply: the crucial change that is being proposed is the move forward along the distribution chain into retailing. Ask yourself what is essential for success in this area and whether the company can do it with its present skills and abilities.

Section A questions: Project management

48 Objective test questions

36 mins

48.1 Which of the following would you describe as most clearly characteristic of the nature of a project?

A   Intended to be carried out on a continuing basis
B   Allocation of resources never exclusive
C   A defined beginning and end
D   No clearly visible end result   **(2 marks)**

48.2 In the PRINCE2 system of project management, what is the name of the process that controls work done by specialist teams by agreeing what work is to be done and ensuring it is carried out to the proper standard?

A   Managing product delivery
B   Configuration management
C   Directing a project
D   Managing stage boundaries   **(2 marks)**

48.3 In the 4D model of the project life cycle, what is meant by 'Develop the process'?

A   The creation of a project brief or terms of reference for the project
B   Detailed project planning
C   The operational phase of the project
D   The completion and review phase of the project   **(2 marks)**

48.4 What was the surname of the man who invented the resource planning chart a century ago?

A   Gant
B   Gantt
C   Gannt
D   Ganntt   **(2 marks)**

48.5 What extra feature does the project evaluation and review technique (PERT) bring to critical path analysis?

A   It incorporate resource requirements usage and availability
B   It allows for uncertainty in determining project duration
C   It enables rapid re-planning
D   It permits the computation of float times   **(2 marks)**

The following data is to be used to answer questions 48.6 and 48.7 below

A company is about to undertake a project about which the following data is available.

Activity	Preceded by activity	Duration Days	Workers required
A	–	3	6
B	–	5	3
C	B	2	4
D	A	1	4
E	A	6	5
F	D	3	6
G	C, E	3	3

48.6 What is the duration of the critical path for this project?

    A   7 days

    B   12 days

    C   10 days

    D   14 days   **(4 marks)**

48.7 What is the minimum number of staff that will be required on day 6 of the project, assuming the critical path is not extended?

    A   9

    B   15

    C   8

    D   12   **(6 marks)**

(Total 20 marks)

49 Objective test questions

36 mins

49.1 Project W is a severely time-constrained research project and must be completed to high quality standards. The project staff all have academic qualifications and a wealth of relevant experience. They are divided into four specialist teams, each working on separate, complex problems. Each team is headed by an expert in the relevant field. The project manager has good experience of the general theoretical background to the work being done but ceased to be involved in practical research some years ago.

Using the Ashridge classification, which management style would you expect to be least useful to the project manager?

    A   Tells

    B   Sells

    C   Consults

    D   Joins   **(2 marks)**

49.2 The project 7S model and the McKinsey 7S model differ in only one particular. Which of the following is not part of the project 7S model?

    A   Strategy

    B   Stakeholders

    C   Systems

    D   Specialisation   **(2 marks)**

49.3   What is the role of the project sponsor?

    A   Provides and is accountable for the resources invested in the project
    B   Communicates the project vision within the organisation
    C   Takes responsibility for delivering the project on time
    D   Represents the interests of the project board   **(2 marks)**

49.4   Which of the following is not a feature of the PRINCE2 project management system?

    A   A project is driven by its business case
    B   The system may be used for projects of any size
    C   The system focuses on the technical processes of project management
    D   A clear management structure is defined   **(2 marks)**

49.5   In *Maylor's* 4D model of the project lifecycle, the components of the delivery stage are:

    A   Planning, execution, handover, review
    B   Startup, execution, completion, handover
    C   Planning, startup, execution, completion
    D   Startup, planning, execution, completion   **(2 marks)**

The following data is to be used to answer questions 49.6 and 49.7 below

Activity	Immediately preceding activity	Duration (weeks)
A	–	5
B	–	4
C	A	2
D	B	1
E	B	5
F	B	5
G	C, D	4
H	F	3
I	F	2

49.6   What is the duration of the critical path for this project?

    A   14 weeks
    B   9 weeks
    C   12 weeks
    D   7 weeks   **(5 marks)**

49.7   What is the free float on activity D?

    A   2 weeks
    B   3 weeks
    C   1 week
    D   4 weeks   **(5 marks)**

(Total = 20 marks)

Section B questions: Project management

50 Project network
18 mins

The following tasks, estimates and precedences have been agreed in a project.

Task ID	Task description	Estimate (in days)	Precedences
A	Write project initiation document	3	
B	Research Site One	4	A
C	Research Site Two	2	A
D	Document requirements – Site One	6	B
E	Document requirements – Site Two	5	C
F	Define non-functional requirements	2	A
G	Define agreed requirements	3	D, E, F
H	Write invitation to tender	4	G

Required

(a) Construct a project network for this project. **(6 marks)**
(b) Which activities are on the critical path of the project? **(1 mark)**
(c) What is the estimated elapsed duration of the project? **(1 mark)**

What would the effect be on the elapsed duration of the project if:

(d) Task C overran by two days? **(1 mark)**
(e) Task B overran by one day? **(1 mark)**

(Total = 10 marks)

The following data are given for questions 51 and 52

You work for a firm of management accountants that specialises in implementing information systems. The latest assignment is to implement new systems at a small chain of ten shops managed by FRS Ltd and to integrate these into the systems of a multinational retail organisation (MRO Inc) that has recently acquired them. FRS Ltd sells a range of wines, spirits and groceries.

Draft implementation plans

The information systems department of MRO Inc had drawn up an outline timetable for the introduction of the new system to FRS Ltd.

The first draft of this follows.

Task	Description	Planned duration (weeks)	Preceding activities
A	Communication – inform staff at each FRS shop and indicate how it will affect them	1	–
B	Carry out systems audit at each FRS shop	2	A
C	Agree detailed implementation plan with board of directors	1	B
D	Order and receive hardware requirements	4	C
E	Install hardware at all FRS shops	4	D
F	Install software at all FRS shops	2	D
G	Arrange training at premises of MRO Inc	3	D
H	Test systems at all FRS shops	4	E and F
I	Implement changeover at all shops	10	G and H

51 FRS 1

18 mins

Required

Describe the major issues to be considered in managing the project to implement the new system at FRS Ltd.

(10 marks)

52 FRS 2

18 mins

Required

Produce a critical path analysis of the draft implementation plan suggested by the IS department manager. (This should identify the critical path and the total elapsed time.)
(10 marks)

53 New activities

18 mins

The diagram below shows a project plan for a systems development project. The project plan is shown in both 'activity on node' and 'activity on arrow' conventions.

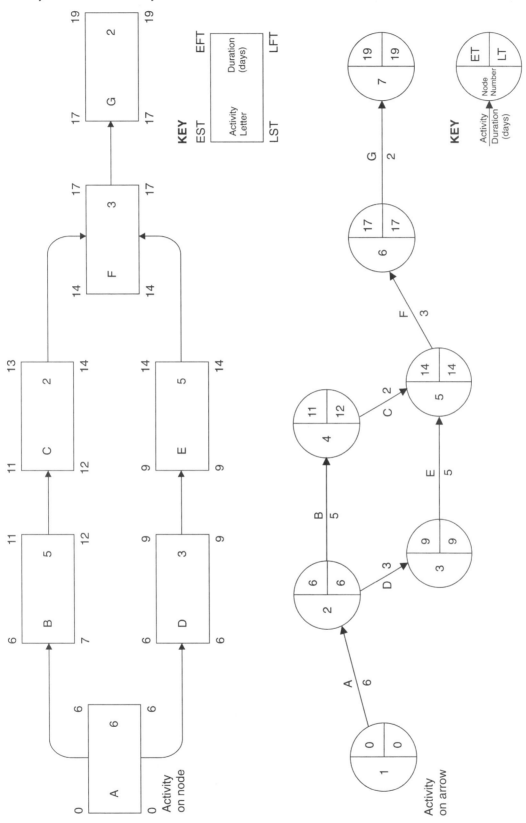

Required

A mistake has been found in the original project plan. The precedences for activities A, B, C, D, E, F, G are unchanged but two new activities now have to be added. No other activities are affected by the inclusion of the two new activities. These are:

Activity	Precedence	Duration
H	D	4 days
I	H	8 days

(a) Re-draw the network (using the notation you are familiar with) amending it to reflect these changes.

(8 marks)

(b) In the re-drawn network, how many days (if any) could activity E over-run without affecting the overall duration of the project? Assume that no other activities over-run. **(2 marks)**

(Total = 10 marks)

54 Question with helping hand: Critical path analysis   18 mins

The following activities, time estimates and precedences have been identified for the selection, purchase and implementation of a software package.

Activity		Precedence	Estimate (days)
A	Define Project Initiation Document	–	5
B	Define requirements	A	8
C	Define training plan	B	3
D	Issue Invitation to Tender	B	3
E	Select Supplier	D	2
F	Install hardware and software	E	5
G	Training course	C,F	3
H	Enter master file data	G	5
I	Convert operational data	F	9
J	Parallel running	H,I	10

Required

Construct a network diagram for this project. Identify the critical path. **(10 marks)**

Helping hand. Most of us have to produce at least one preliminary sketch of a network in order to show the dependencies correctly. Try to allow yourself time to draw a fair copy as this will make the marker's job much easier. Try to draw your event circles neatly: you could draw around a coin or you could prepare a template from a piece of cardboard. Make a point of using a ruler for your straight lines.

55 CityGo   18 mins

The CityGo Bus Company, formerly a regional operating division of a public corporation, has been acquired through a management buy out led by the general manger, Jim Ryan.

Competition will be intense as soon as the routes become fully competitive in January 20X3. The company has a number of weaknesses that have to be attended to immediately.

The most important of these is that its computing systems are totally integrated into the previous owner's systems. Internal management accounts are almost non-existent and most management reports were directed at the corporation's management team not at CityGo's management. It had never been possible to devolve budget responsibility down to key line managers in operations and maintenance.

The privatisation timetable means that CityGo has only a few months to set up new computer based systems.

The requirement will be for a project management process that can deal with tight timescales involving a complicated set of interrelated decisions and actions. CityGo management must realise that effective project planning and control need different management skills than those required to run operational processes.

This is the immediate requirement but in the longer term CityGo must put in place a strategy for managing information resources in ways which enable it to achieve a competitive advantage or at least competitive parity with other bus operators.

Required

Examine the attributes of a project management process and assess the range of project management tools and techniques which are available to CityGo to help achieve an efficient changeover to new financial systems.

(10 marks)

56 Conference network (5/05)   18 mins

R has taken on the responsibility for organising the annual conference for the local Society of Management Accountants. Remembering the project management techniques she came across when studying for her professional qualification, R has decided that critical path analysis may be helpful in planning the conference.

As a start, R has drawn up a list of the activities she must complete in preparation for the conference, she has identified the dependency between the different activities and the time she thinks each will take.

Activity		*Dependency*	*Time (weeks)*
Determine conference theme	A	–	3
Research alternative venues	B	–	6
Identify and book guest speakers	C	A	4
Book venue	D	B	2
Print conference papers	E	C	8
Print and send out invitations	F	D	4
Confirm final arrangements with venue and deliver documents	G	E, F	2

Required

Using the information from the scenario, construct a network diagram and explain how information from this could be useful to R in planning the conference. **(10 marks)**

Section C questions: Project management

57 Project planning and roles (5/05)   45 mins

S Company is a major retailer selling mobile phones. In recent years the Company has opened new outlets and taken on more support staff at the head office. As a result the Company has outgrown its existing headquarters and so the decision has been taken to relocate to a larger purpose-built building.

Although the building work is complete, there are a number of different initiatives associated with the relocation. These include making sure that the premises are ready to move into on time and within budget and setting up a customer service contact team to support the retail outlets dealing with customer enquiries and complaints. In addition, an upgraded office IT support system is to be designed and must be ready for installation in the new premises.

P, the head of facilities management, has decided to establish a project team to ensure that all of the activities associated with the move to the new premises are co-ordinated and within budget. She has the formal role of project sponsor working on behalf of the Board and has appointed D to manage the project.

Required

(a)   Identify and explain the activities that D would need to undertake in the planning phase of the project for re-location.   **(15 marks)**

(b)   Compare and contrast the roles of P, as the project sponsor and D, as the project manager.   **(10 marks)**

(Total = 25 marks)

58 Thurnon   45 mins

Thurnon plc are to initiate a project to study the feasibility of a new product. The end result of the feasibility project will be a report recommending the action to be taken for the new product. The activities to be carried out to complete the feasibility project are given below.

Activity	Description	Immediate predecessors	Expected time Weeks	Number of staff required
A	preliminary design	–	5	3
B	market research	–	3	2
C	obtain engineering quotes	A	2	2
D	construct prototype	A	5	5
E	prepare marketing material	A	3	3
F	costing	C	2	2
G	product testing	D	4	5
H	pilot survey	B, E	6	4
I	pricing estimates	H	2	1
J	final report	F, G, I	6	2

(a)   Prepare a network for the scheme of activities set out above. Determine the critical path and the shortest duration of the project.   **(10 marks)**

(b)   Assuming the project starts at time zero and that each activity commences at the earliest start date, construct a chart showing the number of staff required at any one time for this project.   **(10 marks)**

(c)   Explain what is meant by the term 'project life cycle'.   **(5 marks)**

(Total = 25 marks)

59 Healthweb

45 mins

Project background

Southern Regional Health Authority (SRHA)

The SRHA manages the provision of medical care to the public within its local area. It is responsible for 50 medical centres and 10 hospitals.

You are a senior management accountant working for one of the southern region hospitals.

The 'Healthweb' national information network is a central government-led initiative which aims to provide a secure and dedicated network environment for all medical practitioners and managers, to share and access healthcare information. Other regions within the country have already connected to the network, with 95% of medical centres and hospitals within these regions utilising the facilities.

The SRHA has been sent a target by the central government to have 80% of all medical centres and 90% of all hospitals within the region connected to the Healthweb one year from now. Prior to the project commencement, most information within the hospitals and medical centres was kept by a manual, paper-based system, and all data exchange was done by means of telephone or by post. The senior management team of the SRHA set a project board in January 2002 to oversee the progress of the project and so specify the project objectives.

Project management

 The central government has contracted a large telecommunications company, T, to manage and control the network and to project-manage the regional connection projects. T was contracted to provide all hardware and software systems support, training and maintenance.

The SRHA project team was mainly made up of managers and technicians from T, but also included three doctors and three senior managers.

Project progress

Each medical centre and hospital within the southern region was allowed to discuss terms of usage, (that is, the hardware and software requirements, which aspects of the Healthweb to utilise and the timing of the implementation) separately with the GPC project team.

Financing within the SRHA

Many doctors and senior managers were concerned about the limited resources of the hospitals and medical centres being spent on unnecessary technology and that the disruption of the project might affect the quality of service to patients. Other regions had reported large costs in computer upgrades and facilities, which could have been better spent on direct patient care.

Although the central government has set up a 'Technology Fund', some of which has been set aside for this project, obtaining the funds has proved difficult in other regions. In addition, there has been no previous consistency in financing connection to the network, with some regional health authorities paying all of the costs. Other regions have invested only in the initial technology, with all on-going operational costs being paid by the individual hospitals and medical centres.

The hospital executives at the hospital in which you are a senior management accountant are concerned that the senior managers not involved directly in the GPC project are unaware of its nature and importance.

Required

You have been asked by the executives of your own hospital to prepare a memorandum to the other senior managers in the hospital which should:

(a)   Discuss the relationship of the project manager to:

(i)   The project sponsor (that is, the central government).

(ii)   The project board. - *Overall running smthly. Key targets.*

(iii)   The medical and administrative users (in medical centres and hospitals). *– Best think for admin users – selling it to them.*

Include in your answer a discussion of the potential conflicting project objectives of the above stakeholders.

(15 marks)

(b)   Explain the potential project management problems which might arise from allowing each hospital and medical centre to discuss individual terms of usage of the Healthweb separately with the GPC project team.

(10 marks)

(Total = 25 marks)

Without their support it won't work!

House Project – Part 1

E, a management accountant, and three of her colleagues have decided to venture into the buy-to-rent market. Recently, they set up a company, Enterprise Associates, and purchased a house in which they would each hold a share. E inherited some money and holds a 50% share. The other 50% is divided equally between the three other partners. E, however, will take on much of the responsibility for the company's first venture and she has been given a free hand to develop the property as she thinks fit.

The house purchased by the colleagues is 150 years old and has been poorly maintained. The interior fixtures, fittings and décor are also old fashioned. A survey of the house also reveals that the electric wiring and water piping do not conform to modern standards and that the walls are subject to rising damp. Without extensive repairs and renovation the house would be almost impossible to rent.

With interest rates at an all time low and the demand for rented accommodation at a very high level, E has decided, in consultation with her partners, to renovate the house before offering it for rent.

The easiest option for E would be to employ a builder to carry out all the renovations at an agreed price. After obtaining a number of estimates, however, she decides that she and her husband can carry out some of the basic repairs and manage the decorating themselves at a considerable saving.

E realises that this will make considerable demands on her time and that careful planning will be necessary to fit the work on the house with her demanding job as a management accountant, as well as fulfil her family obligations. Conscious of the need to maintain the quality of her work, E has decided, with the agreement of her employer, to work part-time for the duration of the house project, but she recognises that even with this change she will have to manage her time very carefully.

On this basis, E has agreed with her partners in Enterprise Associates a profit sharing ratio of 70:10:10:10 with all expenses for materials and specialist labour shared equally between the four.

As well as being methodical and hard working, E has developed a number of practical skills over the years while improving the family home. Hence many of the decorating tasks are familiar to her. If E has a weakness, it is that she enjoys conversation and meeting people and often takes more time than is necessary to conduct business and social transactions.

The damp proofing, writing and plumbing will need to be carried out by skilled specialists but E already has contacts with an electrician and a plumber (fitter of water pipes) and they, in turn have contacts with other specialists in the building trade such as carpenters (wood workers) and plasterers (who specialise in covering walls with a skimming of plaster).

Although she has no experience of house renovation on this scale, E has a rough idea of the sequence in which the various jobs – damp proofing, plumbing and so on – will need to be carried out and has received advice from a builder on the estimated time that each job will take to complete. She has also contacted the various skilled specialists for estimates of the cost for each job.

This information is most timely for E because she has just had a firm offer from a prospective tenant, J, to rent the house, provided he and his family could move into the house in three months' time. E, knowing the family, and confident that they would be good tenants, has agreed that she will have the property ready for them in three months and available for rent at an agreed price.

While E naturally wishes to keep costs to a minimum, she also requires that the renovation meets quality standards acceptable to customers who wish to rent property.

60 Enterprise Associates 1

18 mins

Required

Explain to E the benefits of using a Work Breakdown Structure in the planning of the project.

(10 marks)

61 Enterprise Associates 2

18 mins

The management of time is going to be a major issue for E.

Required

Identify the key factors that will have a bearing on E's use of time and explain what action she can take to make the best use of time.

(10 marks)

House project – Part 2: four years later

The renovation of Enterprise Associates' first house went well and the house is still rented by the original family. Four years have now gone by and since then much has changed. Not only has E retired from her position as a management accountant; as Enterprise Associates' Chief Executive Officer she has helped the company to grow very rapidly.

Encouraged by the initial success, by a buoyant housing market, and by low interest rates, E has negotiated a series of bank loans to buy up other old houses in the locality and Enterprise Associates has renovated these and rented them at market rates.

Unfortunately for Enterprise Associates and others in the buy-to-rent business, however, conditions in the housing market have changed since the company rented its first property. Many more people have entered the buy-to-rent property sector, interest rates have increased and are forecast to rise sharply in the next year. This will probably reduce the demand for new houses to some extent, and will also deter some would-be entrepreneurs, who might have borrowed funds to enter the buy-to-rent market.

The central government has acted to increase the amount of building land available and this, in turn, has resulted in a shortage of supply of builders, plumbers, plasterers, electricians and others in the building trades. There is also some evidence from market research that householders have an increasing preference for new houses. Also, in the town in which Enterprise Associates conducts it business, the local government has plans for compulsory purchase and demolition of some of the older properties as part of a new road building programme.

Faced with these changing circumstances, E is not sure what Enterprise Associates' future strategy should be. She feels the need for a better understanding of the changes that are affecting the buy-to-rent market and has asked you, a management consultant, to provide Enterprise Associates with an analysis of the buy-to-rent industry.

62 Enterprise Associates 3

18 mins

Required

Prepare a report for Enterprise Associates which:

(a)   briefly explain Porter's Five Forces model;
(b)   discusses the main opportunities and threats in the buy-to-rent industry.

(10 marks)

Read the following scenario and answer TWO questions ONLY – 25 marks each

The WAM Organisation is one of the most successful supermarket chains in its own country. Its reputation for innovation is unparalleled in its own country with the successful launch of its personal finance, telecom, and internet shopping services.

The WAM Organisation customer focus and its ability to provide value for money through efficient operations and the use of the latest technology has enabled it to gain the largest share of the market.

Following a careful process of internal and external analysis, the senior management of WAM Organisation has concluded that the domestic market for its goods and services has reached saturation point and that the only opportunity for significant growth lies in venturing abroad.

Acting partly on the advice of the central government's Overseas Advisory Board, and using its own research team, WAM Organisation's management has decided to locate its first overseas supermarket in country Y. The location selected is in the suburbs of a growing city, where groceries, clothing and the other non-food products that WAM Organisation intends to supply are currently provided by a large number of small shops.

The new overseas outlet will be staffed initially by managers from WAM Organisation's home country, but other staff will be recruited and trained in country Y. The company has also made it clear that its human resource policy is to provide management opportunities to local people once the business in country Y is established.

The manager for the overall project is Ms D from WAM Organisation's Business Development division, while the project manager for the construction of the buildings, roads and car park that will make up the supermarket outlet is Mr G from the WAM Organisation's Property and Estates division.

The land on which the supermarket outlet will be built has been purchased and following a series of tough negotiations with state and local government officials, planning permission has been granted. Vigorous protest, however, has come from the City's Civic Society, local residents and shopkeepers who are located near to the proposed development.

The Civic Society is concerned about the detrimental impact on the local environment. Residents are concerned about the potential increase in traffic and the danger it poses to the children in the local school. The shopkeepers are fearful about the impact of the new supermarket on their future business prospects.

The media, including television, radio and newspapers, have publicised the fears of the local residents and shopkeepers and these two groups, together with the City's Civic Society, have formed a coalition to attempt to prevent the development.

63 WAM Organisation 1   45 mins

Required

(a)   Explain the approach to strategy formulation and the content of the WAM Organisation's strategy.

(10 marks)

(b)   Identify the secondary stakeholders in the WAM Organisation's supermarket project and explain how the project team should manage these stakeholders.   **(15 marks)**

(Total = 25 marks)

49

64 WAM Organisation 2

45 mins

Required

(a)   Prepare a report for the directors of a major investment bank which explains the resource-based approach to strategic management and analyses the resources/core competences that appear to give the WAM Organisation competitive advantage.

(15 marks)

(b)   Using your knowledge of research findings on international cultural differences, explain why WAM Organisation's management might encounter some problems with managing local staff in Country Y.

(10 marks)

(Total = 25 marks)

65 WAM Organisation 3

45 mins

Required

(a)   Identify the major risks associated with the WAM Organisation's development project.   **(15 marks)**

(b)   Discuss the general negotiating strategy and principles that would be required by WAM Organisation's managers in order to gain planning permission to site their new supermarket outlet in Country Y.

(10 marks)

(Total = 25 marks)

Mixed objective test questions

66 Pilot paper

36 mins

66.1   In a multi-divisional organisation producing a range of products for different markets, the business level strategy of each unit or division is mainly concerned with

A   setting the direction for the organisation
Ⓑ   the competitiveness of a particular division
C   the efficiency of production, marketing and other functions
D   alignment of strategy with other organisations   **(2 marks)**

66.2   In the typical hierarchical organisation, the requirement of a lower-level manager to answer to a higher-level manager in the chain of command is referred to as

A   authority
B   empowerment
Ⓒ   accountability
D   super ordination   **(2 marks)**

66.3   Recent developments towards greater employee involvement, flexible working and flatter organisational structures have placed greater emphasis on which ONE of the following styles of management?

A   Exploitative authoritative
B   Autocratic
C   Participative
D   Benevolent authoritative   **(2 marks)**

66.4   Research on group effectiveness has concluded that the most consistently successful groups

    A   are those in which all members are innovative
    B   comprise a range of roles undertaken by various members
    C   are those in which all members are very intelligent
    D   comprise a range of roles all undertaken by a few members of the group   **(2 marks)**

66.5   When designing an organisational structure, or reviewing the effectiveness of an existing structure, the first thing that must be clarified is

    A   informal organisational relationships
    B   objectives of the organisation
    C   size of organisation
    D   division of labour   **(2 marks)**

The following data is to be used to answer questions 66.6, 66.7 and 66.8 below

Blake plc is a large multi-national designer and manufacturer of specialist road vehicles. Blake plc's products include fire engines, breakdown trucks, rescue vehicles and ambulances. Customer organisations, that are often government-owned, order Blake plc's products in small quantities. Each 'batch' of products is deigned and built by Blake plc to meet a unique customer specification.

Blake plc has been approached by The Armana Airports Authority (AAA) to provide four rescue trucks to carry emergency equipment and personnel at a large provincial airport. This contract must be completed (that is, the trucks delivered to AAA) within 16 weeks of today's date. This is essential, as the trucks currently used by AAA have been deemed unsuitable by the Armana Government Airport Inspectorate (AGAI).

Blake plc has just submitted a proposal to AAA, following an invitation to tender received two weeks ago. The project manager at Blake plc, for the AAA project, is Annie Li. Annie has a meeting scheduled for later today with the Director of Procurement at AAA, Charles Crowe. This is Annie's first meeting with Charles. Annie is aware that Charles is likely to ask for several modifications to the design of the trucks proposed by Blake plc, and that this will have a 'knock-on' effect on other aspects of Blake plc's proposal. Annie is concerned about the impact of any changes on Blake plc's ability to deliver the trucks in 16 weeks.

The normal programme for a project of this scale at Blake plc is as follows.

Activity		Duration (weeks)	Depends on
A	Prepare proposal	2	–
B	Negotiate with customer	6	A
C	Modify and finalise design	4	B
D	Build chassis	3	C
E	Build bodyshell	4	C
F	Paint bodyshell	1	E
G	Assemble, fit out and finish	2	D, F
H	Write manuals	3	C
I	Print manuals	1	H
J	Test	1	G, I
K	Inspect and deliver	1	J

66.6   Based on the normal programme for a project such as this, what is the project elapsed time, from beginning to end?

    A   18 weeks
    B   19 weeks
    C   21 weeks
    D   28 weeks   **(4 marks)**

66.7   Assuming that the durations and dependencies of activities (C) to (K) in the programme cannot be changed, how long can Annie spend negotiating with Charles (Activity B), yet still deliver the vehicles in 16 weeks?

A   1 week
B   3 weeks
C   6 weeks
D   The vehicles cannot be delivered in 16 weeks   **(3 marks)**

66.8   Identify three stakeholders in the project, each of whom is specifically mentioned in the scenario, *other than Annie and Charles*.   **(3 marks)**

(Total = 20 marks)

67 May 2005 examination   **36 mins**

67.1   Identify which ONE of the following perspectives of strategic management is defined by Mintzberg as 'patterns or consistencies realised despite, or in the absence of, intentions'?

A   Rational
B   Local Incrementalism
C   Emergent
D   Positioning   **(2 marks)**

67.2   State which ONE of the following represents the four phases of negotiation:

A   Preparation, opening, bargaining, closing
B   Opening, bargaining, decision, closing
C   Preparation, bargaining, negotiating, closing
D   Opening, negotiating, decision, closing   **(2 marks)**

67.3   Which ONE of the following organisational forms is best suited to a project which requires integration from a number of different functions?

A   Functional
B   Network
C   Divisional
D   Matrix   **(2 marks)**

67.4   Identify which ONE of the following best describes the scope of a project?

A   A statement a client needs
B   The extent of work needed to produce the project's deliverables
C   The specification of resources required
D   The sequence of activities   **(2 marks)**

67.5   Porter's work on industry competition suggests that the strength of market entry depends on the existence of barriers to entry against the entrant. Identify **three** factors that create barriers to entering an industry.

67.6 Identify three missing words (using a, b and c) to complete the diagram of the five process areas of project management proposed by the Project Management Institute.

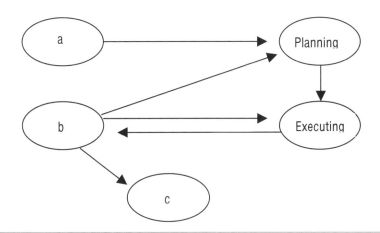

(3 marks)

67.8 List **three** types of feasibility study that might be undertaken as part of project planning. **(3 marks)**

67.9 Blake and Mouton developed the managerial grid to provide a framework for applying effective management. Draw the managerial grid labelling the horizontal axis and vertical axis and identify on the grid where the team management style is located.

Note: graph paper is not required.

(3 marks)

(Total = 20 marks)

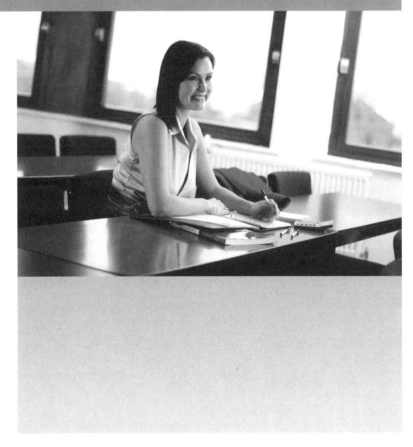

Answers

1 Objective test answers

1.1 C Fact

1.2 B Whistle blowing is informing the public of wrongdoing. Social responsibility is the modification of profit seeking behaviour to support socially desirable objectives. Professional ethics are what the financial director has breached. Internal audit is an example of the mechanisms that support a compliance-based approach to ethical behaviour.

1.3 D *Mintzberg* uses the term 'support staff'. 'Ideology', while not a **structural** component, is part of Mintzberg's model.

1.4 B Fact

1.5 C A and B are part of single loop control. D is an element of feedforward control.

1.6 C A is two of Mintzberg's configurations; B is two of the organisational sub-systems described by *Trist and Bamforth;* D is two other widely encountered forms of organisation structure.

1.7 D While a link between appraisal and reward is played down in many organisations, there is no doubt that it is a valid objective for an appraisal scheme. The other options are uses that may be made of an appraisal scheme, but they would not be described as objectives. Friendly interaction must not preclude hard talk where it is needed Documentation may ultimately be used in court but its generation is not what an appraisal scheme is about; and systems that cannot accommodate individual failings are not themselves robust enough.

1.8 The **shaper** is extrovert, dominant and passionate about the task.

1.9

Configuration	Co-ordination mechanism	Key part
Machine bureaucracy	**Standardised work processes**	**Technostructure**
Adhocracy	**Mutual adjustment**	**Support staff**

2 Objective test answers

2.1 A Fact

2.2 B The fourth style identified was consults. The full spectrum, in order, is: tells, sells, consults, joins.

2.3 D Control might be seen as one of the task needs.

2.4 B The relevant provision actually says that, except for gross misconduct, workers should not be dismissed for a first breach of discipline.

2.5 B Fact

2.6 D The eight original roles were: co-ordinator, shaper, plant, monitor-evaluator, resource-investigator, implementer, team worker and finisher. The specialist joins the group to offer expert advice when needed. A single person may play two or more roles.

2.7 A B, C and D each relate to aspects of the models proposed by *Adair; Hersey and Blanchard;* and *Fiedler*, respectively.

2.8 B A is constructive dismissal. D is wrongful dismissal, D is summary dismissal and may be unfair, wrongful, both or neither.

2.9 B A is direct discrimination, C is positive discrimination, D may be an example of direct discrimination.

2.10 D Many groups exist outside the work environment. Note that 'team' in the sense of a group organised to play a game is a special usage in this context.

3 Objective test answers

3.1   D   A, B and C are all problems typical of large organisations and less common in small ones.

3.2   C   This is not an easy question. Option A might possibly be regarded as a statement of values, but it is more obviously a standard of behaviour. Option B is clearly an operational policy. Option C is undoubtedly a statement of cultural aspiration: it is designed for the long term and deals with relationships between the company and its employees. Option D could be seen as an element of strategy: it could, for instance, be exploited as a unique selling proposition and an element that differentiates the company from its competitors. However, it is best regarded as a policy. The best answer, therefore, is C, the element of culture.

3.3   C   While primary responsibility may lie with the employer, the employee is responsible for such things as operating machinery in a safe fashion (after suitable training).

3.4   C   *Elton Mayo* is regarded as one of the main theorists of human relations.

3.5   B   The relevant learning outcome is: explain the purpose and principles of good corporate governance.

3.6   B   The relevant learning outcome is: evaluate different organisation structures.

3.7   C   The relevant learning outcome is: explain the concepts of power, bureaucracy, authority, responsibility, leadership and delegation.

3.8   A   A wide span of control implies a flat organisation with few layers of management and, indeed, few managers. Career progression is constrained by the lack of posts to be filled and the management of complex work is hampered by the need for work to be largely unsupervised. The contrary of all this is true of tall organisations, which in themselves imply fairly narrow spans of control. Decentralisation may be associated with a range of degrees of flatness or tallness, but implies the existence of a larger number of management posts than would be the case in an equivalent centralised organisation.

3.9   B   The organic organisation is the antithesis of bureaucracy. Procedures, internal rules and hierarchical control are minimised. Innovative ways of working, wide general knowledge, co-operative endeavour and supporting the overall mission are highly valued. Options A, C and D are all typical of the mechanistic approach.

3.10   D   The fourth dimension is individualism – collectivism

4 Objective test answers

4.1   A   Legitimate power is also called position power. Expert power accrues to recognised expertise; resource power derives from control over scarce resources; personal power lies in the manager's personality.

4.2   B   This question requires some discussion. Project management exists when a team is assembled to pursue an identifiable project. It is likely to include specialists from more than one functional area, such as finance and marketing, as here, but there is no project mentioned in the question, so A is inappropriate. Functional departmentation seems to exist at Hydra Ltd, to at least some extent, since the Finance Director is in a position to divert the employment of finance specialists and presumably utilises the services of the management accountants when they are not working for the product managers. However, the narrative clearly indicates a strong element of cross functional organisation. 'Complex organisational form' is a phrase normally used to indicate a degree of boundary-spanning organisation as in, for instance, partnerships, alliances and consortia. There is no mention of this in the narrative. B would appear to be the best option.

4.3   D   Adair's model is connected with his concept of **functional leadership**, which emphasises what leaders *do* rather than what they *are*.

4.4   C   **Authority** in a hierarchical organisation derives largely from the position held: this is **position power** or **legitimate power**. Subordinate managers are **accountable** to their superiors for the way in which they use their authority. **Empowerment** is a process rather than an attribute: it occurs when enhanced authority is granted to those who previously had little or none in order reduce the need for managerial oversight. **Super ordination** simply means being placed higher in any given hierarchy and is not a term commonly used of managers.

4.5   B   **Networks** are usually taken to be groups of suppliers and customers that co-operate on non-core competence matters in order to share benefits. A **functional** structure divides the organisation up by reference to type of work done. A matrix organisation superimposes one hierarchy on another, usually adding a product/market or project based structure to a functional structure.

4.6   D   This is another poor question since, before we can call something effective, we need to know what it is supposed to achieve. Option D is a description of a currently fashionable approach to appraisal but all three other options are features of well-established appraisal systems that meet the requirements of certain organisations. For example, some appraisal systems have the **assessment of suitability for promotion** as a major purpose. Options A and B would be entirely appropriate for such a system.

4.7   C   The wording of the question is almost a definition of the participative style.

4.8   B   *Belbin's* is the best-known work on this topic.

4.9   C   'Procedural justice' *may* be a reference to the need for 'due process' when administering justice, but knowing the way the Examiner's mind works, it is probably just a term he has invented to confuse you. Option B is obviously nonsensical, while option D may be true, but only if the person making the claim is the organisation's PR spin doctor.

4.10   A   *Taylor* was concerned with making the individual worker more efficient. Group working as a subject of study and theory is a post-Scientific management idea. It can be traced back to the work of *Mayo's* team at *Hawthorne*, which laid the basis for the human relations approach and first described the informal organisation. Socio-technical systems is a work-group related idea developed by *Trist and Bamforth* in their study of developments in the UK coal-mining industry after World War II.

5 Code of conduct

> **Top tips.** Ethics is a truly enormous subject and a difficult one to write about succinctly. In this question it is necessary to stick fairly close to the given topic of professional ethics and not wander off into more interesting areas.
>
> Be aware that professional ethics is seen as an increasingly important matter and this is likely to be reflected in your examinations.
>
> Clearly, you must have a working knowledge of CIMA's professional code if you are to tackle questions like this one.
>
> **Easy marks.** The crucial point here is defending the public interest. You can amplify this by saying what it means specifically for accountants.

Ethics is about right and wrong and proper behaviour. While general integrity and correct conduct are important for everybody, members of professional associations are subject to extensive and detailed rules.

The main reason for this is the public interest. The public need to know that persons in responsible positions will behave in an ethical fashion. To this end it is valuable that professional bodies enforce their ethical codes, and that their members support them. The bodies and their members are thus mutually reinforcing. The members are respected because of their affiliation to their professional bodies and the professional bodies are respected because of their members' high standards of conduct.

Like any circular process, this mutual support must be monitored constantly; both good and bad behaviour will rapidly be amplified and a few unethical actions can severely damage the reputation of both a professional body and its members.

As far as chartered management accountants are concerned, employers and clients need to be confident that specific ethical duties peculiar to accountancy will be respected. These include confidentiality, professional competence, due care, financial integrity and trustworthiness. If the public can depend on chartered management accountants in these matters, the economic life of society is enhanced.

6 Question with answer plan: Professional ethics

Top tips. The remarks preceding the answer to question 5 apply equally well here.

Easy marks. It is fairly obvious that codes of conduct should be comprehensive, consistent and legally compliant.

Answer plan

'steps to ensure...take seriously' – important

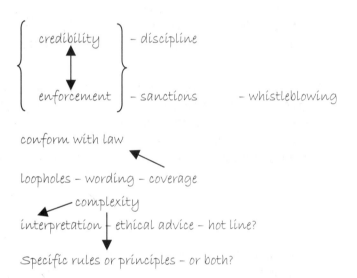

This answer plan is based on brainstorming. The arrows and brackets show the process of building links between ideas generated. The numbers show the way the answer will be structured.

Codes of conduct have become very popular in recent years in organisations concerned about ethical conduct. Where these contain specific clear rules they at least have the value of establishing what correct conduct is in the defined cases. This is both of benefit to the individual and useful at any subsequent disciplinary process. However, such codes have been criticised as tending to be too legalistic and encouraging a compliance-based rather than principle-based approach. Ethics is to some extent a matter of opinion and highly specific codes tend to offer poor guidance in complex situations.

If professional bodies or other organisations have codes of conduct, their first requirement is that they are carefully thought out, with a minimum of loopholes and adequate coverage of the problems they are meant to address. The second requirement is that they should be enforced by a proper system of discipline. Among other characteristics, such a system must conform with over-riding legal requirements, such as, in common law jurisdictions, the rules of natural justice.

Such a system of discipline must be credible. Among other things, that means that it must be administered impartially. For a professional body, this may mean qualified legal input, possibly from a legally qualified president of the disciplinary forum. For a commercial organisation, it may be that non-executive directors can play a part.

The system should also be capable of detecting abuses. One method is a complaint system, to be impartially administered. Another feature would be a facility for 'whistleblowing' by insiders.

Another method of encouraging ethical behaviour would be a means of providing guidance when problems arise. The real difficulties with ethics arise when the rules or principles point in different directions. A telephone hotline to experienced advisers is invaluable in such circumstances.

7 Preparation question: Scientific management

Scientific Management was concerned with the rational organisation of work as a means of increasing productivity. The emphasis was on the problem of obtaining increased productivity from individual workers through the technical structuring of the work organisation and the provision of monetary incentives as a motivator for higher levels of output.

Taylor considered that all work processes could be analysed into discrete tasks and that it was possible to find the 'one best way' to perform each task. Each job was broken down into component parts, each part timed and the parts rearranged into the most efficient way of working.

Taylor believed that a scientific approach to management could make work more profitable for all concerned. Workers could be controlled, not only by giving orders and maintaining discipline, but also by removing from them any decisions about the way their work was carried out. By division of labour and by dictating precise stages and methods for every aspect of work performance, management could optimise work processes. The application of techniques to decide what should be done and how, using workers who are both properly trained and willing to maximise output, should result in maximum productivity. Obtaining the highest possible wages through working in the most efficient and productive way would motivate workers.

The legacy of Taylor lives on. Time study, motion study, standardised tools and materials, methods simplification, careful selection and training, rigorous measurement, payment by results, management by exception, production control, endless and expensive experiments, even benchmarking (although it wasn't called that back then), have all been left to modern management by Taylor and his disciples.

The design of jobs in telephone call centres appears to owe quite a lot to scientific management.

- The operators are carefully selected for their voice characteristics, telephone manner and computer keyboard skills.

- Unskilled operators are trained to be most efficient and effective in providing the service.

- Operators cannot make decisions on how to carry out their work.

- The use of modern technology provides the means for measuring almost every aspect of the telephone operators' work.

- The work is closely supervised with time away from the workstation easily tracked and recorded and the quality of the operators' performance constantly monitored by weekly customer 'call backs'.

- Quantitative and qualitative measures of performance can be used to re-programme work practices and ensure yet more efficiency and effectiveness.

- Performance-related pay provides the motivation to work harder.

There are a number of valid criticisms of Taylor's approach.

- It put the planning and control of workplace activities exclusively in the hands of the management. This reduces the workers' role to that of a rigid adherence to methods and procedures over which they have no discretion

- It led to the fragmentation of work on account of its emphasis on the analysis and organisation of individual tasks or operations.

- It generated a 'carrot and stick' approach to the motivation of employees by relating pay to be geared tightly to output

- It ruled out any realistic bargaining about wage rates since every job was measured, timed and rated by management.

Perhaps the key idea of scientific management and the one that has drawn the most criticism was the concept of 'task allocation'. The criticism of this approach is that it omits the worker's own contribution to the design of work and, thereby, alienates the worker from the job. It is seen as leaving no scope for the individual worker to excel or think. Workers also find the work repetitive, boring and requiring little skill.

Repetitive jobs can cause strain-induced injuries while boredom can lead to accidents and low quality output.

Most of these criticisms can be applied to the work in telephone call centres. The operator's response follows carefully detailed procedures. Performance (and probably pay) is measured by the number of calls taken per operator per hour and there are no opportunities for job enrichment, enlargement or rotation to ease the boredom.

Whilst it is true that organisations the world over have benefited from, and are continuing to use, techniques that have their origins in scientific management, in the West there is a reaction against the basic philosophy. A better educated workforce allows for the re-integration of task components and the exercise of discretion and judgement at the operator level.

8 Dr Strong

Top tips. This question invites a very wide-ranging answer. Note that it is only worth ten marks and do not let your enthusiasm run away with you! There are lots of points to make, but you must try even harder than usual to be concise. Note that a mention of *Burns and Stalker* and the organic-mechanistic spectrum is almost mandatory: their book was called *The Management of Innovation*, after all.

Easy marks. The characteristics of the organic organisation may well be worth up to half of the total available marks.

Dr Strong's system of management clearly does not support the innovatory science that the C Pharmaceutical Company depends on for its commercial success. Dr Strong's system, with its strict financial and personnel discipline, clearly **constrains the creativity** of the R&D unit's scientists.

It is widely accepted that a management system based on rules, procedures and routine (that is to say, a **bureaucratic** system) is unsuited to dealing with new problems and rapid developments. *Burns and Stalker* called such a system a **mechanistic** system and contrasted it with an **organic** (or **organismic**) system. The latter emphasises interactive teamwork, collaborative problem solving, respect for individual expertise at all levels and commitment to the overall task. This is likely to be very effective in contexts such as R&D.

However, such an approach is not a licence for random, unstructured activity more or less directed at a vague objective. There is still a need for **control of resources and effort**. In an organic system this is achieved largely by cultural means. There is a network structure of control, with decisions and plans being made after consultation with all parties concerned. The bureaucratic idea of power flowing down from the top of the hierarchy is largely abandoned: prestige and influence can exist anywhere and tend to revolve around expertise.

It is probably impossible for Dr Strong to preside over such a system, because of his commitment to the more formal current methods. **He may have to go**. However, scientists generally will find a more collegiate approach familiar and easy to operate. If it is necessary to replace Dr Strong, an important criterion for the selection of a replacement will be experience of operating a more organic system of management.

It would then be appropriate to **encourage teamwork and collaboration** within the R&D unit by employing suitable HRM policies. For example, recruitment should emphasise commitment to those ideals, appraisal should be based on actual work done rather than procedures adhered to and remuneration should be include an element of reward for team success. However, none of this should be done at the expense of individual creativity.

Innovation can be encouraged in other ways.

- Leaders must create a **vision and a climate of support** that takes a long-term view of R&D. Suitable targets should be set to cover both short and long-term timescales.

- **Risk** must be accepted. Not all programmes may come to fruition, but there must be no recriminations for failure not caused by incompetence.

- A careful watch should be kept on what is going on in the **wider pharmaceutical development world**. This is not so that so that ideas can be copied, but so that R&D staff can learn from others and are stimulated into speculation and experiment. It is also appropriate to keep abreast of emerging requirements for new products.

9 Virtual organisation

> **Top tips.** This is very much a knowledge-driven question. Either you have an idea of what a virtual organisation is or you don't. The sting in the tail is the requirement to account for the emergence of such organisations. Candidates who regularly read *The Economist* and a broadsheet newspaper would find themselves better prepared for this than those who do not.
>
> **Easy marks.** There are some very obvious features, such as email and other forms of electronic data transfer that could be mentioned here. From this, it is but a short step to deduce that physical products are unlikely to be the most important aspect of a virtual organisation: value added in the form of data, information and knowledge is likely to predominate.

The idea of a **virtual organisation** or **cybernetic corporation** has attracted considerable attention as the usefulness of IT for communication and control has been exploited. The essence of the virtual organisation is the electronic linking of spatially dispersed components. Such an organisation is a temporary or permanent collection of geographically dispersed individuals, groups, organisational units (which may or may not belong to the same organisation), or entire organisations that depend on electronic linking in order to complete the production process.

While there is some disagreement among academics as to a precise definition of the virtual organisation, a consensus exists with regard to **geographical dispersion** and the centrality of **information technology** to the production process. Many also agree that the virtual organisation has a temporary character. Other characteristics are a flexible structure and a collaborative culture.

Virtual organisations have developed for a variety of reasons. One important one is simply the recent availability of the internet computer and communications technology that makes it possible. This has permitted the creation of work networks that otherwise could not exist without physical presence in work premises. Another reason is the modern management tendency for organisations to concentrate on their core competences and buy in a range of services, which has increased the need for close collaboration with entities outside the organisation.

Some firms have entered into complex relationships with customers, suppliers and even competitors, giving rise to what has been called **network organisation**. Such organisations aim to exploit the benefits of collaboration where appropriate, without compromising independence too far. A simple example is the modern tendency to **outsourcing** of non-core activities. On a much larger scale, the *Toyota* system of manufacturing, with its emphasis on JIT calls for a great deal of co-ordination along the value chain. Competitors can collaborate in such matters as R&D and distribution channels, especially internationally. These networks are dispersed geographically and tend to rely to a great extent on sophisticated ITC technology,

However, an organisation is not a virtual organisation merely because it uses IT extensively and has multiple locations. Many academics would exclude organisations that use communications extensively, but not in a way critical to completing the production process.

10 Leadership style

> **Top tips.** This question may seem like an opportunity to discuss the organisational life cycle but such a discussion, no matter how detailed will not score many marks. This question is principally about leadership. Note that *Greiner's* life cycle model, while generally very useful, does not really deal with the phases mentioned in the question: birth, growth, maturity and decline.
>
> **Easy marks.** The phrase 'leadership style' indicates that one of the many spectrum models of leadership, such as that of Likert or the Ashridge College would form a good basis for an answer: an explanation of a chosen model could be worth two or three marks.

When a business is being set up from scratch, it will live almost from hand to mouth, making mistakes, exploiting opportunities and solving problems as they arise. There will usually only be a small group involved. Whether they are partners or a single principal and a few employees, the ethos is likely to be one of vision, creativity, flexibility, and community spirit. Effective leadership is therefore likely to be rather **democratic,** to encourage commitment and make maximum use of the available talent, when possible. However, founders with clear ideas of where they are going may be quite **autocratic,** and **crises are best managed firmly.**

A company that grows successfully will eventually find its progress limited by the **finite abilities of the founders.** They will discover that they cannot do everything and the **skills of professional specialists** like accountants, sales people and production engineers must be obtained if the concern is not to stagnate. Top management will now be at one remove from their staff, operations will be more complex and **a participative style will be more difficult to use.** For many companies this is a time of crisis as the founders lose their way.

If successful growth continues, overall management of the company can develop in different ways. **A simple, stable environment** may allow continuing firm direction from the top. However, a **complex or rapidly changing environment** may require extensive delegation of authority: a laissez-faire style of top management, in other words. On the other hand, severe external threats may still require a firm hand at the top.

A company can **decline** for a variety of reasons, including **management failure.** When decline is identified and acknowledged, hard decisions have to be taken, often redundancy and other severe effects on employees. This requires very competent leadership which can combine firmness of purpose in implementing difficult programmes with a maximum of consultation, communication and sympathy with the victims. The balance is very difficult to strike.

11 Sheila

> **Top tips.** This is a very interesting question, combining as it does business ethics with the concept of power. Both themes are the subject of considerable theoretical and academic attention, but it is important for you to deal with them in as practical a way as possible. Address the scenario!
>
> Candidates often have difficulty applying their theoretical knowledge in papers that require written answers. To help overcome this difficulty, we print the application points in this answer in *italic*. Note that we also continue to use italic for technical references and to indicate a particular emphasis on some words.
>
> **Easy marks.** The simple recommendations of the combined code, such as the appointment of independent and non-executive directors; separation of the roles of chairman and CEO; and the formation of a remuneration committee would provide three or four marks just for a mention, while relating them to the scenario would probably produce a pass mark.

No measures a board may take can **guarantee** that the CEO will not act illegally or unethically. If CEOs are to have the power to control their businesses effectively, they will inevitably have the power to do wrong. All that a board can do is to put in place mechanisms to discourage wrongdoing and to detect it before it goes too far.

A major precaution must lie in the process of **selecting** senior managers. *We are not told, but it may be that an investigation of Sheila's background could have revealed evidence of earlier sharp practice. Taking up references and checking qualifications is an important aspect of personnel selection.*

In the UK, investigations after a series of corporate scandals led to the Cadbury, Greenbury and Hampel reports on corporate governance. These reports made a series of recommendation that are now accepted as best practice and, indeed, are compulsory for listed companies.

One of the most important requirements is that the roles of chairman and chief executive should be **separate**. This acts as a check on the otherwise unfettered power of the person at the top.

Another very important rule is that there should be a substantial number of **non-executive directors** on the board. These non-executives should take responsibility for settling the remuneration packages of the executive directors. *This would have prevented Sheila from bribing Bob with a pay rise.* The non-executives should also form an **audit committee** to liaise with the auditors, and the directors generally should consider the need for **internal audit**. *A strong internal audit department with direct access to the audit committee would have formed a powerful check on Sheila's activities.*

A further measure the board might consider is protection for 'whistleblowers'. Persons within companies who report on the wrongdoing of others are frequently treated as troublemakers, often being dismissed. The establishment of a confidential hotline to an ethics referee would make whistleblowing safer. Such a referee could be an independent non-executive director or an external consultant.

12 Icebergs

> **Top tips.**
>
> - Managers make a major contribution to the informal organisation. *Mintzberg* mentions that managers have many contacts outside the chain of command.
>
> - The informal organisation is key in internal politics. The formal organisation by contrast may be mock bureaucracy.
>
> - A lighthearted survey in the Financial Times suggested that smokers, who congregate outside office buildings where smoking is prohibited, are becoming an informal organisation – the tobacco leaf, perhaps, has replaced the grapevine.
>
> - Do not confuse 'informal organisation' with 'organic organisation' as described by *Burns and Stalker*. Even the most rigid bureaucracy has a network of informal links.
>
> **Easy marks.** The subversive potential of the informal organisation is obvious to anyone who has ever worked in any but the smallest ones.

The **informal organisation** develops within an organisation as a means of communication, often stemming from the **social contacts** within the organisation. It utilises communications and cultural structures which are different from those provided by the formal organisation. If the formal structure does not provide adequate or flexible enough means for employees to get the job done, they will find ways of circumventing it and develop the informal structure.

Informal organisations develop through the social activities that employees carry out together, The informal groups created which then form part of the informal communications network in the organisation. Often peer groups, such as people who joined at the same time, constitute much of the informal organisation. The informal organisation is likely to **span the various levels and boundaries** of the organisation, extending to customers and suppliers, creating a network of contacts.

Disadvantages

(a) **Sub-optimal behaviour** can emerge if the informal organisation creates a culture or way of operating that is not beneficial to the organisation as a whole. This could occur throughout the organisation or as the result of an informal group operating in a part of the organisation.

(b)   **Resistance to management actions** could also cause considerable disruption to operations if the informal organisation encourages resistance.

(c)   **Influence** can be exerted by informal groups which could undermine management direction.

(d)   It is **hard to control**.

(e)   It is a **source of rumour** and misinformation.

Advantages

(a)   It is a good way of **disseminating information**. It can jump levels of hierarchy. Speeding up the communications process in this way may not be possible through the formal structure.

(b)   Although the managers should not use the informal network to manage the organisation, it is useful to be able to tap into the informal network to **keep close to what the employees, colleagues or rivals really think** about an issue.

(c)   Humans are social animals and therefore the informal contact can act as a **morale booster**, enabling people to get matters of their chest without fear of retribution.

13 Question with tutor's answer: Aerospace team 1

> **Top tips.** Another possible approach to 'the essential features of a team' would be to discuss *Tuckman's* roles. After our suggested solution we reproduce another answer to this question. This was prepared by a BPP tutor to illustrate a simple point-by-point approach. It was completed in the recommended time of 18 minutes and is considered to be worth a pass mark. The answer has been lightly edited for slips of the pen that might hamper understanding, but otherwise is printed as it was written.
>
> **Easy marks.** A definition is a good way to start a question like this: it need not be a quotation.

Part (a)

Katzenbach and Smith define a team as a 'small number of people with complementary skills who are committed to a common purpose, performance goals and approach for which they hold themselves basically accountable'.

Team working allows work to be shared among a number of individuals, so it gets done faster without people losing sight of their whole tasks or having to co-ordinate their efforts through lengthy channels of communication.

A team may be called together temporarily, to achieve specific task objectives (project team), or may be more or less permanent, with responsibilities for a particular product, product group or stage of the production process (a product or process team).

Part (b)

There are two basic approaches to the organisation of team work: multi-skilled teams and multi-disciplinary teams.

Multi-disciplinary teams

Multi-disciplinary teams bring together individuals with **different skills** and specialisms, so that their skills, experience and knowledge can be **pooled or exchanged**. Teamworking of this kind encourages freer and faster communication between disciplines in the organisation.

Multi skilled teams

A team may simply bring together a number of individuals who have **several skills** and can perform **any** of the group's tasks. These tasks can then be shared out in a more flexible way between group members, according to who is available and best placed to do a given job at the time it is required.

Team working will offer the T Aerospace Company a range of advantages over ordinary work group methods.

(a) Teamworking increases workers' awareness of their overall **objectives and targets**.

(b) Teamworking aids **co-ordination**.

(c) Teamworking helps to generate **solutions to problems**, and suggestions for improvements, since a multi-disciplinary team has access to more 'pieces of the jigsaw'.

(d) **Work organisation**. Teams combine the skills of different individuals and avoid complex communication between different business functions.

(e) **Control**. Fear of letting down the team can be a powerful motivator, hence teams can be used to control the performance and behaviour of individuals. Teams can also be used to resolve **conflict**.

(f) **Knowledge generation**. Teams can generate ideas.

(g) **Decision-making.** Teams can be set up to investigate new developments and decisions can be evaluated from more than one viewpoint.

Tutor's alternative answer

(a) A team has the following four essential features.

Common goals

Team members have common goals, aims, and purposes resulting in higher levels of goal congruence.

Defined roles

Belbin stated that certain roles must be present in a team in order for it to be successful, and furthermore these roles should be balanced i.e. one leader, one completer-finisher.

Good communication

Team members often share common language and terminology between them, for example an IT support team may talk to each other using technical phrases that non-team members may not , understand.

Cohesiveness

Members of an effective team work well together and are bound to each other by a common set of cultural norms; this increases loyalty and interaction amongst the group.

(b) The benefits that T-Aerospace can expect to see from the adoption of team working may include.

More and faster innovation

As the company will be drawing together different workers with different backgrounds and expertise it is likely that working together these multidisciplinary teams will be able to provide new engineering solutions that working alone they would not have achieved. For example if an electrician works with an interior designer it may be that the new application of electronics is found in some of the interior design of a new aircraft.

This advantage is likely to be particularly important to T-Aerospace as we are told that their "new technology… might provide them with a competitive edge.".

Given the relative importance of innovation in the aerospace industry as noted in the previous point a second major advantage the company may gain would be faster innovation from team working. This appears to be likely given that we are told that this is a benefit gained by some of the company's competitors after adopting team working practices.

Increased staff loyalty

If the company successfully adopts team working practices it can expect its staff to show more loyalty. In addition to the employees having loyalty to the company it is likely that they will also start to owe loyalty to other team members as friendships and personal relationships evolve. The positive impact of this for T-Aerospace may include lower staff turnover and increased morale, which should both lead to higher productivity in the longer term.

Multi-skilled staff

As mentioned earlier, if staff work in teams drawn from different backgrounds it is inevitable that there will be some knowledge and skills transfer. If for example an electrician works closely with a computer engineer they are both likely to learn from each other giving them broader skills set and enabling them to be able to perform a wider range of tasks. The benefit for the company is that it now has a more flexible, highly skilled workforce.

14 Question with tutor's answer: Aerospace Team 2

Top tips. There is a vast amount that could be said about the management of teams because we are talking about complex human behaviour, not just some simple management technique. Try to stick to concrete material in questions about people and the way they behave: there is plenty of experimental material and useful theory to talk about.

After our suggested solution we reproduce another answer to this question. This was prepared by a BPP tutor to illustrate a simple point-by-point approach. It was completed in the recommended time of 18 minutes and is considered to be worth a pass mark. The answer has been lightly edited for slips of the pen that might hamper understanding, but otherwise is printed as it was written.

Easy marks. This is quite a difficult question to answer well, but if you are familiar with the Hawthorne studies you should be able to deal with it quite well.

Management theory has long recognised that work group dynamics can operate against the corporate interest as easily as in favour of it. The classical description comes from the Bank Wiring Room observations during the Hawthorne experiments, where a determination to hold up piece rates by holding down output was noted.

That study also noted another common problem with teams, which is that conflict is inevitable where human beings are concerned. A constant dedication to mutual support is simply unattainable and the potential advantages of team working are undermined as a result.

Another problem with group behaviour is what *Janis* called **group think**. This is a cosy consensus that not only stifles creativity but can actually lead to a confident advance in quite the wrong direction. This is, perhaps, a special case of the common situation in which working in a team simply is not the best way to proceed. Some problems require individual flair and drive if a quick, workable solution is to be reached.

A final problem for T Aerospace is the role of the manager in team working. We are not told the exact nature of the 'negative experiences' some managers have had. However, a common problem is the inability of the authoritarian manager even to understand the potential benefits of a more participative style, let alone implement it. The role of the manager in team working is not necessarily diminished but is changed to one of coaching and facilitating.

These are all problems that managers must solve.

Subversive behaviour must be detected by close observation and tackled by a combination of discipline and leadership. This may take a long time, especially if the T Aerospace workforce has become disaffected by a history of bad treatment, real or perceived. Counselling and intergroup transfers may help.

Conflict between individuals can be tackled in the same way.

Group think and other types of poor performance are partly cultural problems and the remedy must come from the top. If innovation and drive are required they must be encouraged by example and appropriately rewarded. There must be some freedom to fail, where possible and appropriate. An aerospace company may have a particular problem here, with its over-riding need for reliability in its products.

The main problem T Aerospace will have will be with its managers. They will have to implement all these improvements and do it in a new and unfamiliar way. The company will find it necessary to provide extensive training for its managers and may have to recruit some new ones.

Tutor's alternative answer

The difficulties that T-Aerospace may encounter in its management of teams may include;

Resistance from managers

Some of the existing management teams have had negative experiences of team working in the past, as such they are likely to resist any move to implement new working procedures.

The best way to overcome this is likely to involve consultation with these managers. If we could find out what caused their negative experiences in the past and take their views on board when implementing our new system this will help allay their fears as well as possibly getting them to 'buy into' the process.

Lack of team working skills

Team working will require additional and new skills for our existing workforce. If they have previously worked as individuals they are unlikely to be able to immediately work as effectively in teams, causing short-term falls in productivity.

A solution to this problem may well to be to provide teamwork training courses, or to recruit and selection staff with a team working background. It would also be necessary to make senior management aware of the likely impact on productivity, thus ensuring realistic budgets and targets are set during the transitional phase.

Resistance to change

It is well known that people do not like change, and that this intolerance increases with age. A change in working practices will involve physiological, physiological, and circumstantial change for the majority of the workforce, in the form of new working hours, colleagues, shift patterns etc. This could result in staff resistance to change, industrial action if the workforce is unionised, or falls in morale and productivity.

Staff resistance is best overcome by using experts in change management. Appointing an experienced change manager, 'champion of change', will ensure that appropriate levels of communication, counselling, consultation, and coercion are used when necessary. This should help minimise any passive or active resistance to change.

Concern over loss of work specialisation

It appears that the company has a culture that values 'experts', being employees who have highly developed, but narrow skill sets. In an industry where expertise, accuracy, and reliability are crucial a loss of skills will adversely affect the companies abilities to maintain quality and innovate. Again this perception amongst staff over loss of skills could cause a lowering of staff morale or increase staff turnover.

This concern could be allayed by again consulting with staff and management. It is likely that the company will continue to employ people because of their high degrees of specialisation and provide training to support this. However if it can be explained and demonstrated that these skills will be enhanced, rather than degraded by team working then the workforce may see the changes in a more positive light.

Co-ordination of the workforce

The company is likely to move towards a matrix structure in order to create multi-disciplinary teams. This is turn is likely to make it harder to control and co-ordinate its workforce. Additionally this could make the staff a more difficult resource to drive efficiently.

The company may need to invest in new human resource software in order to be able to track and allocate its staff efficiently. A new layer of management may also be required, as a matrix structure requires each team member to report into a project manager as well as their line manager.

15 Joan Timmins

> **Top tips.** This is a simple question about management style that could be answered by reference to any of the style spectrum models.
>
> Candidates often have difficulty applying their theoretical knowledge in papers that require written answers. To help overcome this difficulty, we print the application points in this answer in *italic*. Note that we also continue to use italic for technical references and to indicate a particular emphasis on some words.
>
> **Easy marks.** It would be possible to score close to 50% on this question by setting out an appropriate theory of leadership style and identifying two things: where Joan Timmins style lies on the model, and where her subordinates' expectations lie. You should bring any personal experience you may have to bear in questions like this.

Style is a difficult factor to measure or define. Most of the early theories were based on the different uses made of authority. Some of the leadership theories present two basic choices – a task centred leader on the one hand and an employee-centred one on the other. *Likert's* theory offers four choices and the managerial grid offers five. *Huneryager and Heckman* identified four different management styles.

- **Dictatorial style** – where the leader forces subordinates to work by threatening punishment and penalties.

- **Autocratic style** – where decision-making is centralised in the hands of the leader, who does not encourage participation by subordinates.

- **Democratic style** – where decision-making is decentralised, and shared by subordinates in participative group action.

- **Laissez-faire style** – where subordinates are given little or no direction at all, and are allowed to establish their own objectives and make all their own decisions.

The style of a manager is essentially how he or she operates, but it is a function of many factors – one of which is culture. *Joan Timmins has moved from a military position, with its authoritarian style of leadership, to her current position as Head of the Finance department of the SOFT corporation and is finding that the style of management she is used to is not going down well in the new environment. Her style is still authoritarian. All decisions are taken by her, with little or no discussion with the subordinates, and possibly not even with fellow members of the top management team. Unfortunately for Joan, this style is causing resentment.* What generally happens in this type of situation is that the work gets done, but productivity is both very low and quality indifferent, or it requires a high level of overheads to ensure that there is any output at all.

It is obvious that her new team expect a different, more participative style of leadership. Recommendations should be made to Joan to adopt a participative or democratic style of management.

At SOFT, the leaders share their decision-making activities with their subordinates as much as possible while not compromising their ultimate responsibility or authority. Much decision making, therefore, is done using discussion and consultation, either on a formal or informal basis. This approach permits effective delegation and is thus highly motivational. There must always be scope for individuality of working, and hence idea generation, if a business is to succeed and continue to be successful. The democratic process creates the environment for this to grow. Likert is the leading advocate of this general approach, linking together worker satisfaction and high company effectiveness as resulting from a democratic management approach.

16 Disciplinary procedure

Top tips. This is a fairly easy question to score a pass mark on if you have a reasonable idea of what discipline is and some knowledge of modern disciplinary procedures.

However, note carefully the use of the word 'why' in the question .You are **not** being asked what discipline is, you are being asked **why** discipline is a good idea.

Easy marks. Speed, consistency and fairness are obvious requirements of any disciplinary system.

Discipline promotes order and good behaviour in an organisation by enforcing acceptable standards of conduct. It can be enforced by sanctions, encouraged by example or created by individuals' own sense of what is fitting and proper.

The purpose of disciplinary action is not punishment or retribution. It should have as its goal the **improvement of the future behaviour** of the employee and other members of the organisation. The purpose obviously is the avoidance of similar occurrences in the future.

Disciplinary action tends to generate **resentment** because it is an unpleasant experience. The challenge is to apply the necessary disciplinary action so that it will be least resented. A formal, written disciplinary procedure can enhance and support the maintenance of workplace discipline by ensuring consistency, speed, transparency and fairness of application.

(a) Discipline must be **consistent** in application. Inconsistency is bad for morale and brings the whole system into disrepute. Those responsible for administering discipline must know in detail what is expected of them so that the system runs satisfactorily.

(b) Disciplinary action should be taken as **speedily** as possible, subject to the need to investigate thoroughly while at the same time avoiding haste.

(c) **Transparency** is an important contributor to fairness; people subject to disciplinary rules must not only know what those rules are, but also how they are to be administered and enforced. This is so important that many national legal systems include rules with which the procedures of individual organisations must comply.

(d) **Fairness** is provided for by incorporating legal principles such as proper rules of evidence and natural justice into the organisation's procedures.

There is no doubt that NYO needs a comprehensive and workable disciplinary system. Its business of providing financial advice makes it subject to specific rules relating to investment markets and professional conduct. NYO's employees will be subject to considerable temptation to infringe such rules, especially if they are paid by commission. The continuing investigations and reforms relating to the mis-selling of financial products in the UK illustrate this. It will be essential for NYO to be able to demonstrate to regulators and customers that they have in place an effective and robust system for dealing with transgressions.

A statutory disciplinary procedure exists within the UK. This includes a requirement for careful investigation of any disciplinary incident and gives any work person the right to be accompanied by an advisor at any disciplinary meeting.

17 Preparation question: performance appraisal

(a)   The general purpose of any assessment or appraisal is to improve the efficiency of the organisation by ensuring that the individual employees are performing to the best of their ability and developing their potential for improvement. Performance appraisal may be defined as 'the regular and systematic review of performance and the assessment of potential with the aim of producing action programmes to develop both work and individuals.'

The common objectives of a formal performance appraisal system include the following:

- To enable a picture to be drawn up of the human 'stock' of an organisation – its strengths and weaknesses, enabling more effective personnel planning

- To monitor the undertaking's initial selection procedures against the subsequent performance of recruits, relative to the organisation's expectations

- To establish what the individual has to do in a job in order that the objectives for the section or department are realised

- To assess an individual's current level of job performance. This can be used both as a base line against which performance can be measured in future and as a means of deciding how the individual has improved since the last performance appraisal. It allows managers and subordinates to plan personnel and job objectives in the light of performance

- To identify weaknesses in an individual's performance and identify training needs. Actual performance is compared with pre-defined objectives; shortcomings in performance are then used as indicators of the training required to achieve improvements. Training needs may arise for reasons other than the capabilities of individuals, such as new demands made by changing legislation, new technology and so on. Once training has taken place, performance appraisal enables some evaluation of training effectiveness

- To assess the level of reward payable for an individual's efforts, eg, in merit payment systems. It represents an opportunity to provide positive feedback to employees on their performance and to set new targets and challenges for the coming period along with the a reminder of possible rewards

- To assess potential. At the organisational level this permits career and succession planning. At the individual level it permits superior and subordinate to assess the most effective development plans for the subordinate.

(b)   A problem with many appraisal schemes in practice is that they concentrate exclusively on the individual subordinate. In other words they reinforce hierarchy, and are perhaps unsuitable to organisations where the relationship between management and their subordinates is fluid or participatory. Upward, customer and 360° appraisals address this, but they are not widely adopted.

Appraisal systems, because they target the individual's performance, concentrate on the lowest level of performance feedback. They ignore the organisational and systems context of that performance. For example, if any army is badly led, no matter how brave the troops, it is likely to be defeated. Appraisal schemes would seem to regard most organisation problems as a function of the personal characteristics of its members, rather than as symptomatic of wider dysfunction.

A performance appraisal system is designed by specialists in the technostructure and operated by managers in the middle line. Its effectiveness depends on a number of factors.

- The effort line managers are prepared to put into the appraisal process

- The integrity of line managers

- The ability of line managers to do more than just give good appraisals to people who have a similar personality and background

- The congruence between what the organisation actually wants and the behaviours it is prepared to reward

The effectiveness of any appraisal system relies heavily on the quality and reliability of assessment. Variations in the consistency of reporting standards can quickly lead to a feeling of dissatisfaction and injustice. There are many potential sources of rating errors including, for example, perceptual distortions such as stereotyping and the halo effect. Where a senior manager has the opportunity to confirm the ratings and countersign the appraisal this may help to identify inconsistencies and those appraisers who appear to be too generous or too critical in their assessments.

However well designed the appraisal system it is not possible to apply a completely objective approach to every unique situation. The system should therefore always allow for at least a degree of discretion and personal judgement. The reporting system should give the appraiser an opportunity to record formally any necessary qualifications to the given ratings.

The appraisal may tend to concentrate too much on feedback on past performance and especially on the recent past. The lapse of time between events which occurred early in the reporting period and completing the appraisal may lead to a distortion in the overall flavour of the report. Although reviewing past performance is an integral part of the appraisal system, it is even more important to concentrate attention on the changes required to bring about an improvement in future performance.

In some organisations the problems associated with performance appraisal have been recognised and management have taken steps taken to limit their detrimental effect.

- Competence-based frameworks have been introduced that focus on the performance rather than on the qualities of the appraisee. This can increase the objectivity of the appraisal.

- Appraisal is becoming more recognised by senior management as a benefit to the organisation. This has been driven to some extent by employment protection legislation requiring a less arbitrary approach to such matters as reward, promotion, discipline and dismissal. Schemes of integrated performance management have been introduced, incorporating appraisal within a wider, structured approach to the management of the human resource.

18 Functions

> **Top tips.** The requirement to illustrate your answer with examples from an organisation with which you are familiar is unusual, though by no means unique to this question. What are you to do if you are unable to give examples from an organisation with which you are familiar? Invent some. We have used an entirely imaginary organisation.
>
> Candidates often have difficulty applying their theoretical knowledge in papers that require written answers. To help overcome this difficulty, we print the application points in this answer in *italic*. Note that we also continue to use italic for technical references and to indicate a particular emphasis on some words.
>
> **Easy marks.** You are given the functions of management in the question requirement: do not be tempted to invent two of your own! We deal with all five for completeness.

We cannot do better than to combine and paraphrase the descriptions of these activities provided by *Drucker* and *Fayol*. We illustrate them with examples from the practice of Albert-Delameter Ltd (ADL), a large privately owned machine tool manufacturer specialising in the manufacture of sophisticated spline-shaft broaching machines.

Planning consists of the selection of objectives and the strategies, policies, programmes and procedures for achieving them. Drucker emphasise that targets must be quantified. *ADL do not have a mission statement in the commonly accepted sense but the Chairman regards it as the role of the company to make a decent profit by manufacturing machines of good workmanlike quality for the general engineering industry. Spline-shaft broaching machines are rather specialised machine tools, so ADL works closely with its customers to modify existing designs and create new ones to satisfy their requirements. Manufacture is planned for up to one year ahead, as the lead*

time for a new batch of machines can be several months, and is carried out by a works planning cell whose supervisor reports to the works manager.

Organising, according to Fayol involves establishing a structure of **tasks** to be performed to achieve the organisation's goals, grouping these tasks into **jobs** for individuals, creating **groups of jobs** to create departments, delegating **authority** to carry out the jobs and providing systems of **information**. Organising therefore inherently includes the design of the organisation. *ADL is a hybrid organisation. Its fundamental structure is functional, but superimposed on this is a project organisation for the introduction of new products. These normally appear in response to customer requirements and project teams including representatives of sales, costing, design and production engineering are set up as required.*

Communicating is not specifically defined as a management function in this sense by either Fayol or Drucker. However, Fayol speaks of **commanding** and **co-ordinating**. By commanding, he means **giving instructions** to subordinates to carry out tasks over which the manager has authority for decisions and responsibility for performance. By co-ordinating he means **harmonising the activities** of individuals and groups within the organisation. Drucker speaks of managers communicating **targets** and providing the **information people need** to do their work. *The CEO of ADL has made it his business to ensure that people throughout the organisation are aware of what is going on by means of quarterly face-to-face briefings. There are usually two or three sessions each quarter to ensure maximum attendance. The briefings are held in the works canteen. They rarely last more than half an hour and include a summary of achievements, problems and future prospects.*

For Fayol, **controlling** means measuring the activities of individuals and groups, to ensure that their performance is in accordance with plans. Deviations from plan are identified and corrected. This is a simple description of a cybernetic or feedback control system. *ADL uses a normal system of budgetary control for its continuing operations. The production engineering and works planning staff are able to make accurate forecasts of cost because of their training and experience; the works manager and his assistants use these estimates in a flexible way to control costs.*

Drucker, writing much later than Fayol differs from him in his awareness of the human resource management role of managers. He regards it as fundamental that managers both **motivate** and **develop** their employees. The manager 'brings out what is in them or he stifles them. He strengthens their integrity or he corrupts them'. *ADL's HR manager refined the company's payment scheme to give greater emphasis to individual achievement. The company operates a single-status pay scheme, with all employees receiving a monthly salary. There was already a company-wide bonus scheme in existence, with payment based on annual profits. This has been modified so that managers can recommend individuals for extra bonuses for good performance. In addition to this and the communication programme outlined above, the company also ensures that its managers are trained in the skills of people management, using* Adair's **contingency based scheme**. *Newly appointed managers are sent off-site for two days to HR consultants who provide appropriate training.*

19 Question with analysis: Stress management

Top tips. The scenario is very brief but, even so, the marking scheme requires answers to refer to it in order to score well. Notice how our opening paragraph explains how stress can harm the running of an organisation and how it can be unrelated to work.

Easy marks. Stress is regularly mentioned in the business press and many organisations have undertaken stress management programmes. You should have been able to mention two or three measure that could be taken from your general knowledge.

Examiner's comments. There was some failure to read the question carefully and to discuss the consequences of stress rather than how the problems it presents could be overcome.

People who are over-stressed are likely to display a range of symptoms that can **prejudice the efficient running of the organisation**. These can include deterioration in personal relationships, absenteeism, irrational behaviour and impaired work performance. In an organisation such as a bank, with its emphasis on correct procedure, such effects can be particularly significant. Work itself and workplace relationships can be significant sources of stress, though they are not the only ones: domestic concerns can be equally significant. Whatever its origin, stress is a problem that managers must be prepared to manage.

Part of the problem is that many high achievers cope well with stress. Such people tend to do well and be promoted and, as a result, **it is common for managers to be unaware of the significance of stress** in their organisations or to underestimate its importance. The first step for T to take would be to **promote understanding among managers of its significance**. This could be combined with an acknowledgement of the problem of stress to the workforce at all levels through the launch of a stress management programme. The aim should be to encourage the staff of X Investment Bank to accept the existence of stress as a problem and, in the case of those affected by it and their managers, to take positive steps to deal with it.

T should take a proactive stance and attempt to establish the incidence and effects of stress within the organisation. Such a **stress audit** might be undertaken through a programme of interviews or by means of confidential questionnaires, possibly involving external consultants to ensure confidentiality. It is **unlikely that the appraisal system** would be a suitable mechanism for such an investigation, though managers should certainly be encouraged to use every opportunity to establish the incidence of stress within the Bank.

Workplace stress may be induced by aspects of the job content or the physical work environment and by the formal and informal social aspects of the employment. There are not likely to be any major stress-inducing aspects of the **work environment** in a bank compared with, say, a foundry, but job content or social factors may be significant.

When T has a better idea of the extent to which stress is a problem in the Bank, he might then take steps to deal with it. These might have two aspects: first, removing or reducing as many as possible of the **factors that produce stress**; and second, **ameliorating the effect** of any remaining factors.

In a bank, the need for accuracy, judgement and caution may clash with the drive for expansion and profit, for example, producing stress in the managers responsible for **reconciling these conflicting objectives**. Similarly, unsympathetic superiors and irritating colleagues, themselves stressed by the demands of their roles, can exist in almost any job.

It is unlikely that all stress-inducing factors can be removed from any work and it may be that some degree of stress is an important **spur to high performance**. However, employers must take care that they do not allow stress to have adverse effects on their employees' health. **Counselling programmes** are becoming common: they are a good way to both monitor the incidence of stress and to provide some amelioration where it is required.

20 PB Company

Pass marks. Note the way we have chosen to lay out our answer to this question. This is not the only possibility – you could also set out the agenda and append notes below it – but this has the advantage of dealing with one thing at a time.

Easy marks. Any meeting other than the most informal ones is likely to include simple predictable items such as the minutes of the last meeting. Most of the items in the left hand column of our table are entirely predictable and between them might produce as many as three marks.

Outline agenda for Saturday's meeting

Agenda Item	Reason for inclusion
Open the meeting and welcome representatives	Important because representatives will have given up part of their weekend to attend. Need to recognise this and try and decrease the amount of hostility for being at the meeting.

Agenda Item	Reason for inclusion
Apologies for absence	Some representatives may have wanted to attend, but can't for various reasons. These names should be recorded to show they do have an interest in the proceedings.
Minutes of last meeting	As this is a one-off meeting, there is no need to have the minutes or similar formalities.
Agree items for discussion	The main item for discussion will be the proposed change to working conditions. It is important to confirm this and also produce a longer list of other grievances. If other problems are recognised then these can be left for later discussion and not 'get in the way' of the main issue.
Discuss the proposed change in providing demonstrations to potential customers.	It is important to obtain a detailed list of objections; only then can specific actions be taken to overcome those objections. Record comments on a flip chart so representatives can see what is being discussed.
Agree action plans	For each specific problem area, try and agree an action, although some actions may be very limited where company policy cannot be changed. State trying to be helpful but some items become difficult, if not impossible, to change.
Discuss other issues.	Any other problem areas can be discussed, if there is time.
Confirm dates for action plans	Agree dates when minutes and then actions resulting from the meeting will be distributed to all attendees.
Close the meeting	With thanks for attending and being willing to discuss views openly.

21 Question with answer plan: Workload

Pass marks. This is a very practical question, as questions on this topic tend to be. There is little theory to consider and it is appropriate to plunge straight into sensible recommendations.

Easy marks. Laura's actions to improve her own time management are standard and should be easy to note down if you have done even a little preparation for this topic.

Part (a)

Answer plan

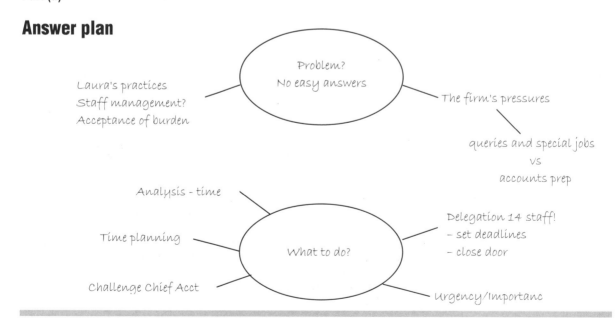

BPP
PROFESSIONAL EDUCATION

Managing Laura's workload

No easy answers. In situations such as this, it is easy to take a one-sided view and either blame Laura entirely for being overworked, or blame her employers for over-working her. In practice, both are probably to blame.

If Laura appears willing to work long hours, then her employers will, inevitably, take this for granted. However, the ability to 'manage the boss' is an important facet of surviving in organisations and Laura should manage her boss and her time more effectively.

(a) **Laura's own approach to time management**

Laura allows herself tends to be a victim of events. She allows events such as interruptions from assistants to happen 'to' her. She does not shape what goes on.

Laura is perhaps not suited to the job. Laura does not appear to enjoy the HRM aspects of the job. If she embraced these more forcefully, she might save time in the end, by matching the development of her staff with a reduction in her workload.

Laura is not using her staff profitably. Laura could make their jobs more interesting, give them more responsibility and save himself time.

Urgency and importance. Laura perhaps does not ask the chief accountant whether the ad hoc projects are as urgent as she thinks they are. They may not need to take priority over other things.

(b) **The firm's approach to Laura**. The firm does not make it easy for Laura to prioritise her time. When she is doing monthly and quarterly accounts, she should not be interrupted with ad hoc projects. The chief accountant should act as a filtering mechanism for these.

Actions Laura should take

(a) As a first step, she should **keep a time diary** over a typical month. Although time consuming in itself, this should enable her to see where particular problems lie. Interruptions are disruptive not only because of the time they take, but also because they interrupt Laura's train of thought and make her work more difficult to complete. Interruption is one of the essential characteristics of a manager's job (according to Mintzberg) – **but Laura's job is not solely managerial, as it has a technical aspect**.

(b) Once she has reviewed the results of her time diary, she can then plan her time better. This means reviewing the extent to which she is available to her assistants (eg to discuss queries, which might all be dealt with together), the importance of deadlines and so on.

(c) She can increase **delegation** – some of the assistants should be suitable candidates, especially if the delegated tasks can be part of their training.

(d) She can institute a **closed door policy** on occasions to let her get on with her technical tasks.

(e) **She should set her team deadlines** and allocate their work so that it ties in easily with her own; in other words she should ensure that, for month-end and quarterly reporting, she is undisturbed and that they are working on other things. She needs to establish a routine for the department.

(f) She should arrange a **meeting with the chief accountant** to **agree priorities**. In the case of ad hoc assignments given to her when she is busy, she should learn to say 'no' on occasions. This means educating her boss into giving adequate notice and details – not the easiest things to do, but necessary nonetheless. The boss can also let her know how long a project will take. She may have no idea as to the complexity of some of the tasks she has asked him to do. Some of the ad hoc tasks can be given to one of her juniors.

(g) She should learn to distinguish **between urgency and importance**. Importance can be assessed in relation to her own mission in the organisation. Monthly and quarterly financial reporting is **always important** and always **urgent** at the month end. Ad hoc projects may appear urgent, if the person requesting it would like an answer tomorrow, but Laura might have to say 'no' – unless of course it is the managing director.

(h) Eventually, she might want to **restructure her job** – but the firm may not take kindly to requests for this nature.

Part (b)

How Laura should delegate. By delegating authority to subordinates, the superior takes on the extra tasks of calling the subordinates to account for their decisions and performance, and also of co-ordinating the efforts of different subordinates.

(a)   The **expected performance levels** (the expected results) of the subordinate should be clearly specified (ie determine the required results). These should be fully understood and accepted by the subordinate. These can be quantified as SMART objectives.

(b)   **Tasks should be assigned** to the subordinate who should agree to do them.

(c)   **Resources should be allocated** to the subordinate to enable him to carry out his tasks at the expected level of performance, and authority should be delegated to enable the subordinate to do this job.

(d)   **Responsibility should be exacted** from the subordinate by the superior for results obtained (because ultimate responsibility remains with the superior).

(e)   The **subordinate's ability and experience must be borne in mind** when allocating tasks and responsibilities, since it is highly damaging to allocate tasks beyond a subordinate's capabilities.

(f)   **Frequent contact must be maintained** between superior and subordinate to review the progress made and to discuss constructive criticism.

(g)   **The delegate must be properly advised** as to what is wanted and when.

A subordinate **may** have written or unwritten authority to do the job. Written authority is sometimes preferable because it removes the room for doubt and argument. Authority may also be general or specific.

(a)   It is general if the subordinate is given authority to make any decisions with regard to a certain (specified) area of the operations – **he or she is put in charge**.

(b)   It is specific if the subordinate has authority to make certain limited and identified decisions within that area of operations. General authority gives the subordinate greater discretion and flexibility.

As has been suggested above, Laura can, by delegating, cover two aspects of her job at once. Not only can she make her own life easier, but she can contribute to the development of her assistants. She is responsible for their professional development: delegating tasks to them, with appropriate supervision, satisfies this requirement.

22 ICC

> **Top tips**. A difficult question – ICC already has some of the features of a matrix structure, outlined in part (a) at international level, but, within each country, the two divisions operate separately. So part (b) implies that the matrix structure should be taken further at country level.
>
> **Easy marks.** This is quite a complex technical problem. However, like all questions it has its easy marks. These revolve around the nature of the matrix structure, the organisational problems it addresses and the extra complexities it introduces. This is all basic theoretical material that you should be familiar with.

Part (a)

Why ICC has chosen a matrix structure

For many years it has been the principle of organisation design that there should be a **direct line of command**, with one person having one boss. How jobs were distributed in that particular hierarchy varied from business to business: some might have arranged their organisational hierarchies by job specialisation (functional organisation), others by geography (every body reports to local, area, regional managers etc) or by product divisionalisation or market.

In practice, most firms employed a **hybrid approach**; some functions (eg research and development) were centralised, whereas others (eg manufacturing and marketing) might have been arranged on an area basis. **ICC has faced the classical disadvantages of such an approach, and these are the reasons why it perhaps has chosen the matrix structure**. There might be very good reasons for hardware to be structured by product division, and equally sensible reasons whereas service contracts, dealing with the firm's relationships with its customers should be structured in another way.

Whilst **ICC is a global company**, it chooses to co-ordinate some of its activities by country. Because S&M and SES operate as divisions, it is likely that the **actual power of the country vice-presidents to set strategy is very limited**.

The **matrix structure** is more than just a co-ordination mechanism or a system of internal politics. It is consciously adopted as a structure, because **any other type of structure over-simplifies an essentially complex decision system**. For example, the needs of customers differ from country to country, and each country itself may be seen as a market in its own right with its own characteristics. Simply running S&M and SES from the US without regard for the context in which they will operate is not optimal; a local supplier can always come up with a product that might be better tailored to the local market. Furthermore, the **customer does not see S&M and SES as two separate entities but as two faces of one corporation**. To refer all co-ordination to a distant head office in the US is clearly impractical.

ICC's arrangements fall down because SES and S&M are largely independent of each other, and report back to separate offices. It features **two lines of authority, only loosely co-ordinated at country level**.

Part (b)

Changing the structure at country level

Currently, at **country level, the two divisions act independently**, although each reports, at a senior level to the country vice president, as do other business functions such as finance.

The **problems described are not necessarily caused by poor organisation structure**. Perhaps in their zeal to sell more, S&M have **not been selling entirely appropriate products** – if their performance is based on sales, they would have an incentive sell whatever they could, especially if another division is left picking up the costs and clearing up the mess. Not enough is known about the system of **performance assessment and incentives**.

The S&M function should have correctly ascertained the performance levels required by the clients – this seems like a failure of management and market research not co-ordination as such. However, certain **types** of system configuration might be particularly difficult to maintain.

Possible structural causes of these problems

(a)   **Hoarding of information** by different divisions; information is not seen as a corporate resource in a heavily bureaucratic organisation

(b)   **People not knowing** who to direct sales leads to: an excessively vertical chain of command leads to information going up the chain of command rather than horizontally along the gangplanks. There might be reasonable co-ordination at strategic level, but a lack of it at implementation level.

(c)   **Sales leads are not really seen as SES's responsibility**.

Advantages of introducing a matrix structure.

(a)   **Better co-ordination** across the value chain – in this case, sales and after-sales service would be better co-ordinated, as far as the customer is concerned.

(b)   **Greater awareness** of the strategic realities facing the different activities. S&M staff would not sell systems which SES find hard to maintain – S&M staff can communicate the necessary performance standards to SES staff.

(c)   Any **potential problems are flagged in advance**, as the maintenance implications of any contract can be described before the final proposal to the client. This will lead to increased customer satisfaction and lower costs in running the maintenance department.

(d)   There should be better management. People are not classified according to the functions they fulfil but their role in promoting the wider success of the organisation.

Drawbacks

(a)   Introducing a complex matrix system at country level will almost certainly lead to a **greater level of bureaucracy**, in that decisions will have to be co-ordinated. Decision-making might be slower than before.

(b)   Inevitably this will give **greater power to the country managers** and will weaken the reporting links within S&M and SES globally.

(c)   ICC may have **clients** who themselves are global companies. They may prefer to **deal with the divisions on a product rather than on a country basis**.

Part (c)

Management problems of the matrix form.

(a)   A greater **capacity for conflict**, between departmental and project managers. There is more scope for internal politics if there are many sources of authority.

(b)   **Wasted management time** and slowness of decision-making as many different people have to be consulted.

(c)   **Confusion as to who has the final say** in areas of disagreement.

(d)   **Stress**, as many people do not like working in environments of ambiguity.

(e)   **Difficulties in measuring performance** and reward.

(f)   Managers have to spend **more time consulting** and negotiating with equals than giving orders to their juniors, or taking them from their superiors. Their juniors have other people to appeal to.

Given these problems, the success of matrix management cannot be guaranteed. Success can, however, be made more likely if the following are in place.

(a)   Visible **senior management commitment** to the new organisation structure.

(b)   **Clear briefing and management training**. Training courses will cover the reasons for the new structure, together, perhaps with lessons from other successful users of the matrix form. The new management environment will be very different.

(c)   **Clear guidelines for responsibility and accountability**, especially with regard to profit centres and so on. In such cases, an attractive grand plan can be fatally undermined by poor implementation. This means that the costing and accounting systems should be in place. It is possible that a new profit centre organisation may have to be introduced.

(d)   **Appropriate information systems** so that functional managers can get some idea how the resources under their command are going to be used.

(e)   A culture which encourages more **open communication**. Although matrix organisation does not necessarily encourage the development of an organic culture, such a culture applied in certain areas of BMC (not throughout the whole company).

23 Work performance

Part (a)

An interview is an important managerial task and should be planned and conducted carefully so it achieves its purpose.

The first arrangements to be made are the logistical ones of **place and time**. If Jane does not have her own office, she must make arrangements for the use of a private room were they will not be interrupted. Even if she does have an office, she should consider this option as being more likely to ensure privacy. She should also decide what to do about the **telephone.** The meeting should have been arranged for a time convenient to both parties. Jane should attempt to be disciplined in her use of time, but in a case like this where personal problem may be involved, it would be prudent to allow for an over-run.

Jane must be sure what her objectives are holding this interview. Her overall objective is to guide the staff member back to acceptable performance but it is probably too much to expect that this can be achieved with one interview. Her first aim must be to discover what has led to the deterioration in performance. Only when she knows that can she formulate a plan. It may be possible to glean a good deal of information from colleagues before the interview; this may enable her to prepare a choice of **possible approaches** if the situation becomes clear. These could range from counselling through offering advice and giving instructions to referring the matter to a higher authority if it warrants it.

Jane must control the interview. Her first objective will be for the staff member to communicate as much as possible. This implies a **careful use of questioning and listening skills**. She must establish the legitimacy of her concern about the deteriorating performance and then use open questions to persuade the staff member to speak. These are questions which cannot be answered with simple affirmatives or negatives. An example would be 'please tell me what is on your mind'. Full answers can be encouraged by attentive body language and interjection such as 'I see' and 'go on'.

If Jane obtains sufficient information to make her feel that the matter can be dealt with there and then, she can become more direct in her approach.

Part (b)

Formal appraisal interviews are often used to **sweep up** a number of minor points which have occurred in the previous period. This is because managers' time is always limited, especially when they have their own professional responsibilities, as is always the case in accountancy. However, it is really only appropriate for non-urgent matters, which the present case is not. **Managers should not limit their supervisory input to formal appraisal only.** They must be prepared to deal with problems of performance quickly. The next formal appraisal interview is three months away and Jane must tackle this problem in the immediate future. This is partly because the staff member's behaviour is unacceptable and partly because it is atypical and may be a good opportunity to review progress.

Part (c)

Discipline promotes good order and behaviour in an organisation by enforcing acceptable standards of conduct. There is a possibility in this case that the staff member's behaviour may eventually lead to a disciplinary procedures must be carefully **controlled** so that there can be no subsequent accusations of **unfairness** or **justice**. The UK has a statutorily prescribed disciplinary procedure. Among other provisions, this gives an employee attending a disciplinary meeting the right to be accompanied by a trade union official or other supporter.]

There is thus a considerable difference between the informal interview which Jane is planning and a disciplinary meeting. The one is largely about communication and, possibly counselling and problem solving; the other is the culmination of a **formal procedure of investigation.**

Nevertheless, because any staff problem may eventually lead to disciplinary action, Jane should put a **summary of the interview** on the staff member's **personal file.**

24 PSTV

Top tips. This question is a gift for the well prepared candidate since it deals with very basic structural theory. However, it is **essential** to pick up on the use of the work 'organic' in part (b) and recognise that *Burns and Stalker's* model is required.

Easy marks. The basic characteristics of bureaucracy as defined by *Weber* would be worth at least three marks in part (a). Similarly, in part (b) pointing out the contrasting features of the organic approach would be valuable basis for an answer.

Part (a)

Bureaucracy is a form of structure to be found in many large-scale organisations. *Weber* suggested that the decisive reason for the advance of bureaucratic organisation is its purely **technical superiority** over any other form of organisation.

The term has always had connotations of red tape and rigidity; though in the study of organisations and management it is important that the term is used objectively, meaning certain structural features of formal organisations.

Bureaucracies have a **formal structure**, and operate by well-established **rules and procedures**. Job descriptions establish definite tasks for each person and procedures are established for many work routines, communication between individuals and departments, the settlement of disputes and for appeals.

(a)   The organisation structure defines the **authority** and **responsibility** of individual managers, who enact the role expected of their position.

(b)   Individuals are required to perform their jobs to the full, but not to overstep the boundaries of their authority. Line management will accept advice from the technostructure when such advice seems necessary or appropriate.

(c)   Since a wide variety of people are capable of doing the same job, the efficiency of this organisation depends on the **structuring of jobs** and the **design of communications** and **formal relationships**, rather than on **individual personalities**.

(d)   Individuals who work for such organisations tend to acquire expertise without experiencing risk; many do their job adequately, but are not over-ambitious. Psychological sensitivity is a feature of this culture.

The bureaucratic style can be very efficient in a **stable environment**, when the organisation is large and where the work is predictable. This is of course why PSTV has adopted a bureaucratic structure but is also the reason why they may have difficulty coping with the rapid changes now taking place in the media industry.

A bureaucratic approach to strategy would be **rational and deliberate**. Typically, a head office department would co-ordinate functional departments and assemble budgets detailing the plan for future performance. Unfortunately, PSTV has to compete at present in several markets – TV, books, videos, radio, the Internet, digital broadcasting and so on – all fast-moving markets requiring faster responses than PSTV is capable of. However, preserving the status quo is not an option: the organisation has to adapt to the new environment.

Miles and Snow categorise organisations into three basic types in terms of how they behave strategically. Historically PSTV are **defenders** with a desire for a secure and stable niche. Their preferred strategies are specialisation and cost-efficient production. Their goals have been internally focused. To compete in the current market would mean changing its **defender** strategy by changing its structure and using task-centred cross-functional teams in a matrix or a hybrid kind of organisation. However, the organisation would still find it difficult to change to a prospector because this would be such a cultural change.

Part (b)

Burns and Stalker's research was primarily concerned with how firms coped with **technological change**, although market change was also considered. They concluded that systems could be categorised along a continuum ranging from **mechanistic** (bureaucratic), at one extreme to **organic** at the other. Firms could operate at different points on this continuum at one and the same time.

Environment is significant in that the **stable** environment can be dealt with by a relatively rigid **bureaucratic** structure but this is not the case with a **volatile**, **rapidly changing** environment. This will require a flexible organic structure, which can respond quickly and relevantly to the changes in the environment.

The bureaucratic type of organisation has proved very efficient and successful in static environments. However, it is difficult for this type of organisation to perceive the need for change, and achieve that change. Bureaucratic organisations tend therefore to exist where the organisation can control its environment by exerting its monopoly power, or where the market itself is very stable, perhaps because the product life is very long. A bureaucratic organisation such as PSTV will fail if flexibility and innovation are important.

In contrast to a bureaucratic organisation, an organic organisation thrives on the **power of personalities**, lack of rigid procedures and communication and can **react quickly and easily to changes in the environment**.

The characteristics of an organic structure include the points below.

- Skills, experience, and specialist knowledge are recognised as valuable resources.
- Formal and informal communication channels exist.
- Leadership styles based on consultation and involvement are normal.
- Commitment to task achievement, survival and growth are more important than loyalty and obedience.

The organic system is seen to be more responsive to change, and is therefore recommended for organisations moving into periods of rapid change in technology, market orientation, or tasks. Rapid change in the technology and regulations affecting PSTV means that it needs to be flexible and decentralised in its structure. This will allow it to respond appropriately to changes in environmental conditions.

Mintzberg would describe the structure as having a large corporate **strategic apex** and a large **technostructure** with a craft-based **operating core** to physically transform its products and participate fully in the new technologies. Here organic structures would be particularly appropriate.

PSTV also needs a distribution system of technical excellence to enable the transmission of its programmes through the mushrooming variety of media. This means a mechanistic element must be incorporated.

Part (c)

> **Top tips.** This is quite a difficult part of the question, partly because it gives you the opportunity to range widely over the topic of control. You must take a disciplined approach to questions like this and avoid producing a list of unrelated jottings.
>
> Also, you really have to have some notion of how non-bureaucratic approaches to structuring organisations have led to the development of new ideas about control. *Ouchi* is the name to conjure with here.

In order to ensure the organisation is operating in line with its agreed strategy, control mechanisms need to be developed to provide data that allows the organisation's activities to be monitored. These can take a variety of forms depending on the emphasis of the organisation's activities. *Ouchi* outlines three types of control.

Bureaucratic control represents a formal approach to control consisting of policies, procedures, hierarchies of authority, specialists and defined roles, which govern all that the organisation does. Bureaucratic control works well in stable environments, but as these type of formal control systems are relatively inflexible and slow to change, they do not suit unstable environments.

This type of control suits organisations such as PSTV with its bureaucratic system that allows any type of control system to be set up and outputs measured easily, but would not be suitable for an integrated multi-media corporation which does not have the same structure to support the control systems.

Clan control is based on corporate culture, with a group of related people (the clan) behaving in a commonly agreed way due to shared values, beliefs and traditions. *Child* noted that effective control can only really take place in organisations if there is positive commitment from employees. There are four aspects to this.

- Shared values, beliefs and traditions, which means that similar types of people are recruited
- A common understanding and acceptance of the organisation's vision and mission
- A common set of standards in terms of acceptable and desirable behaviour
- Respect for the head of the 'clan'

Traditional Japanese companies exhibit these characteristics. These organisations judge themselves by results and are tolerant of the means of achieving them.

Market control is based on pricing to control organisational behaviour from both an internal and external perspective. This approach can only be used where it is possible to price the output in line with the organisation's needs and customer demand, taking into account competitor's pricing strategies.

Clan and market control affect integrated multi-media corporations (IMMC), more readily than bureaucratic control. This is because of their wide geographic spread and the range of different products and markets. Clans can be created for each environment or product based on market control.

However, it is important that acceptance of organisational variety does not permit the growth of internal rivalry and conflict: the organisation as a whole must pull together and not be allowed to disintegrate. There is thus an important responsibility laid on the corporate headquarters and the division chiefs. One approach to integrating the macro-organisation is a system of cross-positing for executives with potential for senior appointments, so that a variety of experience is acquired and a common basic loyalty is fostered.

25 S Company

Top tips. Candidates often have difficulty applying their theoretical knowledge in papers that require written answers. To help overcome this difficulty, we print the application points in this answer in *italic*. Note that we also continue to use italic for technical references and to indicate a particular emphasis on some words.

Easy marks. This is quite a demanding question, with carefully worded, complex requirements. The closest the question comes to offering easy marks is in part (a) (ii) where an explanation of the nature of bureaucratic control would go a long way towards satisfying the requirement.

Part (a)

Top tips. The key words in the question are '**grows**' and '**diversifies**'. Growth and diversification are important influences on the way organisations develop. You could make a good stab at answering this part of this question by thinking about and summarising the general implications of having more people, a more complex pattern of transactions, more products of greater complexity and a larger number of more diverse customers.

Small organisations can often be run with a simple combination of co-operation, *ad hoc* decision-making and informal supervision. In such an organisation, it is usually clear who is in charge of the various aspects of the operation and problems of co-ordination tend to be simple. This is because few people are involved and the operation itself is uncomplicated.

If such an organisation enjoys substantial growth, it is almost inevitable that the things it does will become more **diversified** and **complex**; and that it will employ **more people** in a wider variety of **specialised roles**. If this happens, it is likely that informal methods of co-ordination and supervision will be found to be inadequate. In particular, it will no longer be possible for the small number of people forming the strategic apex to have detailed knowledge of everything that is happening and to exercise direct control over all of the organisation's activities.

Under these circumstances, it becomes necessary to establish both a **structure of subordinate managers** and a **system of rules and procedures** to guide and control the activities of staff at all levels. *We are told that S Company has been through this process. We might expect that S Company will have instituted normal administrative and accounting procedures such as clear terms of service for staff, a functional or project based organisation structure and proper procedures to safeguard assets, for example. We would also expect suitable task-based rules and procedures to be established, dealing with such matters as quality control and the security of the intellectual capital that forms the company's chief asset.*

As outlined above, the introduction of rules, procedures and structures of managerial accountability and responsibility allows a larger, more complex organisation to be controlled effectively by its strategic apex. Unfortunately, it is very easy for such developments to have a deadening effect on **creativity** and **innovation**.

These techniques enforce conformity and adherence to established practice. However, where there is a requirement for an organisation to respond to a **dynamic or complex environment**, new ideas and methods are critically important if the organisation is to survive and prosper. Such ideas and methods will be stifled if rules and procedures are sacrosanct. Also, and probably more important, the **motivation** of the people responsible for developing those new ideas and methods will be adversely affected. A further important consideration is that a formal, hierarchical structure tends to constrain **lateral communication** between peers in different areas of the organisation. Such communication on an informal basis is an important source of new ideas and approaches. There is thus a tension between the organisation's need for control and its need for independent thought and different approaches.

S Company is typical of organisations that find themselves in this dilemma, operating as it does in the rapidly changing world of software development. It may be necessary for S Company's software engineers to ignore existing rules about how things are done in order to produce solutions to new problems. Even in the apparently simple area of accounting procedures, different customers may require different approaches to things like credit terms and transaction processing.

Part (b)

As outlined above, a degree of autonomy in working practice contributes to workplace motivation and creativity; *it is particularly relevant to the staff of S Company and their work.*

Nevertheless, control must be maintained if the company is to be successful.

This **trust-control dilemma**, as Handy names it, can be tackled in several ways. The simplest is **delegation** of decision-making authority to the lowest hierarchical level at which it can be usefully employed. This is so common an approach that it is widely accepted as a fundamental of good management practice. Control is achieved through the accountability of decision-makers to their superiors for the results of their decisions.

The process of delegation can be extended into a wider **decentralisation**, which has implications for organisational structure. Decentralisation is most useful in large organisations with a number of disparate operations, geographically dispersed sites, or both. *It is not clear whether or not S Company is of a size to warrant full decentralisation of control, but it may be able to make use of a looser structural approach.*

Burns and Stalker examined this problem in detail. They identified two basic types of organisation: the **mechanistic** and the organismic or **organic**. They found that where an organisation had to respond to conditions of change (as S Company does), it was less likely to do so successfully if it adopted the mechanistic (or bureaucratic) approach.

If S Company is to continue to prosper it will probably have to adopt some of the characteristics of the organic organisation, such as a focus on overall objectives rather than conforming with procedure and a loose, network structure of control and communication. *S Company is probably already doing this to some extent, since the formation of project teams is a natural approach to developing new products. A matrix organisation structure would also allow the close integration of customer requirements with technical possibilities.*

Ouchi described a system he called **clan control**. While this is most applicable in societies and organisations that value family relationships and solidarity, *it can be useful to companies such as S.* Clan control is based on largely cultural artefacts.

- Shared values and traditions
- Commitment to the organisation, its goals and its customers
- A sense of common purpose

A further technique that can be used is **empowerment**. This is often seen merely as a way of reducing managerial headcount, but properly employed it pushes the motivating effect of delegated authority further down the scalar chain. There are significant implications for the selection and development of the staff concerned, *but S Company is likely to be employing the type of well-educated and intelligent staff that can respond to this challenge.*

26 Group roles

Part (a)

> **Top tips.** There is really only one way to answer this part of this question and that is to explain *Belbin's* ideas about group roles. There are other authorities and approaches, but they are all rather obscure, at least when compared to Belbin. An important point to bear in mind is that merely expounding Belbin's taxonomy of roles will not be sufficient to earn good marks. The question asks you to 'explain why an understanding of group roles **is important**', not just to explain the **nature** of the various roles you know about. The essential point here is that you make a link between the role structure of the group and its effectiveness.
>
> Another important point to be aware of is that the Examiner does not want you to look at roles from the point of view of the individual: a discussion of ideas such as role set, role conflict and role expectations, while interesting, would not really answer the question.
>
> **Easy marks.** Fairly clearly, in part (a) there will be some easy marks for identifying Belbin's roles and more for a brief summary of the characteristics of each. Probably not more than one or two sentences will be required for each role. There might be as many as six marks available for the information we give in our table below.

Formal work groups exist in order to bring the skills and experience of a number of people to bear on a task that a single person could not perform, either because of its magnitude or because of its complexity. Clearly, in the case of tasks whose complexity requires a group approach, the effectiveness of the group will depend on the variety and sophistication of the **task-related** skills and experience present in the group. This is true to some extent of all but the most undemanding physical tasks, where a group provides more muscle than a single person.

What is not quite so obvious is that group effectiveness also seems to depend on the presence of **group-related** skills and experience: a range of individual contributions to the way the group functions provides the environment necessary for the task-related factors to be deployed.

Belbin drew up a list of the most effective character-mix in a team. This involves eight necessary roles which should ideally be balanced and evenly spread in the team.

Member	Role
Co-ordinator	Presides and co-ordinates; balanced, disciplined, good at working through others.
Shaper	Highly strung, dominant, extrovert, passionate about the task itself, a spur to action.
Plant	Introverted, but intellectually dominant and imaginative; source of ideas and proposals but with disadvantages of introversion.
Monitor-evaluator	Analytically (rather than creatively) intelligent; dissects ideas, spots flaws; possibly aloof, tactless – but necessary.
Resource-investigator	Popular, sociable, extrovert, relaxed; source of new contacts, but not an originator; needs to be made use of.
Implementer	Practical organiser, turning ideas into tasks; scheduling, planning and so on; trustworthy and efficient, but not excited; not a leader, but an administrator.
Team worker	Most concerned with team maintenance – supportive, understanding, diplomatic; popular but uncompetitive – contribution noticed only in absence.
Finisher	Chivvies the team to meet deadlines, attend to details; urgency and follow-through important, though not always popular.

The **specialist** joins the group to offer expert advice when needed. Notice that one team member may play two or more roles.

The implication of Belbin's work is that managers responsible for assembling work groups should endeavour to ensure that all the necessary roles are played by the group members. This is of particular importance in organisations making use of a fluid organic structure to deal with a dynamic and complex environment: the implications for **project teams** are obvious.

Part (b)

Top tips. This part of the question covers much more ground than part (a). This means that discussion must be brief if it is to be comprehensive. We have used *Handy's* contingency-based summary of the factors affecting team success, though the Examiner's post exam guide indicates that a less structured approach would be quite acceptable.

Handy takes a contingency approach to the problem of team effectiveness.

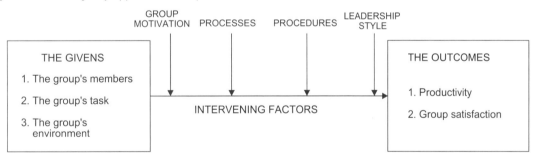

Management can operate on both givens and intervening factors to affect the outcomes.

The givens

The group. We examined the roles that group members play in effective groups above. It is important to be aware that there are also **self-oriented roles** that members can play that are potentially damaging to performance. These roles place the member in opposition to the group and include such behaviour as promoting disagreement, attempting to manipulate or dominate and refusing to focus on the group task. Task effectiveness will also be affected by such matters as the size of the group and its experience of working as a team.

The task. The nature of the task influences both how a group should be managed and the challenge it must overcome.

(a)   If a job must be done urgently, it is often necessary to dictate how things should be done, rather than to encourage a participatory style of working.

(b)   Jobs which are routine, unimportant and undemanding will be insufficient to motivate either individuals or the group as a whole.

(c)   On the other hand, complex and ill-defined tasks increase the effort that must be expended on task definition, planning and control.

The environment. The team's environment relates to factors such as the **physical surroundings** at work; the **resources** available to the group; the **culture** of the overall organisation; and the degree of **synergy** achieved during interaction with other groups. Such factors will inevitably have an impact upon the effectiveness with which the group discharges its responsibilities.

Intervening factors and outcomes

Processes and procedures. Research indicates that a team that tackles its work systematically will be more effective than one that lives from hand to mouth, and merely muddles through. This means that the group must **communicate** effectively, both internally and externally; make **decisions** and implement them in a rational and robust fashion; and keep track of essential **information** as it is produced.

Motivation and leadership style. High productivity outcomes may be achieved if work is so arranged that satisfaction of individuals' needs coincides with high output. Where teams are, for example, allowed to set their own improvement goals and methods and to measure their own progress towards those goals, it has been observed (by *Peters and Waterman* among others) that they regularly exceed their targets. The style of leadership adopted by the team leader can also affect its outcome. This depends on the circumstances.

27 Configurations

> **Top tips.** Candidates often have difficulty applying their theoretical knowledge in papers that require written answers. To help overcome this difficulty, we print the application points in this answer in *italic*. Note that we also continue to use italic for technical references and to indicate a particular emphasis on some words.

Part (a)

> **Top tips.** It is fairly obvious that you should not expect to score good marks with this question unless you are familiar with *Mintzberg's* typology! In addition to that, you have to be sure that you know it well enough to produce a logical recommendation for each organisation mentioned in the question. Unusually, there is a great deal of prescriptiveness here, in that there is really only one solution appropriate for each organisation. You have to get them right to score well: there will be few marks available for the candidate who knows the basic Mintzberg diagram inside out but cannot recognise which configurations are applicable here. Indeed, a good answer would omit any general description of the components of the basic Mintzberg organigram and proceed directly to making correct use of it.
>
> One final point – make sure you use the correct letter labels for the organisations in your answer! It might be safer to talk about 'the restaurant', 'the university' and 'the manufacturer'. Another approach is to deal with each organisation under its own heading. We have used both of these approaches.
>
> **Easy marks.** This could be a useful question to tackle if you are short of time, looking for easy marks and know one or two of Mintzberg's organisational types reasonably well. The marking scheme indicates that the question is really three mini-questions, so you could snap up three or four marks by producing a good answer for just one of the organisations, or even five or six for dealing with two of them in a basic way.

The restaurant

*The **simple** or **entrepreneurial** structure is probably appropriate for organisation X, the restaurant business.* This structure consists of the **strategic apex** and the **operating core** only. It is typical of small organisations run by a very small group, or possibly by just one owner-manager. The high degree of centralisation reflects the expertise of those at the strategic apex and allows full use to be made of it in the processes of planning and control.

The simple structure is well-suited to a business such as a restaurant that has to deal with a **fast-moving but essentially simple environment.** The strategic apex can exercise direct control over all mission-critical activities without becoming over-stretched; communication can be face-to-face and therefore rapid, two-way and as urgent as required. Wider co-ordination of longer-term plans is equally easy to arrange.

The simple structure has its limitations, however. There is little if any hierarchy, so **span of control** tends to be wide, which increases the burden of supervision. Also, it **depends heavily** on the expertise of those at the strategic apex: sickness or death can lead to the break-up of the organisation. Finally, the simple structure effectively places a **limit on growth**, since when a certain size is reached, delegation and thus the introduction of a **middle line** become necessary.

Middle line can become necessary.

The university

*Y university would probably be organised as a **professional bureaucracy**.* This displays a **strategic apex**, **support staff** and **operating core.** *In Y university, academic staff would form the operating core, with a small number of them emerging as the strategic apex, probably by informal consent or direct election. The role of the strategic apex would be to deal with higher co-ordination, such as setting overall budgets. Administrators and ancillaries would form the support staff. They would have their own, better developed hierarchy.*

Middle line and **technostructure** are largely absent from this form because the operating core sets its own standards. In Mintzberg's terms, it exercises a 'pull to standardise' (that is, to professionalise) its skills and cultural values. Also, the type of work performed by professional bureaucracies is generally too complex to be easily standardised by a technostructure. Professionalism is relied upon.

In a university, we would expect that any new academic appointees would possess formal qualifications fitting them to carry out teaching and research. Peer pressure would tend to ensure that they continued to work to appropriate standards. Very little supervision would be required and what power was exercised would be based on expertise rather than formal hierarchy.

The manufacturing company

Middle line + Auto-nomy

*The manufacturing company, Z, is already configured in the **divisional form**, and this seems appropriate to its size and the diversity of its products.* Mintzberg regards the divisional form as satisfying the desire of the **middle line** to achieve as much autonomy for itself as possible. It is a common solution to the problem of combining overall central control with the enterprise and motivation that comes from a high degree of independent decision-making.

In the divisional form, each division tends towards configuration as a **machine bureaucracy**, since it must behave in many ways as though it were a truly independent entity. The divisions thus require their own strategic apex, middle line and operating core and at least some support staff, though some of the latter may be centralised. The prime co-ordinating mechanism is **standardisation of outputs**, using performance measures such as ROCE. This will require an element of technostructure, such as an accounts department to prepare the necessary reports.

Within the overall organisation, all five main structural elements are present, though the technostructure tends to be fairly small because of the system of control by standardisation of outputs: divisions have their own technostructures suited to their own operations. Overall control is exercised by the strategic apex in two main areas: it retains the power to **hire and fire** the divisional chief executives and it controls the **allocation of resources** within the wider organisation.

Part (b)

> **Top tips.** First of all, note that there is no opportunity to score application marks in this part-question, since there is no scenario.
>
> **Easy marks.** The Examiner specifically mentions the work of *Burns and Stalker* in his 'suggested approach' and we would agree that this is the obvious basis for an answer. Nevertheless, it would be possible to produce a reasonable answer without mentioning *The Management of Innovation*, so long as you explained the fairly simple relationship: dynamic environment > new problems > rapid response > expertise and flexibility. Also, as an alternative to the mechanistic/organic dichotomy, you might just be able to use *Mintzberg's* model of the **adhocracy** as a basis for an answer.
>
> **Examiner's comments.** The Examiner remarked that a common failing was simply to discuss the nature of environmental uncertainty to the exclusion of any consideration of its implications for the organisation and its structure. **Answer the question!**

The structure of an organisation is determined by a number of influences, including the history and development of the organisation, the need to combine control with a degree of management autonomy and initiative and the nature of the organisation's activities. The environment is also an important influence, sometimes in a negative sense when a benign environment allows other factors to predominate; and sometimes in a more active way when environmental complexity or rapid change constrain the organisational choices available.

If an organisation is to deal successfully with an **uncertain environment**, it must be capable of **rapid and agile response**, adjusting its operations and even its overall strategy as conditions change. Behaviour typical of bureaucracy, such as reference to precedent, reference up the hierarchy and deference to seniority are unlikely to lead to rapid and innovative action. The agile company tends to display more fluid and responsive systems, delegating decision-making authority downwards as far as possible and reconfiguring itself in an *ad hoc* fashion to bring the most appropriate combination of personal expertise to bear on a new problem.

Burns and Stalker described such an approach and labelled it **organic** or (organismic). The organic organisation has few formal rules or procedures and trusts its members to take effective action on their own initiative. Authority is tightly linked to **specialist expertise** rather than to hierarchical status and organisation structure is **loose** and **flexible**. Co-ordination is by **mutual adjustment** rather than formal direction and control depends on a network of interactions. The lack of formal controls is made up for by a kind of **cultural control** under which staff understand and are committed to the overall mission rather than to a narrow interpretation of specific responsibilities.

28 Key influences

> **Top tips.** All the professional accounting bodies are concerned about the recent decline in ethical standards in commercial organisations. This decline undermines public confidence in both the profession and the wider world of business. The Examiner for Paper 11 reflected this concern in his later exam papers.
>
> **Easy marks.** Generally, in questions with an ethical theme, it is appropriate to take a high moral stance. Do not propose the utterly impractical, but emphasise the need for lawful conduct and to be fair to all stakeholder groups. Note that this does not necessarily involve an unquestioning acceptance of the 'social responsibility' case: hard decisions may have to be made.

Part (a)

Influences on ethical conduct can be divided into two groups: positive influences and negative ones.

Positive ethical influences

It is possible to discern an **ethical climate** in a society, that forms part of its culture. Notions of right and wrong tend to be conditioned by history, the behaviour of respected leaders, the tenets of the dominant religion and so on.

It is possible to discern subtle differences between societies in this respect, and some that are not so subtle. It has been reported, for example, that there is concern in Western Europe at the less rigorous attitudes to corrupt practices in business that Eastern European countries may bring with them when they join the EU. *The Times* reported that 'former communist states have been tainted by corruption since bribery and the black market became a means of survival in over-regulated, centrally planned economies.'

Organisations tend to have ethical climates too, just as they have their own cultures, and like its culture, an organisation's ethical climate is heavily influenced by its external environment. Thus we may discern an important difference between employers in the USA and those in Europe in relation to ideas of corporate social responsibility. It is inappropriate to overemphasise extremes of behaviour, but we might consider the different attitudes that prevail concerning job security on opposite sides of the Atlantic, for example.

Within an organisation, an ethical influence is the **behaviour of senior managers**, to the extent that the influence of artefacts such as corporate **codes of conduct** and **ethics** hotlines can be completely neutralised by unprincipled behaviour. This was a major problem within *Enron*, which paid extensive lip service to ethical behaviour.

Professional institutions have their own codes of **professional ethics**, such as CIMA's own code, the ethical demands commonly made on auditors and the specific requirements for objectivity and impartiality made by their own professional bodies. These codes can put members under considerable strain when they demand behaviour that is at variance with what is accepted in an organisation. As CIMA's code says, sometimes a professional may have no alternative but to resign.

Negative ethical influences

Personal amorality is likely to exist in any organisation to a greater or lesser extent, quite apart from actively immoral or illegal behaviour. Such amorality, or lack of care about right and wrong must inevitably lead to unethical conduct.

Financial pressures will be a major problem. These may take the form of personal financial problems resulting from, for instance, gambling, drug use or simple over-spending. Such problems drive individuals to a range of unethical behaviour, ranging from inflated expense claims to outright fraud.

Financial pressures leading to fraud also exist at the **corporate level**. External pressure from shareholders or markets to improve profitability can lead to **bribery** to win contracts and all kinds of **creative accounting**, for example. It is also a specific threat to auditors, since efforts may be made to undermine their impartiality and objectivity. The methods employed may range from simple friendliness and the provision of agreeable lunches for the auditors on site, to threats to take more lucrative consulting business elsewhere if the audit is qualified.

Under such circumstances, unprincipled demands for improved performance are likely to filter down through the organisation as each level of the hierarchy comes under pressure from the one above. CIMA's own code specifically identifies **pressure from a superior** as a potential cause of ethical conflict.

Part (b)

'It is men and arms that make the force and power of the law'   Hobbes, Leviathan

Coercion is the fallback position of all systems of behaviour control, including law and ethical codes. If organisations and professions want their people to behave in accordance with a particular set of rules, they must be prepared to **enforce** them. Professional bodies, such as CIMA have a set of law-based procedures for doing just that; you may occasionally find reports of CIMA's internal disciplinary proceedings in '*Financial Management*'.

Organisations, too, are capable of enforcing their ideas about ethics. An allegation of unethical behaviour at *Boeing* in late 2003 led to the dismissal of the head of finance and subsequently to the resignation of *Phil Condit*, Chairman and Chief Executive.

If a willingness to enforce them exists, **codes of ethics** can have an effect, both in organisations and in professions. If breaches of such codes are ignored or condoned, they will be treated with contempt and be worse than useless, since they will demonstrate that senior officers are hypocrites as well as unethical in their behaviour.

Ethics management has several tasks.

- To define and give life to an organisation's defining values.
- To create an environment that supports ethically sound behaviour
- To instil a sense of shared accountability amongst employees.

There are two approaches to the management of ethics, according to *Paine*, the **compliance-based** and the **integrity-based**.

A **compliance-based** approach is primarily designed to ensure that the company **acts within the letter of the law**, and that violations are prevented, detected and punished. Some organisations, faced with the legal consequences of unethical behaviour take legal precautions such as those below.

- Compliance procedures to detect misconduct
- Audits of contracts
- Systems to protect and encourage 'whistleblowers'
- Disciplinary procedures to deal with transgressions

Corporate compliance is limited in that it relates only to the law, but legal compliance is 'not an adequate means for addressing the full range of ethical issues that arise every day'. This is especially the case in the UK, where **voluntary** codes of conduct and self-regulation are perhaps more prevalent than in the US.

The compliance approach also overemphasises the threat of detection and punishment in order to channel appropriate behaviour. Furthermore, mere compliance with the law is no guide to **exemplary** behaviour.

An **integrity-based** approach treats ethics as an issue of organisation culture. It combines a concern for the law with an **emphasis on managerial responsibility** for ethical behaviour. Integrity strategies strive to define companies' **guiding values**, **aspirations** and **patterns of thought and conduct**. When integrated into the day-to-day operations of an organisation, such strategies can help prevent damaging ethical lapses, while tapping into powerful human impulses for moral thought and action. Such approaches assume that people are social beings with values that can be supported and refined. They attempt to integrate ethical values into the organisation (or profession) by providing guidance and consultation and by identifying and resolving problems.

29 Question with analysis and helping hand: Structure and innovation

Top tips. Notice the breakdown of marks in this question. Part (a)(i) is worth only seven marks and part (a)(ii) only six. There is a very great deal that could be said on the topics introduced but there is not much time in which to say it. The mark allocation is an indication of the depth and extent of the answers the Examiner wants and also of the amount of time you have available for your answers. Do not get carried away!

Perhaps the most difficult element of part (a)(i) is the requirement to 'compare and contrast'. This term means 'show the similarities and/or differences between', so something more than descriptions of the two structures is needed. Using words and phrases' such as 'like', 'unlike', 'by contrast', 'similarly' and 'in comparison' can help you to satisfy this requirement. You would be well advised to start with the entrepreneurial structure, since this is the simpler of the two, and then go onto combine a description of the functional structure with comments on how it differs.

Easy marks. The easy marks, as is often the case, are available in part (a) and particularly in part (a)(i): the simple structure and functional structure are perhaps the simplest types of organisation and the ones that most people are most familiar with.

It is reasonable to use *Mintzberg's* terminology, as this is widely understood.

Examiner's comments. In part (a)(ii), there was a tendency to be prescriptive about future changes rather than to explain what the current problem was.

Part (a)(i)

An entrepreneurial structure is very simple, with a **small strategic apex** (often consisting of a single owner-manager) and an informal system of control. It is suited to new, small organisations in which the founder knows all the details of what has to be done and runs everything by **personal supervision**. While there may be specialist members such as accountants and designers, coordination is centralised and there is no **middle line** or **technostructure**. In *Harrison's* terms, this is organisation falls into the **power** type.

By contrast, a functional structure is more commonly found in **larger organisations** dealing with **greater complexity**. This complexity makes personal supervision by a single person, or even a small group, impossible and **managers with specialist expertise** have to be employed. Specialised technical expertise forms the basis for departmentation and hierarchy, since **expert supervisors are needed** and **delegation** is only possible if subordinates themselves possess a degree of technical competence. **Communication and control** are vertical, rather than fluid and free as in the simple structure and there may be little contact between departments. Technostructure and support staff emerge. There is a tendency to formalise work and the organisation displays a **role culture**.

Part (a)(ii)

> **Top tips**. It is questionable whether the current organisational approach was *ever* appropriate for L Company, never mind whether it may *no longer* be appropriate. However, this is more a matter of the trend towards ' bureaucratic and rigid control methods' rather than simply the functional structure. The two do not inevitably go together.
>
> To answer this part of the question, concentrate on the features in the scenario that are constraining innovation and enterprise in L Company.

L Company is part of an industry that is constantly introducing new products and ideas; continuing technical innovation and a high degree of enterprise are essential if it is to survive and prosper. *Burns and Stalker* described both L Company's earlier informal and creative approach to business and its current rather bureaucratic methods in their book *The Management of Innovation,* calling them **organismic** (or organic) and **mechanistic** styles respectively. They had no doubt that the organismic style was best suited to a rapidly changing technical environment.

The mechanistic style, rooted in procedure and functional structures tends to be slow to change because of its **focus on specialist responsibilities**. It does not have sufficient people taking a broad view of what is going on and what should be done and it tends to become slow in its responses because of **poor cross-functional communication and decision-making**. Innovation depends to some extent on the **free exchange of ideas and responses** between people of differing backgrounds and specialities: functional organisation tends to inhibit this and may actually reduce cross-functional co-operation and increase conflict.

Part (b)

> **Top tips**. There is a very large number of things that can be discussed in this part of the question. We have tried to give reasonably full coverage in our answer: for the twelve marks available, a good discussion of four points should suffice.
>
> **Easy marks**. The fact that you have spent some time discussing structural matters in part (a) does not disqualify you from proposing structural changes in part (b).
>
> **Examiner's comments**. We constantly reiterate the importance of making your answers relevant to the question scenario: in his comments on this part of the question, the Examiner stated clearly that a pass mark would only be awarded if suggestions were explained in terms of how they could make a difference at L Company.

As discussed above, L Company's current organisational approach may well be inhibiting creativity. A should review the existing structure and methods used to see if suitable changes could be made. The aim would be to encourage cross-functional communication; devolve power and responsibility; and reduce formality of structure and procedure where appropriate.

An overall **matrix structure** might be considered as a way to enhance customer focus and encourage cross-functional liaison. However, L Company's range of products is now quite diverse and a better approach might be **divisionalisation**. While there is plenty of scope for innovation in basic products such as kettles and vacuum cleaners, it is likely that the main managerial emphasis would be on cost-effective manufacturing. PCs and media equipment, on the other hand, would probably require much greater investment in new product development if market opportunities were to be seized. A policy of devolving responsibility on a product line basis should be considered, divisions being set up to design, manufacture and market compatible groups of products. **Team working** and matrix approaches may then be useful within divisions.

Control systems should be examined alongside the structure of the organisation. Any organisation will have areas, such as financial reporting compliance, that must be subject to strict control; however, if creativity is to be encouraged, such control should be restricted to the areas where it is necessary and a **looser approach** used elsewhere. **Cultural forms of control** should be developed, perhaps based on devolved budgets and performance measurement in terms of results rather than procedures. A **balanced scorecard** approach, with its emphasis on customer service and innovation and learning, may be useful.

Linked to culture is **management style**. A should satisfy herself that individual contributions are not being stifled by an over-authoritarian style of management. Creativity generally thrives best when there is a degree of empowerment and participation in the development of the organisation.

Rosabeth Moss Kanter's general prescriptions for encouraging organisational creativity provide a good summary of what can be done.

Accept change

Encourage new ideas

Permit interaction and communication

Tolerate failure

Reward creative behaviour

30 Question with analysis: Departmental conflict

Part (a)

> **Top tips**. This is quite a complex question because the scenario, for all its apparent simplicity, deals with some fairly complex behavioural topics in the sources of the conflict. We explain these in our answer.
>
> There is also the word 'nature' in the requirement. The Examiner is actually using the word with a specific meaning: he is asking you to put conflict that is taking place into some sort of classification of type or category. As you will see in our answer, we classify the problems at M Company as **horizontal conflict**.
>
> **Easy marks**. There are few easy marks in this requirement. You would glean a mark or two for pointing out the different attitudes of the departments, but this would not count as a full analysis since both **goal incompatibility** and **cognitive and emotional orientation** are involved.
>
> **Examiner's comments**. Perhaps unsurprisingly, many candidates found it difficult to provide the detailed analysis required and merely repeated the detail of the scenario.

M Company is suffering the effects of **horizontal conflict**: that is, the conflicts are arising between groups and individuals that do not have a hierarchical relationship and are of more or less equal status in the company.

The various disputes have occurred for several reasons.

Operative goal incompatibility: the primary goals of the various departments involved, rather than supporting the overall objective of successful NPD, are themselves effectively incompatible. For example, the apparent slowness of the R&D department may reflect a goal of high technical excellence, while the anxiety of the sales department ad the frustration of the marketers may, in turn, reflect goals of continuing growth and good customer relations.

Emotional and cognitive orientation: People working in different functions tend to have rather different personal priorities, interests, attitudes and values. For example, the perception of the finance department as unhelpful controllers of resources may say more about the attitudes prevailing in the other departments than the actual nature of the finance department's motivation.

Task interdependence: it is necessary for all the departments to cooperate closely if successful NPD is to take place, since information, in particular, must flow effectively back and forth between them. Any lack of co-operation from any department, perhaps rooted in one of the other causes of conflict mentioned here, is likely to produce significant frustration and further conflict as a result. This may be behind some of the production department's complaints about lack of co-operation from the R&D people.

Work pressure: M Company is facing difficult business conditions, which is likely to produce stress effects all responsible members of staff, both because of awareness of the need for improved performance and as a result of pressure from above. Conflict is a possible symptom of this stress.

Part (b)

> **Easy marks**. As with any question on teams, when thinking about this requirement, your mind should instantly make an agile leap to the work of *Tuckman* and that of *Belbin*. In fact, the Examiner's marking scheme indicates that discussing these two topics could almost take you to a pass mark. Naturally, you would not overlook the fact that the leader is part of the team and a consideration of management style would provide the remaining marks required.
>
> **Examiner's comments**. Answers were generally good, confirming our impression that this is a friendly, manageable question. However, some candidates missed the point of the wording of the requirement and discussed project management rather than building a team.

The task of developing a new team might be considered under three headings: the individuals needed, the functioning of the group, and the leadership of the team.

The individuals

V must ensure that the members of the new project, between them, possess the skills, experience and aptitudes necessary to develop successfully his new range of luxury foods. Past disputes mean that perhaps the most important personal quality the team members will require a **commitment to working productively together**. They must retain their orientation towards the role of their own departments, but they must supplement that with a willingness to understand the needs and priorities of their colleagues. The emphasis must be on a judicious **balance of departmental concerns** in order to **support the overall goal**.

Belbin suggests that the effective functioning of a team depends, at least in part, on the ability of the members to play a range of important team roles. These roles are co-ordinator, shaper, implementer, monitor-evaluator, resource investigator, team worker, specialist and finisher.

> **Top tip**. The Examiner's own suggested solution does not include an explanation of these roles: we think that it would be appropriate for you to include such an explanation if you wished to do so.

The group

A successful group will develop its own internal life that will help its members to work together. The development process was described by *Tuckman* as taking place in four stages.

- **Forming** is the process of bringing the group together and beginning to work out its aims, structure and processes. The team members are likely to be wary of one another and social relationships will be unformed.

- **Storming** is a period of open conflict between members about objectives, methods and relationships. It should lead to a robust basis for co-operation in the future.

- **Norming** is a period of settling down with the development of group norms about work requirements and methods and social expectations.

- **Performing** productive work follows as the final phase.

Leadership

Leadership style will be important. The project team will include experienced professionals with their own competences and expectations. An autocratic style is unlikely to be the most productive when working with such people. In *Hersey and Blanchard's* terms the **maturity** of the team is high, therefore a low degree of directive behaviour on the part of the leader will be appropriate. **Participation in decision-making** and a high degree of **delegation** will be important.

The complexity of the task and the need for a wide range of co-ordinated inputs will make **communication** very important. Providing for this will be a major leadership role. V must, in the first place, ensure that he communicates effectively with his team himself. He must provide clear objectives and decisions, brief future activity and plans clearly and give feedback on progress. He must also ensure that the team members communicate effectively with each other. No doubt much important communication will be **verbal, face-to-face and informal**, but there should also be **meetings** held at suitable intervals to ensure that important matters are not overlooked and there is general understanding of work and progress.

31 Objective test questions

31.1 C Accounting software could conceivable offer a strategic advantage but it is much more likely to be a routine matter within the finance function.

31.2 C A is internal: a weakness. B is also an internal weakness, which interacts with the environment but is not part of it. D is a policy and therefore part of the mission.

31.3 B A and D relate to overall corporate strategy, while C is about functional or operational strategy.

31.4 C

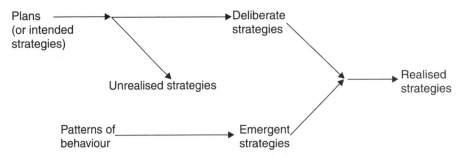

31.5 B A and D relate to the degree to which subordinate objectives support mission. C has much in common with *Kaplan and Norton's* internal business perspective but is not the phrase they use.

31.6 A This is *Daft's* analysis.

31.7 D A and C are internal stakeholders; B is an external stakeholder.

31.8 B 'Shared values' is one of the elements of the model.

31.9 B A is **corporate strategy**, C is **functional strategy** and D could be regarded as one aspect of corporate strategy.

31.10 A The groups in option B are all **internal stakeholders**; suppliers are regarded as **connected stakeholders** so options C and D contain mixed groups of stakeholders.

32 Objective test questions

32.1 B Vertical integration. Some assets have little or no value outside a given contractual relationship that requires their use. Firms may therefore be reluctant to invest in such assets, making it necessary for firms at a different stage in the value system to extend their operations upstream (or even downstream) in order to secure access to such assets.

32.2 B Both approaches are built around deliberate decisions by managers. Neither emphasises the possession of core competences and, of the two approaches, only the rational model is dependent on detailed medium-term forecasting and deals with a wide range of strategic possibilities.

32.3 D Growth is identified by *Mintzberg* as 'the natural goal of the manager': managers benefit personally and directly from growth in terms of salaries and status and in reduced vulnerability to the environment.

32.4 False. **Satisficing** is one possible response to goal conflict. *Daft* also identifies **bargaining, priority setting** and **sequential attention**.

32.5 True. Both display fluid structures in which expertise is more important than status, and commitment to the task more important than correct procedure, for example.

32.6 Market share and market growth.

32.7 B Procurement is a support activity. The value chain model does not include 'functions' either in terminology or in the sense of 'departments'.

32.8 Threat of new entrants; threat of substitute products; bargaining power of customers; bargaining power of suppliers.

32.9 *Mendelow* proposed classifying stakeholders in terms of their level of **interest** and **power**.

32.10 C The others are support activities.

33 Fast food culture 1

Top tips. This is a very simple question based on culture in its widest sense, though management culture also rears its ugly head. You would be equipped to produce a pretty good answer to this question if you merely read a decent newspaper regularly.

Easy marks. Differences of national culture and *Hofstede's* model of management cultures are obvious bases to build an answer on. There is no need to go into great detail about the latter in particular, however.

The managers of FFC are unlikely to be surprised by the reactions of their customers in country C, since the subjects of complaint are common points of differentiation of national culture.

There can be wide cultural differences even between neighbouring countries that are part of the same basic society; if country C's national culture is significantly different from that of country S, it is inevitable that there will be complaints. This is particularly so as customs and taboos associated with food are particularly strong. These problems will be exacerbated by the current tendency to decry 'globalisation' as an evil and to denounce cultural insensitivity and even cultural imperialism whenever there is the slightest excuse.

Management culture is a specific part of wider culture and a similar disparity of approach is to be expected between countries. The very notion of a fast food chain is typical of Western industrialised society and, indeed, within that society, of 'Anglo' society specifically. The general approach of management in that society is quite different from that of other societies, even within the industrialised world, as *Hofestede* pointed out. Even more to the point are the typical human resource management policies of the fast food industry.

FFC's management have presumably decided to standardise as much of their operation as possible in order to enhance control and brand image and to achieve economies of scale. It seems likely that they will have to make some adjustments to this rather ethnocentric approach to their operation in country C if it is to prosper.

34 Fast food culture 2

Top tips. This is a very practical question and requires only that you think carefully about what FFC could do to improve its position.

Easy marks. Easy marks will be available for references to market research and promotion techniques such as advertising and PR.

FFC have a major policy decision to make, assuming they have not already made it. That is, they must decide whether they are going to persist with their existing policy, and rely on a process of familiarisation and perhaps something like cult status to save their venture, or whether they are going to adjust to local norms. Note that neither of these positions need be extreme: some elements of compromise could be present in both.

In either case FFC must do some market research into the tastes and preferences of its target market. It will also be necessary to undertake some skilled promotional work to build the desired image. It is likely that local input will be indispensable here.

The complaints about architecture present a particular problem, since fast food restaurants often have some important aspect of their brand included in their premises' design. McDonald's 'Golden Arches' are an example.

Presumably country C has inadequate planning controls; otherwise, FFC would not have been able to build a structure that most people disliked. FFC should consult a local architect to discover if anything can be done.

The problem of management culture must first be understood in detail. FFC will be unwilling to compromise on essentials such as accountability and operation of accounting controls, but it may be that some compromises can be achieved here also. Recruitment and training policies may have to be adjusted in order to obtain a more motivated workforce.

35 Sam and Frank

Top tips. Interestingly, the Examiner's answer to this question makes no reference at all to the contentious nature of T Inc's product. Many people would consider that the addictive nature of tobacco and its proven threat to the health of its consumers would be important considerations in any discussion of T Inc's goals and responsibilities.

Easy marks. The Friedmanite or ownership interest approach is quite easy to describe and is a good way of starting your answer.

Sam's view of the business

Sam could support his view that the purpose of T Inc is to make money for the shareholders to the exclusion of any other interests, by using the arguments below.

- A business is **owned** by its shareholders. Property rights are fundamental to a free society and an efficient economy and should not be infringed without very good reason. Such infringements must be sanctioned by law. If the aim of maximising shareholder value is subordinated to any other goal, the shareholders' assets are being misused.

- Even if it is accepted that groups other than shareholders are intimately affected by a company's behaviour, many of those groups' **legitimate concerns** are satisfied by their contractual relationships with the company. Staff are paid salaries. Suppliers are paid for their supplies. Customers are provided with the products they require and pay for. Taxes are paid to central and local government.

- Other groups may feel that they have an interest in what companies do. In the case of a tobacco company, which may source its raw material from poorer countries, **exploiting cheap labour** in the process; which may cause **pollution** in its manufacturing operations; and which may be accused of **marketing dangerous substances** without proper controls, there is likely to be a large, vocal, well-organised and powerful body of opinion about its activities. The **anti-smoking lobby** will do what it can to hamper T Inc's activities. The correct response to such action is to point out the legal position. It is for government, not pressure groups, to decide what is legal and what is not and the extent to which companies have responsibilities to society at large.

Frank's view of the business

The stakeholder view of organisations' social responsibility is based on the idea that people have inalienable natural rights in addition to any granted by the law as it exists from time to time. Frank might argue along the lines below.

- Employees' relationship with their employment is such that **they establish greater rights** than simply the right to remuneration. They **invest a great deal of their lives and personal consequence** in their work and deserve to be treated with care and consideration.

- Large companies, in particular, control so much in the way of resources that their conduct has **wider implications** for society than just its commercial effects. They also do not bear the total cost of their activities, since many **externalities** exist This should be recognised by the companies themselves and they should acknowledge their duty to society.

- Corporations' relationship with government through the mechanism of tax is subject to **manipulation**. Many companies do not pay a fair amount of tax. An acceptance of social responsibility can go some way to compensate for this.

36 Engines 1

Top tips. This is a simple question and revolves around knowledge of simple definitions of the three terms for which explanations are required.

Candidates often have difficulty applying their theoretical knowledge in papers that require written answers. To help overcome this difficulty, we print the application points in this answer in *italic*. Note that we also continue to use italic for technical references and to indicate a particular emphasis on some words.

Easy marks. As usual, the easy marks here are for providing simple definitions of the three terms used in the question.

Examiner's comments. The Examiner identified a lack of detail as the main failing in answers to this question. It is important here to understand just what the Examiner wants: clearly, definitions of the three levels of strategy are not going to earn you ten marks. To *explain* the differences between the three levels of strategy you really need to **compare** them and draw out the **contrasts** between their natures. This is something that is actually made easier if you use concrete examples from the scenario, as we do in our answer.

Note also that the marking guide for this question specifically mentions the need for the three levels of strategy to be **linked**. An important aspect of the nature of the three levels of strategy is that they support one another: each higher level sets the context and basic premises of each lower one, while the strategies at the lower levels each amplify and implement some aspect of the higher ones.

Strategies at the corporate, business and functional levels form a hierarchy, each level having its specific function and relating up and down to the others.

Corporate strategy is decided at the strategic apex and 'is concerned with the overall purpose and scope of the organisation'. This is the level of strategy that directly addresses the **purpose** for which the organisation exists: in a business organisation, success at this level will be measured in terms of shareholder benefit. The **deployment of financial and other resources** within the organisation will form a major component of strategy at this level. A typical corporate strategy decision is which product-markets to compete in. In very large organisations, this may effectively become a **portfolio management** activity, with the organisation moving into and out of product-markets as seems advantageous from time to time. *The E company's corporate strategy appears to revolve around high quality engine design and production.*

Business strategy 'is about how to compete successfully in a particular market.' In a small business operating in a single market, this level of strategy will be very closely related to the overall corporate strategy. A bigger company might be made up of largely autonomous **strategic business units**, each responsible for developing and implementing a strategy to compete within a given market.

*In the case of the E company, there are clearly three product-markets to consider: automobile engines, marine engines and aerospace engines. It would be possible to have a **distinct strategy** for each. In fact, we are told that the company has emphasised design and quality; presumably that applies in all three major product groups. Other examples of business strategy that the E company could have pursued would include: concentrating on design and development in order to build a reputation for advanced engineering; and building market share in the automobile market by producing engines for less expensive cars.*

Business strategy is thus an amplification of corporate strategy: it lays down the general methods that will be used in the given product-market.

Functional strategy (or operational strategy) flows from business strategy and supports it. This level of strategy is concerned with the optimum use and deployment of the **resources used within a given business strategy**. *For example, within the E company's marine engine operation, there might be separate functional strategies for R&D, sales and production. To take the example of production, strategies might range from in-house manufacture in a single integrated factory; through dispersed assembly plants, each intended to service one segment of the global market; to complete sub-contractorisation of production.*

Note, however, that functional strategy must **support** business strategy and, ultimately, corporate strategy. *For example, if the E company were determined to maintain its reputation for quality, it is unlikely that it would contract out much of its core manufacturing work: control is much easier to maintain over in-house activities.*

37 Engines 2

Top tips. It is worth noting that, while the mark scheme for this part of the question simply mentions explaining the two approaches, the Examiner's 'suggested approach' includes this: 'deduce from these explanations why manager C emphasises environment and D emphasises resources and competences'. In our opinion, this a bit rich, as there is no mention of such a requirement in the question itself.

However, you can insure yourself to some extent against such things by making it a rule always to include some reference to the setting in your answer. The last paragraph of our answer shows how we have addressed this need.

Candidates often have difficulty applying their theoretical knowledge in papers that require written answers. To help overcome this difficulty, we print the application points in this answer in *italic*. Note that we also continue to use italic for technical references and to indicate a particular emphasis on some words.

Easy marks. It is not often the Examiner asks you to explain a piece of theory, so this question might have attracted the candidate who finds application difficult.

The strategic analysis phase of the **rational model** of strategy includes consideration of both environmental factors and those internal to the organisation. These two categories, internal and environmental are divided respectively into strengths and weaknesses; and opportunities and threats. The aim of strategy development is to take proper account of these four sets of factors, so that strategy exploits opportunities and strengths, evades or combats threats and minimises the effect of weaknesses.

There are two schools of thought about the strategic impact of the two main categories of factors to be taken into account.

The first approach seeks to achieve a **strategic fit** with the environment. The organisation that responds best to the pressures generated by its customers, its competitors and its wider environment is the one most likely to achieve a strategic advantage. Strategy here consists of developing the strengths needed to exploit opportunities and combat threats. This is sometimes known as the **positioning** approach.

A more recent development is the **resource based** or **core competence** approach. This proceeds from the view that strategic advantage is most robust when it is based on hard-to-imitate corporate capabilities. Exploitation of such capabilities gives the organisation a long term boost in the market place simply because rivals find it difficult to compete effectively.

*It is clear that manager C tends towards the **positioning view** of strategy, while manager D is more inclined to support the **core competence** approach. This may reflect their personal exposure to strategic considerations: manager C may be a marketing specialist and manager D an engineer, for instance. Alternatively, the difference may simply arise from their exposure to strategic theory, the core competence approach being more recent in origin than the positioning approach, as mentioned above.*

38 Question with helping hand: Screen

Top tips. We have identified four important stake-holder groups below. However, you might have chosen others. Local government perhaps has similar expectations to central government, but sees the Cinicentre as a major local employer and an attraction for people to visit the borough. Local residents are probably concerned about traffic noise and security.

Easy marks. Our short note about the ways *Mintzberg* says stakeholders exercise power is a simple piece of knowledge that is relevant to the question and probably worth a mark.

Stakeholder expectations and interests

(a) **Members**. People join such societies for a **variety** of reasons. Some **active members** may want put themselves up for election, providing a suitable number of secondments can be found. Other members may simply be pursuing a **vague interest** in films, and are chiefly interested in the publications and discounts that membership can bring. Members who feel that the Screen is becoming too commercial have protested – however the **deficit** should concern them too.

(b) **Employees and staff.** Their interest is in **continued employment** and the continued interest in the job. Obviously they must love film, particularly in the Film Archive Unit, where specialist expertise is highly valued. Staff in the museum must also enjoy and be skilled at dealing with the public, as expectations of quality rise.

(c) The **government** funds Screen as it is a public benefit and there would be a major protest, especially in the media, were the Cinicentre to close. It is a tourist attraction to London, it provides jobs, it is prestigious for Britain, and it supports education. Funding Screen is perhaps similar to funding museums, art galleries, orchestras the National Theatre and so forth. There are many calls on government spending, and the government will be concerned about financial efficiency.

(d) **The media.** Although this might seem surprising to list as a stakeholder, British media firms may see Screen as a resource for programming ideas. Certainly, the film industry will be keen to promote an interest in the cinema, both as art and as entertainment.

Stakeholder power

Mintzberg suggests that stakeholders can exercise power in three ways: loyalty, exit or voice (ie interfering with what is done so as to change it). The extent to which they can exercise power depends on the sort of relationship they have with the managers.

(a)   **Membership**. Members have little power as individuals, unless they are distinguished film-makers, producers, actors etc. Exit is relatively easy for them: they can simply resign or allow their subscriptions to lapse: in the long term this will threaten the existence of the organisation; in the short term, they do of course have the vote, and in theory are able to exercise voice through their representatives on the Board of Governors. This power is probably latent rather than active for the individual. Presumably, at elections, the Governors have to submit a manifesto as to what their main priorities are.

(b)   **Employees and management**. In the short term, the staff can disrupt totally the operations of Screen even if in the long term this would be self-defeating. On the other hand the staff at the FAU have little power in the short term – other than resignation – but they could do long – term damage to Screen's reputation and mission.

(c)   **Central government's** power is large, as it provides most of Screen's revenue, covering most of its overheads. Its power of voice is significant.

(d)   **Media**. The media have no direct power. They contribute no regular income, other than fees to use films from the archive. But they are powerful nonetheless in that they can mobilise the attention and interest of the public. They have the capacity for setting the agenda in terms of public policy. As Screen is a multi-stakeholder institution, such power is important.

39 Question with answer plan: Social responsibility

> **Top tips**. There is no scenario here, so you are free to expound the theory you have learned. In essence, this question is asking what the proper purpose of business is: is the traditional view correct, that the pursuit of personal interest automatically produces the best possible outcomes for society? Or is it more effective to pursue non-profit objectives directly? There are compelling arguments for both points of view.
>
> **Easy marks**. There are some fairly complex arguments to this debate, but don't overlook the simple things like the extra cost imposed by, for example, supporting community activities or the PR value gained by the same sort of thing. Some basic ideas from economics could be deployed, including, on the one hand, the view that free markets maximise output and minimise waste; and the existence of externalities on the other.
>
> **Examiner's comments**. Some candidates neglected the arguments against the idea of socially responsible actions. Remember, this debate is still in progress.

Answer plan

Traditional View		Stakeholder view
Profit ←————————— Costs		Natural law –rights
Production		Unrestrained power
Employment		Externalities
Ownership rights		Commitment

PR   *Brent Spar*
Fair trade

This answer plan is based on the clear split of arguments into two general positions of principle, with the practical matter of PR and image as a further consideration.

Against social responsibility

The traditional view is that business is undertaken to increase the wealth of the owners by **generating profit**. Business undertaken on this basis benefits society by providing goods and services, by creating employment, by funding tax revenues and, it is said, by means of a 'trickle down' of wealth from the rich to the poor.

Milton Friedman said that businesses do not have social responsibilities, only people have them. He asserted that managers who disburse corporate assets for social purposes were **failing in their duty to their employers**, usurping the role of government and furthering politically collectivist ideas.

It must be acknowledged that socially responsible activities are likely to directly disadvantage a business's owners by incurring **extra costs**, or by **sacrificing profitable turnover**. Such activities must at the very least, have the potential to **reduce stakeholder value**, though it can be argued that compensating effects can make them worthwhile from this point of view, as we shall see.

It must also be made clear that this view does not envisage business being run in any way that is either illegal or unethical.

For social responsibility

The opposite view, that business should not simply pursue profit but should undertake socially responsible actions can be supported on both **practical** and **philosophical** grounds.

Philosophically, the case for socially responsible action derives from natural law theory and is based on the idea of **individual and collective rights** that go beyond those currently recognised by existing legal systems. This approach suggests, for example, that businesses should recognise obligations to a range of **stakeholders**, such as to provide continuing employment and not to make profit or reward executives to a degree that could be called excessive. Such a **stakeholder view** holds that modern businesses are so powerful that unrestrained use of that power will **inevitably damage other people's rights**. This extends the traditional economic concept of **negative externalities**.

This general body of opinion is now widespread and cannot be discounted by those responsible for running businesses. They must be particularly alive to the **PR implications**. Bad publicity can cause severe damage to a business as *Shell* found when it took action to dispose of the *Brent Spar* oil production platform by sinking it in the North Atlantic.

On the other hand, actions of corporate social responsibility **can generate very good PR** that can, in turn, enhance competitive advantage and shareholder value. A good example of this is found in *Fairtrade* coffee products that retail at premiums many times larger than the extra margin they provide to the growers concerned. A good corporate image thus not only avoids difficulty but also attracts customers who take an active interest in such things.

40 Company J 1

> **Top tips.** This is a simple question. We use the list of factors that influence culture given in the BPP Study Text for Managerial Paper 5. The McKinsey 7S model could also form a basis for an answer, but if you have any knowledge of organisations you could almost invent your own list.
>
> For completeness, we give details of *Hofstede's* findings on regional differences in culture rather more fully than you would have time to do in the exam
>
> Candidates often have difficulty applying their theoretical knowledge in papers that require entirely written answers. To help overcome this difficulty, we print the application points in this answer in *italic*. Note that we also continue to use italic for technical references and to indicate a particular emphasis on some words.

> **Easy marks.** *Hofstede's* model of cultural differences is a little complex, but a statement of the axes of difference would be simple and worth a couple of marks. Be careful with the punctuation of the terms: only 'masculinity' has quotes and only individualism-collectivism has a hyphen.

An organisation's culture is influenced by many factors.

The organisation's founder. A strong set of values and assumptions is set up by the organisation's founder, and even after he or she has retired, these values have their own momentum. *Peters and Waterman* believed that 'excellent' companies began with strong leaders.

The organisation's history. *Johnson and Scholes* state that the way an organisation works reflects the era when it was founded. The effect of history is indicated by stories, rituals and symbolic behaviour. They legitimise behaviour and promote priorities.

Leadership and management style. An organisation with a strong culture recruits managers who naturally conform to it.

Structure and systems affect culture as well as strategy. *Handy's* description of an Apollonian role culture (bureaucracy) is an example (among others) where organisational form has cultural consequences.

In addition to these elements, there is the wider social and cultural setting, which is particularly relevant here, since we are concerned with transplanting Japanese managers and methods into a Western country.

Hofstede explains national cultural differences by identifying **key dimensions** in the value systems of all countries. Each country is represented on a scale for each dimension so as to explain and understand values, attitudes and behaviour. Global businesses have to be sensitive to these issues.

In particular, Hofstede pointed out that countries differ on the following dimensions.

(a) **Power distance**. This dimension measures how far superiors are expected to exercise power. In a high power-distance culture, the boss decides and people do not question.

(b) **Uncertainty avoidance**. Some cultures prefer clarity and order, whereas others are prepared to accept novelty. This affects the willingness of people to *change* rules, rather than simply obey them.

(c) **Individualism-collectivism**. In some countries individual achievement is what matters. In a collectivist culture people are supported and controlled by their in-group and put the interests of the group first.

(d) **'Masculinity'**. In 'masculine' cultures assertiveness and acquisitiveness are valued. 'Masculine' cultures place greater emphasis on possessions, status, and display as opposed to quality of life and caring for others.

Hofstede grouped countries into eight clusters using these dimensions. Here are some examples.

Countries in the **Anglo** group (the UK, the USA)

- Low to medium power-distance
- Low to medium uncertainty avoidance
- High individualism
- High 'masculinity'

Countries in the **Nordic** group (Scandinavia and also The Netherlands)

- Low power distance
- Low to medium uncertainty avoidance
- Medium individualism
- Low 'masculinity'

Countries in the **more developed Asian** group (ie Japan)

- Medium power distance
- High uncertainty avoidance
- Medium individualism
- High 'masculinity'

Countries in the **more developed Latin** group (including Belgium, France and Spain

- High power distance
- High uncertainty avoidance
- High individualism
- Medium masculinity

Countries in the **Germanic** group (including Germany and Italy)

- Low power distance
- High uncertainty avoidance
- Medium individualism
- High masculinity

We cannot say which group W would fall into, but it seems likely that it would differ from Japan on some if not all of these dimensions. Hence we might expect a certain amount of culture-based puzzlement if not actual conflict between management and workers in the early days of the new plant. Eventually, management power being what it is, we might expect normal rates of staff turnover to produce a workforce that could operate under largely Japanese cultural norms.

41 Company J 2

> **Top tips.** This question is a little more difficult than the previous one. To begin with, if you have no experience of the particular situation described (and very few candidates will) you must pause, think and imagine what the implications of *Hofstede's* model are for the running of a factory and what reasonable recommendations you might make.
>
> Candidates often have difficulty applying their theoretical knowledge in papers that require entirely written answers. To help overcome this difficulty, we print the application points in this answer in *italic*. Note that we also continue to use italic for technical references and to indicate a particular emphasis on some words.
>
> **Easy marks.** Basic knowledge of Hofstede's results will enable you to give a general introductory sentence or two to each section.

As we pointed out earlier, we do not know just where W would fall on *Hofstede's* dimensions, but we could suggest some ways in which differences might have practical implications.

Power distance

The Japanese managers and supervisors may be expected to display a medium degree of power distance. Workpeople whose cultural base includes a low score on this dimension may disconcert their managers by a familiar attitude and tendency to treat instructions as a basis for discussion. On the other hand, in cultures where a high degree of power distance is common, the Japanese managers may be disappointed at the apparent unwillingness of the work force to make suggestions, even when they are called for.

Uncertainty avoidance

Uncertainty avoidance is about the desire for **clarity** and **order** and tolerance of confusion, ambiguity and variety of process. *The Japanese managers would tend to value standard procedures and predictable organisational responses. An 'Anglo' or 'Nordic' workforce would be less likely to place such a high value on these things and may be quite happy with fluid, ad hoc arrangements. They may even assume that such flexibility is normal and find the Japanese approach over-restrictive, unimaginative and unpleasant to work under. This could be a cause of friction, possibly aggravating any industrial disputes that might arise.*

Individualism

The Japanese management style is widely perceived as placing a very high value on **consensus** and **group cohesion**. Behaviour prompted by individual ambition or inclination may be seen as a threat. *Such behaviour by members of work groups may cause some concern to the Japanese managers from the beginning of operations; it is likely to be even more of a concern later on, when it starts to become appropriate to appoint locally recruited supervisors and managers to work alongside Japanese expatriates.* A high degree of **individualism** is common among the 'more developed Latin' and 'Anglo' countries.

'Masculinity'

The Japanese display a high degree of 'masculinity', as do the 'Anglo' countries. Status symbols are very important in these societies: a good example of this is the British manager's company car, which, in many organisations, reflects fine gradations of status and success. *We might expect Japanese managers and 'Anglo' workpeople to have similar attitudes to such matters, but a different situation is likely to prevail in 'Nordic' countries, where 'masculinity' is low. This difference might be apparent in the workforce's attitude to status-enhancing incentives (which might not be very effective) and its failure to appreciate and recognise distinctions of status between managers and other staff.*

42 Supreme football

Top tips. The examiner has been quite careful in his choice of organisation for this question: clearly, the fans of the club will expect that their interest and loyalty will be reciprocated. They are more than customers but their continuing adherence to the club cannot be taken for granted. In part (b), there is not necessarily a correct answer. It will be possible for you to sit on the fence or choose one particular group. However, you *must* substantiate your position.

Easy marks. This question is a good example of the very common type in which part (a) is simple and part (b) requires a little more judgement. However, even in part (b), identifying the most important stakeholders should be quite easy.

Part (a)

Any organisation has many stakeholders and all have their own views on what they are entitled to expect from the organisation. *Freeman* defines stakeholders as 'any group or individual who can affect, or is affected by, the performance of an organisation'.

Stakeholders may be classified as falling into one of three categories. These include:

- internal stakeholders such as employees and managers
- external stakeholders which include pressure groups, government and the community
- connected stakeholders like shareholders, providers of finance, customers and suppliers.

Internal stakeholders of the Supreme Football Club (SFC) include the club's directors, the club manager, the players, the ground staff and other employees such as those employed in sales, marketing, finance and administration.

For internal stakeholders the relationship with the club is likely to be strong and long term. Both management and employees look to the club for their livelihood, for career development, for the opportunity to achieve something, for status and to associate with others.

- As well as guiding the affairs of the club, the directors are often major shareholders with a financial interest in its success.

- The players are key stakeholders because the club provides both their incomes and their careers.

PROFESSIONAL EDUCATION

- Managers and other employees will have a financial interest in the club and also have individual interests and goals such as:
    - security and increases of income
    - a safe and comfortable working environment
    - a sense of community
    - career development
    - a sense of doing something worthwhile

Connected stakeholders include shareholders, sponsors, bankers, fans and their parents and suppliers. Like internal stakeholders, the relationship with the organisation may also be long term and strong but it is different. Shareholders, bankers, fans and other customers and suppliers do not work directly for the club – although some may do as in the case of employees who hold shares – and so their concern is not with the day-to-day operations of the club as it is for the managers and employees.

- For the shareholders a major interest in the club is a return on their investment, but they are almost certainly also emotionally involved as fans.

- Sponsors provide funds for football clubs as a way of showing their interest and also as a means of advertising. They are interested in the club because of the media interest when the team is successful.

- Bankers who have provided loan finance will be interested in the club for both security on any loans granted and the interest they will receive.

- Fans are customers and are interested in the club as a source of leisure interest and pleasure. Parents of younger fans are stakeholders as a result of their children's interest. As customers they buy the club's merchandise and have an interest in good quality products at reasonable prices.

- Suppliers are interested in additional orders from the club and payment for what they supply.

- The mass communication media such as TV and radio companies, newspapers and magazines have a financial interest because football is a game of worldwide interest and attracts millions of viewers, listeners and readers. For satellite-broadcasting corporations with specific rights to film the games, this provides direct income from pay-to-view charges and indirect income from the advertising income attracted by a wider TV audience.

External stakeholder groups interested in the club include the government, local authorities, the community at large and the governing bodies in football.

- The government and local authorities have an interest because they tax receipts from the games and the club's merchandise. The government has a duty to see the club complies with various aspects of legislation including health and safety.

- The community at large and especially those near the stadium are interested from the point of view of parking, pollution, crime and crowd problems.

- The football governing bodies are required by their constitutions to regulate the game and see that it is not brought into disrepute.

Part (b)

All of the stakeholders will have an interest in the outcome of the bid for the club but the ones that are likely to influence the outcome will be those directly involved in the negotiations. These are the directors, the representatives of the satellite-broadcasting corporation and the football authority.

The directors are the legal representatives of the shareholders of the club. In many circumstances they will also be shareholders themselves. They have significant influence because they must recommend whether or not to accept a bid. The shareholders will determine whether or not the bid is accepted by voting in a ballot, but they are likely to follow the directors' advice.

The representatives of the satellite-broadcasting corporation are able to exert influence by how much they are prepared to offer for the club. As is often the case, the satellite company making the bid may not be the only interested party wanting to take over the club. There may be other companies waiting until negotiations start to find out how much is at stake; once this is known better offers might be placed before the directors. Until this happens they are not key stakeholders in the situation.

The football authorities that regulate competition in the industry will also influence the decision. They will wish to promote competition in the industry and avoid over-concentration of ownership.

Although they are not party to the negotiations, other stakeholders will have influence. The sponsors of the team may be direct competitors of the satellite broadcasting corporation or may not agree with the principles involved and decide not to continue with their contract when it comes up for renewal. The supporters may try to influence the decision by exploiting media interest.

43 Bureaucracy

Top tips. Candidates often have difficulty applying their theoretical knowledge in papers that require written answers, to help overcome this difficulty, we print the application points in this answer in *italic*. Note that we also continue to use italic for technical references and to indicate a particular emphasis on some words.

Part (a)

Top tips. Generally speaking, it is inappropriate to expound well-known theory in detail in your answers. The Examiner expects you to name the theory or writer you are going to refer to and then make it clear by the way you apply it that you know what you are talking about.

However, when you get a question that makes a specific reference, it is a good idea to follow it up. Here we build our answer around *Weber's* ideas about bureaucracy. If you cannot remember the model mentioned and it is a compulsory question, don't worry: you will probably only lose a few marks if you can make use of something equivalent, or at least related, such as *Burns and Stalker* in this instance.

Easy marks. The examiner mentions *Weber* in the question requirement. If you know how Weber defined the characteristics of bureaucracy you can obtain some easy marks by providing this information. Such basic ideas would probably be worth up to a third of the total marks available for this part of the question.

The consultant is right: all of Sunil's problems could be tackled by instituting aspects of bureaucracy.

Max Weber's description of bureaucratic methods offers several possible solution elements.

(a)   **Hierarchy**: each lower office is under the control and supervision of a higher one. *Sunil makes most of the decisions at the moment. This may have something to do with his current problems, in that he is too busy to give proper attention to all the demands made on his time. If his organisation grows, this problem will intensify. It would be appropriate for Sunil to think hard about appointing one or more subordinate managers who he could trust to take responsibility for some aspects of operations and the less important decisions. The problem of late deliveries and slow response to customer queries and complaints sound like failures of management: the appointments discussed above might help here.*

(b)   **Specialisation and training**: there is a high degree of specialisation of labour. Employment is based on ability, not personal loyalty. *It may be that some of Sunil's current problems occur because he is employing the wrong people, or because, while the people are potentially competent, they do not have the proper training, supervision and experience to get things right.*

(c)   **Impersonal nature**: employees work full time within the impersonal rules and regulations and act according to formal and impersonal procedures. *We are not told how big Sunil's company is, but if it continues to grow, Sunil is likely to find that allowing people to do things their own way makes for confusion and*

PROFESSIONAL EDUCATION

inefficiency. **Mintzberg's** idea of co-ordination by **mutual adjustment** really only works when a few people are involved. *Sunil's major current problem is one of product quality. Proper standards for manufacturing and inspection would help. A TQM approach would be more complex, but might be worth investigating.*

(d)   **Rationality:** the hierarchy of authority and office structure is clearly defined. Duties are established and measures of performance set. *This aspect of bureaucracy would help Sunil to avoid the potential for dispute about methods and authority that exists within his company today.*

*In addition to these rather theoretical matters, it is clear from the description of Sunil's current problems that a coherent set of **procedures** would go a long way to solving them. For example, lost invoices (presumably creditor invoices) is a clerical problem and proper clerical procedures would help to solve it.*

Procedures offer a number of advantages when what is essentially the same task has to be performed many times with only variation of details.

- The most efficient method can be clearly specified

- Time is saved by not 'reinventing the wheel'.

- Co-ordination between departments and people is easier if everyone knows what is supposed to happen.

- Supervision is made easier if reference can be made to an established procedure, perhaps published in a manual.

Sunil could thus make plenty of profitable use of the bureaucratic approach within his organisation.

Part (b)

Top tips. Despite the reference to Sunil in the question, the Examiner's answer to this part-question contains no more than a single fleeting reference to Sunil. Sometimes it is very difficult indeed to *apply* theory to the scenario and this would seem to be the case here. We do our best, as you will see.

The idea of bureaucracy is often associated with **negatives** like inertia, inflexibility, lack of imagination, inaction, delay, indecisiveness and ineffectiveness. This is largely due to the poor performance that seems unavoidable in large public sector organisations such as government departments and nationalised industries that are not subject to the need to make a profit. *Sunil is quite right not to want to import these features into his organisation.*

Such problems arise for a number of reasons. One has already been mentioned: when profit and commercial survival need not be considered because political motives guarantee the continuance of the organisation, there is no **external check** on the proliferation of unnecessary procedure, hierarchy and so on.

Indeed, the motivation becomes one of proving that exhaustive consideration has been given to all angles on a problem and that mistakes have not been made. This encourages a **defensive culture** and rigid adherence to the rules.

To this end, discretion is removed and decisions must be made in strict conformity to established **precedent**. Many decisions will have to be referred upwards through layers of hierarchy, with consequent loss of time and distortion in transmission. The organisation moves slowly and responds poorly to changing circumstances.

Bureaucracy is not very good at dealing with an environment that **changes** rapidly or in important ways: it takes too long to reach suitable conclusions about what the proper course of action is and its decision-making capability may be overwhelmed. In a commercial organisation, such poor responsiveness may be fatal.

*In Sunil's organisation, for example, **customer complaints** are a problem. It would be very difficult to establish procedures to deal with all the variations of problems that might arise; far better to allow a responsible customer services officer to make an appropriate response within general cost guidelines. The guidelines would represent the full extent of the application of the bureaucratic method in this instance.*

44 Question with analysis: GIC Insurance

> **Top tips.** A sound knowledge of the four cultural models we mention below is essential for this paper. It is likely that one of these models will help you answer at least one question on every paper, even if only as an analytical tool to help you think about the question topic.
>
> *Other ways of approaching the question*
>
> You could have focused on *one* cultural model rather than the many we have described. Moreover, these are not the only ways of characterising culture.
>
> **Easy marks.** This is quite a difficult question, involving familiarity with general models of culture.

Organisation culture

Part (a)

The cultural features within GIC

Corporate culture is influenced by the history of the firm, its founder, the structure of the firm, the environment, leadership and management style. Each organisation may have a dominant corporate culture, but different departments, especially where people are socialised in professional occupational cultures, may have their own.

Many models have been proposed to describe culture.

(a)   *Harrison's* approach (better known as *Handy's* 'gods of management') focuses on organisation structure and practice.

(b)   *Miles and Snow's* focuses on strategic decision making (analysers, defenders, prospectors, reactors).

(c)   *Denison's model* (consistency, mission, involvement, adaptability) focuses on the organisation's orientation (internal and external) and the environment.

(d)   *Hofstede* identified characteristics of culture which can be related to different countries.

Cultural features within GIC

(a)   **Strategic planning**. GIC features a combination of **defenders** and **analysers** (moving into new areas which others open up.). The change to a plc status throws all this open. **The company is in a state of change – but too much of this seems to stem for a 'reactor' mentality on behalf of senior management.**

(b)   **Values, beliefs and guiding principles**. As a mutual organisation, GIC existed for its **policy-holders**. The sales force were customer orientated to the extent that they maintained personal contact. There might have been aspects of the **mission culture**, with an ethos based on mutuality, rather than the satisfaction of demanding shareholders. However, as no single policy holder can exert control, the organisation may well have been run by management in their own interests – this might have been why managers took the decision to de-mutualise and to become a public limited company. **Significantly, no mission statement is provided.**

(c)   Structure of the organisation and the type of work it does

    The **branches** where the personal sales force are sited featured a combination of two cultures.

    (i)   A **power culture** (Zeus) centred round the branch manager, who was supposed to inspire and control the sales force.

    (ii)   A **person/existential culture** (Dionysus) in which people use the organisation to further their own goals. Salespeople who are independent and on commission were left to their own devices. Paid entirely by commission, some would have welcomed a low level of involvement.

    Elsewhere in the organisation, **routine administration** is carried out to maintain the policies and ensure that statutory and regulatory requirements are adhered to. Such a department would have had a **role culture or consistency culture** to ensure that everything is in its proper place. However, other cultures (such as the involvement culture, which is very much concerned with human relations) might have played a role in this particular division. Again, although concerned with administration, it will still feature the 'service' ethos, given that policyholders are the main reason why the business exists.

Part (b)

Changes in culture: more of a role culture

For the time being, one of the major **influences** on organisation culture, in both the sales and administration is the **business strategy**, such as it is, and the structural changes which are supposed to support it.

Most importantly, the mission of the firm have changed from **satisfying policy holders to satisfying shareholders**. Hence the need for cost-cutting, which will change the possibly cosy ethos of before.

The new management team has moved in this direction: whether it will develop from a **reactor** into an **analyser or prospector** (Miles and Snow) is not certain.

This go-getting ethos at strategic level arguably replicated certain aspects of the **salespeople's** approach. They were paid entirely by commission, and so profit-orientation should not be beyond them. However, the **new salary structure, designed to enforce standards, appears like overkill. A greater commercial ethos at board level might meet with its dilution at the level of the sales force**. There are other approaches to operationalising business ethics (eg codes of practice).

The newly expanded **compliance department** will promote certain aspects of a role culture. This influence is reflected in rules and procedures, and will be reinforced by the new salary-based reward system which is taking over from commission.

Not mentioned are the **rituals and symbols of the firm**. At times of change, some firms choose to embody these in a new mission statement – to communicate the emphasis on shareholder value – and a new corporate identity to indicate that the change has been made.

To summarise, the firm will probably take on some of the functions of a **bureaucracy**, internally, although the business and strategy is more commercial and entrepreneurial – the directors are, of course, taking a risk by setting up a telesales operation when so many other firms have done so.

45 J & T

> **Top tips.** Answering this part of the question will require not only careful reading of the setting but also the deployment of some background knowledge about globalisation. You can obtain the latter from regular selective reading of a quality newspaper.
>
> Remember also to think about the practicality of your suggestions.
>
> **Easy marks.** This is a demanding question and there are not too many easy marks beyond those available for the outline of cultural theory.

Part (a)

Choices open to IC plc

(a)   The group of suppliers has developed through **horizontal integration** and now is proposing a strategy of **vertical integration**, by suggesting a takeover of J & T, presumably with the hope that it will be able to keep J & T's customers and lock them in.

     (i)   J & T had a reputation of going to the best source of supply. The takeover will reduce competition. Customers will have to go to suppliers directly. IC plc is thus erecting a small **barrier to entry** round the UK market, by making it impossible for its competitors to use J & T as a distribution mechanism.

111

(ii)   J & T has a great deal of **market knowledge**, however, which needs to be exploited by the new entity, to make the acquisition worthwhile.

(b)   IC plc will have to respond to the **globalisation** of the industry, although this has some way to go. It benefits, for example, from being physically close to its customers. If firms adopt just-in-time production systems, IC plc's physical proximity can be a useful source of product differentiation, as well as saving money on the distribution costs of bulk materials.

Differentiation

(i)   What this means, therefore, is that IC plc should differentiate itself in the home market on the basis of its **local knowledge and speedy service**.

- This might require substantial investment in research and development into new production systems, market research and customer relationships.

- This entails the recruitment and development of technical specialists, whilst retaining a marketing orientation.

(ii)   The firm may need to differentiate itself on grounds of **quality**; although it has to be said that quality is less a differentiating factor than a requisite for being in some businesses at all. Any deficiencies on this score must be addressed.

(c)   The company has to respond to **globalisation**.

(i)   **Multinational firms have taken over many of J & T's former customers**. These large firms will have more clout than J & T's previous customers ever did. As multinationals, they are able to call on a much wider knowledge of suppliers worldwide. IC plc's customers might therefore be keen to gain economies of scale by global sourcing. This means that for certain materials, J & T will never be able to compete on price (unless transportation costs make a difference).

(ii)   There is no reason to suppose that these multinational customers will necessarily keep their UK subsidiaries open, especially with the Channel Tunnel and the development of pan-European distribution centres.

IC plc will therefore be **driven to pursue a global strategy**, in order to avoid being squeezed by its customers.

(i)   At present IC plc is based only in the UK, which could make it **vulnerable to customer decisions** to move elsewhere.

(ii)   IC plc needs to consider **expansion into overseas markets**. To this end, it needs personnel who are knowledgeable about exports, international marketing and IC plc's business.

(iii)   IC plc could explore the possibility of **joint ventures** with overseas companies in a similar position, to share markets and customers.

(d)   **Changes to organisation structure** are required by these developments..

(i)   The firm will need to employ a number of skilled personnel, who can provide expertise in R & D and in marketing. There is thus an enhanced role for the **technostructure** and **support services** in the organisation. Strictly speaking, a powerful technostructure tends to lead towards bureaucracy, as work becomes standardised and technicians control production. The work of the technostructure needs to be designed so as to become a factor which improves operations rather than merely controls them. Support services, on the order hand, lead to adhocracy.

(ii)   The strategic challenges of globalisation also requires an organisational response. The firm should set up an **international marketing division** to research and then to enter new markets. In particular, the firm needs intelligence as to the likely needs of its multinational customers.

(iii) The company should ensure it gains any economies of scale from the mergers, without sacrificing flexibility and responsiveness.

Part (b)

Culture can be defined as the sum total of the beliefs, knowledge, attitudes of mind and customs to which people are exposed. The basic assumptions of J & T, which guide individual behaviour, include **quality** and the establishment of close **long-term relationships** with customers.

Harrison analysed culture into four types, which bear some relationship to the structure of the organisation.

J & T's old culture would have been a **power culture** which *Handy* characterises, in his book **Gods of Management**, by **Zeus**. The other cultures mentioned by Handy are the role culture or bureaucracy (Apollo), the task culture (Athena) and the existential culture (Dionysus).

(a) J & T's decentralised structure was based on the **expertise** of each partner who employed up to forty sales staff. This relatively loose structure would imply that a partner had all the responsibilities for contracts in that area, for developing the business and so forth.

(b) The partner would be the source of all authority, and there is no suggestion that each local office was bureaucratic or proceduralised. Each partner would try to build up bridges with local suppliers.

(c) The lack of a rigid structure and the fairly small size would promote **flexibility and informality**.

(d) The **personal element** is also a feature of the power culture. The partners, in their recruitment practices, are obviously concerned to find the right sort of person, irrespective of his or her technical qualifications for their job: an ethical stance was mentioned. The partners therefore share many of the same assumptions, even those not related to their approach to business. The employment of like minded people is characteristic of a power culture.

For the company as a whole, does this framework still apply? Arguably it does: the founders, Jones and Thompson, are still in charge of the business, having remained senior partners since the firm was founded. Although there is more than one person in this power culture, the nature of the business and its organisation structure would suggest that this culture was prevalent.

The principal **changes** faced are to do with the structure of the industry, and incremental improvements to technology, rather than any radical changes in the relationship the organisation has with its clients. The industry still provides a commodity manufactured product to its customers. The changes in industry structure have been generated by increased competition, and the obvious need for economies of scale. As the market has grown, so too has the size of the organisations within it. The market is now international rather than national.

46 Imperial traders plc

> **Top tips.** It will then be necessary to differentiate carefully between the topics that are relevant to part (a) and those that are relevant to part (b), since the effects of relocation and the benefits of thinking about it are clearly entwined. In essence the answer to part (a) is that a sensible decision can be taken, while that to part (b) is a discussion of the balance of considerations leading to the decision in part (a). This kind of complexity in the logic of a question is, unfortunately, not particularly unusual.
>
> **Easy marks.** In part (a), some easy marks will be available simply for explaining the nature of a position audit.

Part (a)

A position audit is 'Part of the planning process which examines the **current** state of the entity in respect of:

- resources of tangible and intangible assets and finance;
- products, brands and markets;
- operating systems such as production and distribution;

- internal organisation;
- current results;
- returns to stockholders.

The question asked is **'Where are we now?'**. It is the beginning of the long term planning process, on the assumption that in order to reach a desired objective you need to have a good idea as to where you are starting from. This will enable Imperial Traders plc then to assess the extent to which continuing operations can contribute towards the goal, and to develop strategies to fill the gap between the goal and what is currently achievable.

The proposed move to a Pacific Rim location. The position audit will deal with **all** the factors noted for:

(a)   **The company as a whole**
(b)   **The Head Office entity** in particular.

- The position audit covers the unique functions as a head office in the context of the firm's internal operation, and in its relations with the wider commercial environment and with investors and bankers. (No other strategic change in the company's **operations** is being contemplated. The entity under discussion, therefore, will be Head Office.)

- The gathering of comparative cost information for London and various regional sites

- The current role of Head Office in its existing location

Only after such a position audit is carried out, can management decide:

- Whether to move at all
- If a move is desirable, where to go to
- How the move will be implemented successfully

Benefits in carrying out a position audit in respect of this decision revolve around the **role of Head Office**.

(a)   **Head office might simply set financial targets** and **let subsidiaries get on with meeting them**, avoiding interference with tactical or day to day decisions. In this case the role of Head Office will be to communicate with the investment community, to be a central location for financial reporting, and as a domicile for the company so that it can take advantage of a favourable tax regime. Thus it might be **better to keep it in the UK** for the benefit of the company's investors. Moreover, the City of London is a centre of world finance, and if the firm's activities require a great deal of financial sophistication, London might be the place to stay.

(b)   The **Head Office may take a hands-on approach** to the running of the company. If all its activities are heavily interrelated, Head Office coordination may be essential for the company's successful functioning. A position audit of the company as a whole would identify those **regions which are most critical to its long term success**. If that region is Japan, for example, this might be a good reason for relocating to that country.

(c)   The position audit should identify all the major costs and benefits of such a move, in a formal way, and so should result in a better decision.

Part (b)

Effects of relocating to a Pacific Rim country

(a)   **Choice of country.** The term **Pacific Rim** is normally held to encompass the west coast of the USA, Indonesia, the Philippines, and the rapidly growing region of southern China as well as the area of Imperial Traders plc's current operations which comprises Japan, Korea, Malaysia, and Australia. The final choice as to which of the latter countries will be the site of the new Head Office will be as significant as the decision to move away at all. Recent financial crises (eg in Korea) do provide opportunities for expansion.

(b)   **Tangible assets**

(i)   **Imperial Traders will need to sell its London accommodation.** The price it receives may be a major factor in the economic benefits of the relocation decision.

(ii) **Imperial traders will have to buy office space**. The **relative price** of office space in each country will differ significantly. Japan, despite the current slump in land prices, is still extremely expensive. Perhaps an Australian location would be cheaper.

(c) **Finance**. Imperial Traders will be moving from London, which has one of the world's most developed capital markets. It must ensure that its needs are as well satisfied in one of the Pacific Rim countries? A country with a relatively **open financial system**, such as Australia, might be a better than, say, Korea. The company will already deal with providers of trade finance, so this should not be any great problem.

(d) **Products, brands, and markets**.

(i) **Products and brands.** We do not know which products are Imperial Traders plc's particular speciality. It might specialise in trading commodity products (like wool from Australia to textile factories elsewhere) or it might specialise in trading manufactured goods. It might not specialise at all.

(ii) **Markets.** If Imperial Traders plc is basically a transport and distribution company, active in several areas, then the domicile of its Head Office is unlikely to matter very much in terms of the goods it trades, nor in attracting business. However, moving Head Office closer to its main markets may **enhance head office's market knowledge**. If Head Office plays a coordinating role, it might be able to develop a better strategic vision as to where it wants to be if this function is located in its **main market**.

(e) **Operating systems**. The firm will have to arrange appropriate and secure **telecommunications links**, especially for the transfer of commercial documentation by fax or email. If most of its activities before the move were based in the region, changes should not be too drastic, but the firm will need to develop the right system for the Head Office function.

(f) The **internal organisation**. This is where the difference will be greatest.

(i) Many of the London based staff may not wish to be relocated, and might leave the company.

(ii) The company, moreover, might wish to avoid the expense of relocation, and prefer to **recruit staff locally** or transfer staff from the company's divisions in the regions to the new head office function. There are likely to be redundancy costs in the UK, and the cost of hiring and training staff in the area.

(g) **Current results**. There will be a number of **costs** entailed in the move, and perhaps some loss of efficiency in the Head Office function. Careful planning should minimise this risk. It is possible that the firm might receive **relocation subsidies** from some countries, or it may be able to negotiate a tax holiday if the country wishes it to locate there.

(h) **Returns to stockholders**

(i) Initially, there might be an adverse effect, owing to the **costs of the move**.

(ii) Later, if the move of Head Office significantly **affects the firm's trading patterns** or financial arrangements, the effect could be large. For example, the firm might have used Sterling more often than necessary as there was a London Head Office. As currency flows are likely to remain within the Pacific Rim region, the **currency risk will be different**. This might significantly affect the reported returns to stockholders, who are based in the UK. Furthermore, if the company can find capital at cheaper rates than in the UK this will reduce its interest charge, and might make certain activities appear more attractive.

Part (c)

Cultural differences. Imperial Traders plc's activities are divided between two Commonwealth countries (Australia and Malaysia) and two countries (Japan and Korea) where the UK had no formal colonial presence. Some existing staff may move to the new location, with the consequent disruption to their personal lives.

(a)   **Language**. If the Head Office staff relocate to Australia, there will be no problem with language, as English is spoken there. English is used widely in Malaysia. In Korea or Japan, however, while English is taught, staff will find it hard to get by without a good working knowledge of Korean or Japanese.

(b)   **Business culture**. Different cultures have different ways of doing business, arranging deals and so forth. UK staff will have to get used to this in all of the countries mentioned.

(c)   **Different legal systems**. Australia's legal system is probably most like the UK's.

(d)   **Women**. The relative inequality of women in Japanese society is greater than that of the UK. Female executives may find it harder to be accepted by Japanese counterparts. (At the same time, this is an **opportunity** for the firm to recruit talented female employees who might be ignored by more chauvinist local managers.)

(e)   **Personal problems**

    (i)   Newly expatriate staff will need to adjust to different climate, diet and working hours.

    (ii)   Those with **families** will have to find education provision for their children, and perhaps employment for spouses. The firm might have to run a cultural adjustment program to help them cope. People might have initial difficulty in forming friendships if social mores are very different.

47 Bowland carpets

Top tips. It is very important in a question like this not to generalise but to relate the answer to the scenario. Marks were specifically awarded for Bowland's competences, entry barriers for Bowland and Bowland's strategy.

Easy marks. Competences and critical success factors are difficult and complex topics. However, a little background economic knowledge and clear thinking should enable you to come up with a few barriers to entry. Try using the value chain as a model of a business to focus your thoughts on how and where such barriers might arise.

Examiner's comment. The first part of the question revealed some confusion between competences and critical success factors. Better candidates spotted how the use of competitive forces/barrier models and PEST analysis could be used to good effect in structuring their answers

Part (a)

An organisation's **distinctive competences**, highlighted in its internal analysis, are those features, skills or processes that differentiate it and its performance/products attractively from its competitors and enable it to obtain a special sphere of influence or a strong competitive position. Competences derive from experience, staff skills and the quality of co-ordination. **Strategic strengths** (in which the organisations excels), are superior to those of competitors and provide a base of advantage.

Critical success factors.

Critical success factors are those things the organisation must do well at if it is to succeed. They are not the same thing as competences: competences may allow the organisation to achieve its critical success factors. For example, a factor critical to business success is satisfactory cash flow. This might be achieved in a number of ways, such as good credit control or the availability of high margins. It would not be satified by the competence in a special technology.

Mismatches between competences and success factors

Most organisations doing a SWOT analysis will find a mismatch somewhere. A company may be successful at establishing a strong position during the early stages of market development, only to lose ground later when the key success factors have changed. With **consumer products** marketing and distribution skills are dominant during the early phases but operations and manufacturing become more crucial as the product moves into the maturity and decline stage.

Bowland's new strategy. The management at the US parent company of Bowland Carpets have come up with a new strategy in an attempt to solve the problem of the declining carpet sales in the UK, mainly in the domestic market. The **contract** and **industrial carpet** segment will not be affected radically as the distribution network generally uses **direct sales**.

Bowland UK's competences are the ability to:

- Offer a wide range of high quality products at **competitive prices**.
- Sustain **powerful brand names**, presence in different market segments.
- Sustain **good relationships** with distributors.

Success factors for retailing

The proposed option of vertical integration into retailing will require a set of key success factors which will include some of these competences. However, there are **gaps** which are a cause for concern.

The **key success factors** for vertical integration into retail sales which have been **developed in the US will not be totally transferable to the UK** and the domestic company has no expertise in this field.

(i)   **Distribution.** It is not clear whether the intention is to introduce this strategy as an addition to the current distribution network or instead of it. Both of these options would affect the **relationship with distributors** that has built up over a period and could be very **damaging to sales**. To compensate for this loss, Bowland Carpets would need to have a strong **geographical** presence either in High Street positions or in out of town developments. This could be **very costly** in both site selection and development.

(ii) **Expertise** in **retailing** and **distribution**. Staffing and servicing the retail outlets and training the staff in the skills required will be time consuming and expensive. When customers buy carpets they expect a measuring, fitting and laying service as well as after-sales support. It may be that the UK company can learn from the USA but the culture of marketing household durables is different in both countries.

(iii) The **ability to provide a choice of products and services for the customer**. If there is insufficient choice, Bowland Carpets will have to find competitive manufacturers to fill the gap. This action may defeat the strategy to raise the sales in the **domestic** carpet market.

Conclusion. Bowland's distinctive competences are not appropriate to the key success factors required for retailing.

Part (b)

Entry barriers prevalent in the carpet retailing sector.

- The number of established carpet retailers in an already mature market
- The variety of own brands available in dominant department stores
- The cost, availability and maintenance of suitable retail sites
- Suitable suppliers and reasonable terms
- The retailing skills which will need to be developed
- Marketing investments (research, staffing)
- The ability to offer a broad product line
- The level and nature of the service offered
- Brand loyalty

Part (c)

An external environmental analysis identifies emerging trends, **opportunities** and **threats** created by the forces outside the organisation.

(a)   Firms must avoid major surprises by anticipating major changes in their business circumstances.

(b) Firms must make daily responses to changes among their customers, suppliers and workforce. Those who discover the longer-term patterns can decide whether they pose a threat or an opportunity and can gain a head start on their competitors.

Contents

(a) The **competitive** environment. Knowledge of the reactions of the other players in the market, both manufacturers and retailers, could be crucial to the success or otherwise of a new entrant's plan. Established businesses can adopt **retaliation strategies** to make it difficult for new companies to enter the market.

(b) **Economic** factors include the **rate of growth** and the associated increase/decrease in **disposable income** the **rate of inflation**, the state of the domestic housing market (house moves are often associated with new refurbishments) unemployment, interest rates and the availability of credit, taxation levels and incentives.

(c) **Political** factors include laws on the safety of the product, town planning, selling practices adopted and the way a firm treats its employees.

(d) The **social, demographic and cultural** environment analysis would highlight issues such as: the growth or decline in population; changes in ages when people leave home and start their own household; trends in house refurbishments; trends towards car-centred shopping in superstores and out of town shopping 'cities'.

(e) The **technological** environment. Consumers expect modern carpets to have properties which keep stains and insects away. The manufacturing environment is undergoing rapid changes with the growth of advanced manufacturing technology. Retail outlets are using point of sale equipment which can be used for stock control and to analyse the customer trends. Some DIY stores allow customers access to large cutting machines to avoid expensive cutting and laying services.

48 Objective test questions

48.1 C Projects will usually be unique; will have resources specifically allocated to them; and will have clear objectives; so options A, B and D are not typical of projects.

48.2 A Configuration management is a *component* rather than a *process:* it controls the processes by which projects evolve. Directing a project is the responsibility of the project board and consists of the higher aspects of control and decision-making. Managing stage boundaries ensures that one stage of a project is properly completed before the next one begins.

48.3 D Options A, B and C are aspects of the first three phases: define the project; design the project and deliver the project, respectively.

48.4 B Henry Gantt was the man. Some people find it extremely difficult to spell his name correctly.

48.5 B Option A is a summary of the purpose of a resource histogram; option C is a characteristic of the use of project planning software; the computation of float times (option D) is possible with the basic techniques of critical path analysis.

48.6 B 12 days are needed for the critical path A-E-G.

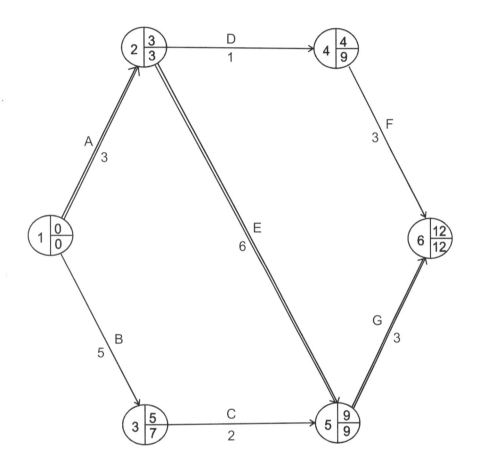

48.7 A   The dependencies given mean that the activities can be thought of as forming three main strands as shown in the Gantt chart below. Two of these strands can be manipulated to reduce the staff requirement on day 6 to the five people needed for activity E.

(a)   Activity B is started on day 1 and is therefore complete by the end of day 5

(b)   Activity C, which depends on activity B, is not started until day 8. This allows it to be completed by the end of day 9 so that activity G is not delayed.

(c)   Activity D can be undertaken on any day from day 4 to day 9 inclusive. We show it happening on day 9.

The disadvantage of this manipulation is to produce a requirement for thirteen staff on day 9.

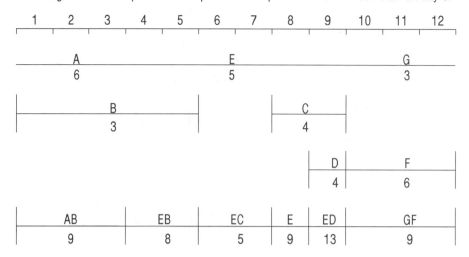

49 Objective test questions

49.1 A This is a tricky question. The characteristics of the project staff are such that a **consultative** or even **democratic** style might be recommended. However, the time and quality constraints mean that the project manager is likely to have to exercise firm control on occasion. This would probably be best done in a **persuasive** style. The conclusion is that the **autocratic** style will probably be of least use.

49.2 D Specialisation appears in neither the project 7S nor the McKinsey 7S model.

49.3 A Communicating the project vision within the organisation is the role of the project sponsor; the project manager is responsible for delivering the project on time; the project board represents the interests of the project sponsor.

49.4 C The system focuses on products rather than processes.

49.5 B Fact.

49.6 C 12 weeks are needed for the critical path B-F-H.

49.7 A

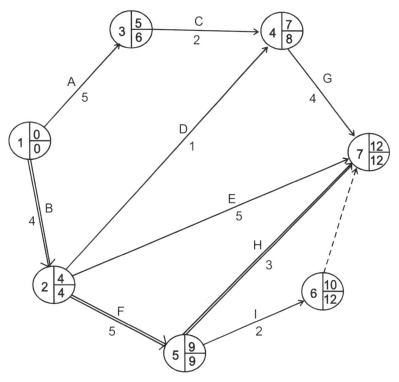

Total float is time available less duration. For D this is $(8 - 4) - 1 = 3$.

Free float is the delay possible assuming all preceding activities started as early as possible and all subsequent activities also start at the earliest time. For D this is $(7 - 4) - 1 = 2$.

Independent float is the delay possible if all preceding jobs have finished as late as possible and all succeeding jobs start as early as possible. For D this is the same as free float, since activity B is on the critical path and therefore cannot be delayed.

50 Project network

> **Top tips.** Your diagram may differ from ours in layout, but you should obtain the same information from it.
>
> **Easy marks.** If you draw the diagram correctly, you already have the answers to parts (a) and (b).

(a)   Either of the following diagrams.

Activity-on-node style

Activity-on-line style

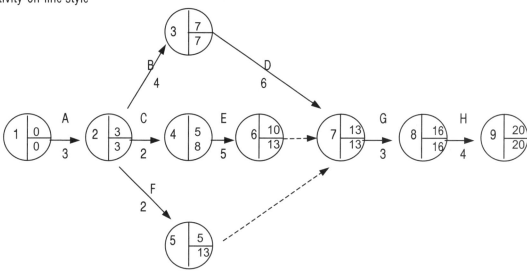

(b)   Activities on the critical path are A, B, D, G, H.

(c)   20 days.

(d)   Task C overrunning by two days would not change the elapsed duration.

(e)   Task B overrunning by one day would increase the elapsed duration to 21 days.

51 FRS 1

To: Management team of FRS Ltd
From: Management Consultant
Date: 29 April 200X

The major issues to be considered in managing the project to implement the MRO Inc system at FRS Ltd are outlined below.

The project manager and the project team

It is important to establish who has overall responsibility for a successful implementation. The scope of the project needs to be established, and then a person with the required motivation and skills appointed as project manager. The composition of the project team is vital – particularly ensuring sufficient user representation. (Including actual 'hands-on' users, ie not only management.)

What the implementation hopes to achieve

The project team requires a focus. What the implementation is supposed to achieve should be spelt out clearly. The statement may seem like stating the obvious, but it provides a reference point for which all issues that arise should take into account.

How successful completion will be achieved

The project must be properly planned and controlled if it is to achieve completion on time, within budget and to required performance specifications. The availability of required resources must be established. Tasks need to be scheduled and allocated providing a framework for monitoring progress and exercising control.

Communication

Communication between developers and users is essential. The project team must establish lines communication between team members (eg meeting, e-mail links) and between the team and all personnel affected. What the implementation hopes to achieve, from both a users and an organisation-wide perspective, should be communicated to the personnel of FRS Ltd.

User training

The survival and prosperity of FRS Ltd is dependant on shop transactions. It is therefore essential staff are able to use the system before it 'goes live'. Training requirements should be planned as part of the overall implementation plan. 'Hands-on' sessions using the new system in a test environment are vital.

Method of implementation

How will the new system be implemented? Will a phased implementation be followed or is it practical to have a straight cut-off of the existing system. Will all shops change over at the same time?

Contingency plan

A contingency plan must be drawn up that enables business to continue in the event of system failure. This may involve utilising the old system or reverting to manual procedures.

52 FRS 2

Top tips. Concentrate on getting the logic of activities E, F, G and H right.

Easy marks. Activities A to D plot themselves!

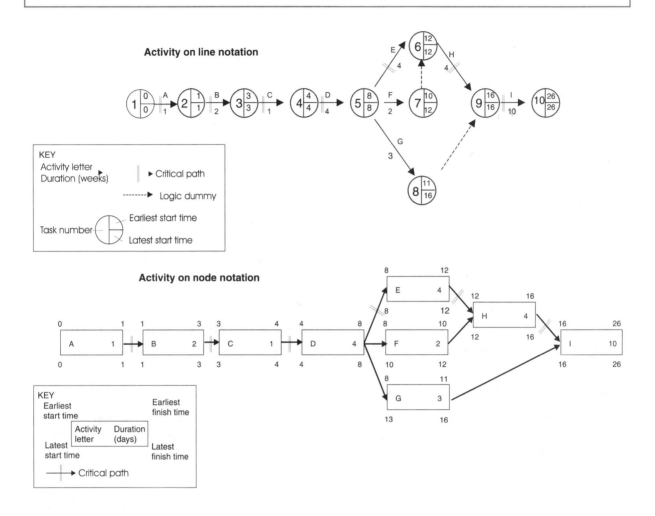

The critical path is A, B, C, D, E, H, I. The total elapsed time is 26 weeks.

53 New activities

Top tips. Use the diagram in the question to position the two extra activities. Then make a fair copy of the whole thing.

Easy marks. If you understand how the diagram conventions work, part (b) is easily answered by reading off the data in the event circle at the end of activity E.

(i)   *[One of the following]*

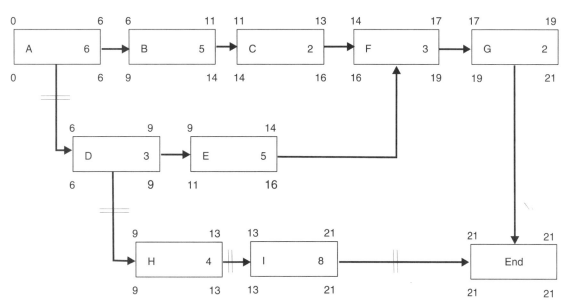

(ii)   Activity E can overrun by up to 2 days.

54 Question with helping hand: Critical path analysis

Top tips. This diagram illustrates how float time may be shown on a network. This is for interest only: do not attempt this in the exam.

Easy marks. This is quite a tricky network; you must recognise the logical requirements of activities G, H and I.

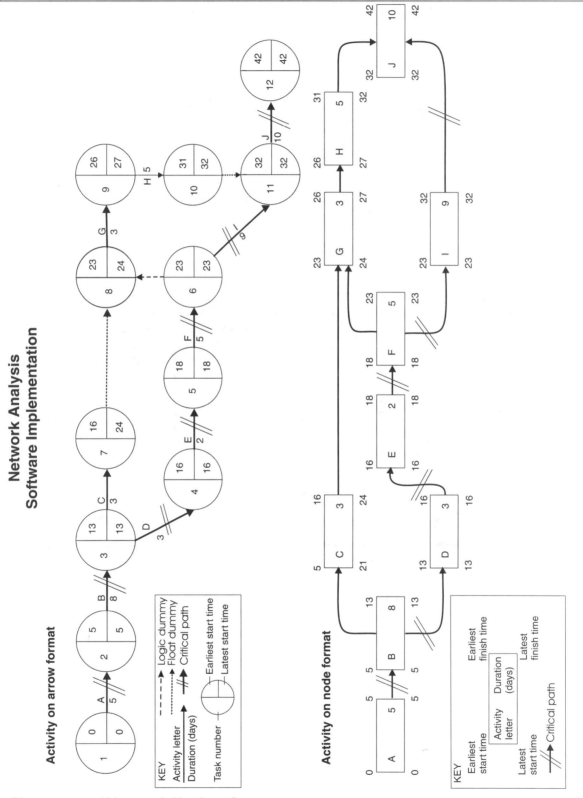

[Your answer could have used either format]

55 CityGo

Projects in general

The implementation of its own financial systems will require the management at CityGo to set up a **project management process** which can deal with tight timescales involving a complicated set of interrelated decisions and actions.

(a)   **Project management** differs from the management of resources which is attempting to achieve specific objectives within set **timescales** and **budgets** – a one-off activity.

(b)   **Functional management**, on the other hand, is concerned with providing an on-going service.

A project has boundaries and it is one of the activities of the project management team to set and keep the project within those boundaries. The set of attributes that are needed to achieve the project's objectives are shown in the diagram below.

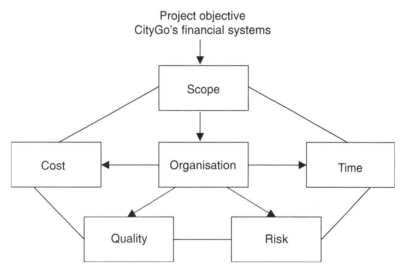

The **scope** of the project is to ensure that the project's purpose is achieved by specifying the work that must be done and excluding superfluous or otherwise unnecessary work.

The project **organisation** assembles the appropriate resources required to undertake the project.

- Approving plans
- Monitoring progress
- Allocating resources (human, technical, financial and material)
- Assessing results
- Recommending continuance or termination

Cost, time and **quality** can be juggled to produce the optimum result. For example, decreasing the cost to deliver the optimum result without compromising the quality objective might mean allowing more time for the project. In the case of CityGo the time element is crucial. They only have a few months to set up these new computer based systems.

Risk. The project manager can then determine how the risks can be lessened, deflected or avoided and draw up a risk management plan, including contingency plans.

Using project management techniques

Project techniques can be managed under suitable project management software, which incorporates most of the techniques familiar to project management.

(a) **Scope**

    (i)   **Project definition**. A precise definition as to what is expected of the project is required.

    (ii)   **Work breakdown structure (WBS)** defines the scope of the project in detail by breaking it up into smaller parts. This is the best way of discovering the work that must be done, as well determining the resources required.

(b) **Organisation**. The roles and responsibilities between the parties at the different levels must be identified, as well as the level and competence of the resource to be used.

(c) **Cost**. The WBS can be used to analyse direct and indirect costs of each activity. This structure can then be used for estimating or tendering for the project.

(d) **Time**. Tasks need to be scheduled and planned in order to make the most effective use of the resources available. **Scheduling techniques** use the work breakdown structure to plan the time required to complete each task. **Network analysis** identifies the dependence of one task on another. A **critical path** will exist throughout the project. If activities differ in their actual time from their estimated time, these differences can be entered into the computer and a recalculation of the critical path takes place. (Project managers may also use **simulations** to assess possible outcomes for alternative assumptions, seeking the best combination with the existing time and cost constraints.)

(e) **Quality**. CityGo management should state their precise requirement for the financial systems so that the standards against which the quality is measured are clear.

(f) **Risk**. The team can attempt to reduce the risk through good work practices, quality specifications and standards, backup systems and contingency plans. The remaining risk may be an **insurable risk**.

56 Conference network

> **Top tips**. There are clearly two parts to this requirement:
>
> - Construct a network diagram.
>
> - Say why it is useful.
>
> However, they are not worth equal marks. The first part is worth six marks and the second is worth four. To score full marks for the first part you not only have to draw the network, you also have to identify the critical path and give the project duration. A properly drawn network will do both of these things, but you should remember in particular to mark the critical path by the use of hash mark or doubling the lines. To be on the safe side you may care to provide a small note of the kind we show in our solution.
>
> **Easy marks**. The basic network is extremely easy to draw. However, do not fall into the trap of numbering the critical path events consecutively from start to finish and then numbering the remaining events on the other path: this would lead you to give a higher number to the last non-critical event than to the event that follows it, which is, of course, by convention not done and might cost you a mark.
>
> **Examiner's comments**. The Examiner found that this question was generally done very well, but some candidates failed to say how the network information could be used.

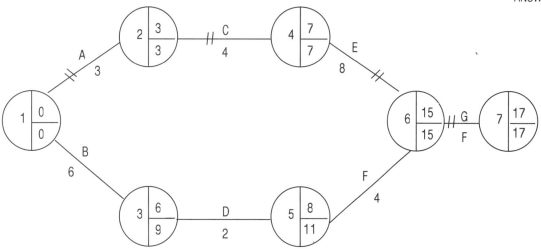

The critical path is activities A–C–E–G and last 17 days.

The network diagram provides several pieces of useful information.

(a)   Knowledge of the **duration of the critical path** will provide R with a latest time by which she must have started work on her project.

(b)   Knowledge of which **activities make up the critical** path will assist R in checking progress along it and in prioritising the work that has to be done on them.

(c)   The two separate paths through the network show the activities that may be undertaken at more or less the same time, which will help with the **planning of resource utilisation**. This process would be further aided by the use of a **Gantt chart**.

(d)   Awareness of the three weeks **float time** available on the non-critical path will allow R some flexibility in the management of her resources.

57 Project planning and roles

Part (a)

> **Top tips**. This is a very practical question, so you will have to try hard to avoid talking about the many interesting but rather theoretical aspects of project management, such as the project life cycle and project stakeholders. Stick very much to what the project manager has to do.
>
> Notice that we make an assumption in response to the ambiguous wording of the requirement. Should you find that you are not quite sure what is required, choose the simplest option and state the assumption you have made.
>
> **Easy marks**. You have been given some clear indications of the matters the project manager has to deal with: make sure you include these topics and the work related to them in your answer, if only as examples of work to be done.
>
> **Examiner's comments**. Some candidates lost their way , going into too much detail on specific planning phases rather than giving an overview of the whole planning process

(Note. We have assumed that the requirement for 'setting up a customer service contact team' means bringing the existing team to a state of operational readiness in the new premises rather than setting up a new team from scratch, with all that that implies in the way of recruitment, selection, training and development.)

Very little planning can be done for any activity without a fairly clear idea of the **objectives** that are to be achieved. In this case, the overall objectives are indicated quite well and we might say that the aim is to prepare for and execute the move of S Company headquarters staff to their new premises. This overall aim will be supported by several **subsidiary or enabling objectives**.

- Ensure that all necessary and appropriate building services and facilities are in place and functioning properly.

- Design, install, test and commission an upgraded office IT support system.

- Close down the existing headquarters building.

- Move portable equipment to the new building and install it.

- Brief and execute the transfer of existing staff to the new building.

- Deal with any HRM problems arising from the move.

The subsidiary objectives listed above give a fair idea of the **scope** of the project; that is to say, the overall amount and type of work that has to be done to complete it. Establishing the project's scope in detail is the first step towards the **work breakdown structure** necessary for detailed project planning.

It is clear that the project has, effectively, already been authorised by the board of S Company and will be undertaken. Nevertheless, there will still be a need for a clear statement of roles and responsibilities in a **project authorisation document** (or project charter), so that all concerned know what is to be done and who is responsible for which parts. This will be particularly important in relation to the IT system, since its development must involve specialists who are likely to have their own ideas and priorities. If **external contractors** are involved, clear objectives and standards must be set for them from the outset.

Once the objectives are in place and the scope of the work is agreed, detailed planning can commence. This will require the establishment of a **project team**, which should include an appropriate level of project dedicated staff and representatives from the various headquarters departments. For a project of this size, D will probably be able to manage with an assistant, so long as he or she can call upon departmental representatives for advice when required.

The detailed planning of the work to be done to enable the move to take place will revolve around three main areas of work: the IT system, the new building and the details of the move. **Network analysis** and **Gantt chats** will be useful for establishing time and resource requirements and constraints. The use of these methods also provides for detailed progress control by the project manager and the establishment of major review gates at which progress can be checked by P.

Other important aspects of planning are **risk** and **cost**. Costs must be estimated and a **budget** created so that expense can be monitored. Risk assessment leads to **risk management actions**, such as avoidance, minimisation and insurance.

Part (b)

> **Top tips**. This is a rather easier question than part (a), dealing as it does with a much more specific and limited aspect of project management activity. Try to provide something more than two lists of bullet points by giving overall accounts of the two roles and, in particular, the ways in which their general natures differ.
>
> **Easy marks**. Some of the project manager's tasks, such as monitoring progress and leading the project team, are fairly obvious.
>
> **Examiner's comments**. Unsurprisingly, candidates tended to do quite well with this question.

The project sponsor is the person whose **overall authority** requires and permits the project to be undertaken. P will initiate the project, appoint the project manager and provide the resources used in the project.

P will exercise **general supervision** over the progress of the project without becoming involved in the detail of project management. This will involve giving **approval to plans, budgets and specifications**; receiving and approving **progress reports** and bids for changes; and ensuring that a clear focus is maintained on the project's **objectives and priorities**.

A further possible role for the project sponsor is that of '**project champion**', promoting and defending the project and providing moral support to the project manager D, particularly when delays occur and problems arise.

D, as project manager is responsible to the project sponsor for the **success of the project**. This means delivering the required results in accordance with planned requirements for **cost, time and quality**. To do this D must **manage and lead the project team** and may have a hand in its selection. He or she must also be responsible for the proper **planning** of the project; the **management of the resources** allocated to it; overall **progress management** and control; and reporting on progress to the project sponsor, P.

D will also have to **manage the expectations** of the various project stakeholders. These include P, the various headquarters groups that are involved in the move and any external contractors or consultants involved in the project. This is likely to involve extensive communication, negotiation and dispute resolution, especially when there are delays or changes of plan become necessary.

58 Thurnon

Part (a)

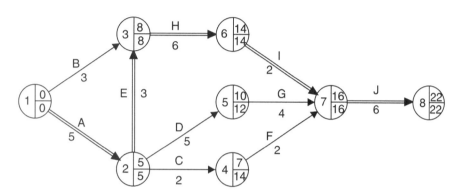

The critical path is AEHIJ, and the minimum total duration is 22 weeks.

Part (b)

To construct a Gantt chart we need to list all possible paths through the network.

A E H I J
A D G J
A C F J
B H I J

Then using the critical path as the basis, we can construct the Gantt chart as follows.

Part (c)

Part of the accepted definition of a project is that it has a beginning and an end; the term 'project life cycle' simply means the succession of stages or processes the project moves through on its progress from one to the other. *Maylor*, in his book *Project Management*, tells us that the projects can be thought of as having four phases or stages: this is the **4-D model**.

Stage in project life cycle	Component	Activities
Define the project	Conceptualisation Analysis	Produce a clear and definitive statement of needs Identify what has to be done and check its feasibility
Design the project	Planning Justification Agreement	Show how the needs will be met Compute costs and benefits Obtain sponsor agreement
Deliver the project **(Do it!)**	Start up Execution Completion Handover	Assemble resources and people Carry out planned project activities Success or abandonment Output passed to sponsor/user
Develop the process	Review Feedback	Identify outcomes for all stakeholders Document lessons and improvements for future use

Define the project

Projects start when someone becomes aware of the need for one. Larger projects are likely to involve the creation of a **project brief** or **terms of reference** for discussion. A **project initiation document** may be prepared.

Design the project

There are several aspects to detailed project planning. Maylor categorises the various techniques used for scheduling, such as network analysis and Gantt charts as **time planning**. He also deals with the need to plan for **cost**, **quality** and **risk**.

Deliver the project

This is the operational phase of the project. Planning will continue as required in order to control agreed changes and to deal with unforeseen circumstances, but the main emphasis is on getting the work done.

There are several important themes.

(a) **Management and leadership**: people management assumes a greater importance as the size of the project work force increases.

(b) **Control**: time, cost and quality must be kept under control , as must the tendency for changes to proliferate.

(c) **Supply chain**: all the aspects of logistic management must be implemented, especially with projects involving significant physical output.

(d)   **Problems and decisions**: problems are bound to arise and must be solved sensibly and expeditiously. Complex problems will require careful analysis using the scientific tools of decision theory.

Develop the process

Because project management is episodic in nature, it is difficult to improve. The lack of continuous operation means that the skills and experience developed during a project are likely to fragment and atrophy after it is complete. This is especially true of organisations that do not have many projects or manage them on an *ad hoc* basis. The completion and review phase involves a number of important but often neglected activities.

(a)   **Completion**. All activities must be properly and promptly finished.

(b)   **Documentation** must be completed.

(c)   **Project systems** must be closed down. In particular, the project accounts and any special accounting systems must remain in operation and under control until all costs have been posted but must then be closed down to avoid improper posting.

(d)   **Immediate review** is required to provide staff with immediate feedback on performance.

A thorough review is the organisation's opportunity to make significant improvements in how it manages its projects: appropriate quantities of management time and attention must be allocated to the review process and to the assimilation of its results and recommendations. Longer-term review is useful for the consideration of **lifetime costs**; which should be the eventual criterion for project success.

59 Healthweb

Top tips. Both the May and November 2005 exams included 25 mark questions as project management. Such a question is therefore likely, especially if a network diagram requirement is included. In any case, you must be prepared to discuss the nature of project management in some depth.

Easy marks. The relationships the project manager must establish and maintain are basic aspects of your syllabus and you should have a good idea of the sort of interests that have to be dealt with.

Part (a)

MEMORANDUM

To: Senior Management Team
From: Management Accountant
Subject: The GPConnect (GPC) project

This memo outlines the nature of the GPC project in relation to two areas; the relationship of the project manager to key stakeholders and potential project management problems.

1   Project manager relationships

1.1   Project manager and project sponsor

Central government provides the funding for the GPC project, and is therefore the project sponsor. The project manager is employed by T, the company responsible for carrying out the GPC project.

Central government will be concerned with how the project impacts upon the achievement of long-term strategic objectives. They will be keen to ensure that the project is not seen to waste public resources, so the project manager will need to work with the sponsor to resolve potential conflict over project costs. The role of the central government in this project as a fund provider may also cause conflict between central government and the SRHA.

With regard to the day-today running of the project, it is unlikely that the project manager would have significant direct contact with central government, as project progress will be reported mainly to the project board.

1.2 Project manager and the project board

The project board is responsible for the overall running of the project and will be concerned with the achievement of management/business level objectives, in particular that the project improves business efficiency and effectiveness. The board is ultimately responsible for the achievement of the sponsors' targets. The board delegates authority to the project manager who is responsible for achieving objectives set by the board.

Regular, direct communication between the project manager and the project board is necessary, for example regular project milestone review meetings.

1.3 Project manager and medical and administrative users

The project manager is responsible for delivering a system that meets user requirements. User objectives in the GPC project would be for the system to facilitate effective patient care whilst minimising staff workload. Administrative and medical staff will be use the completed system to help them perform their day-to-day duties. Good communication between users and the project manager is essential to ensure user needs are understood – and to prevent unrealistic expectations.

The project manager should 'sell' the benefits of the new system to users, as, without user backing, the project is unlikely to succeed. The project manager is responsible for ensuring the system is designed to meet the needs of all users, as far as is practically possible within the project budget and schedule, and for planning user training.

1.4 Possibility of conflicting objectives   *- Everyone has their own say - have their own Inputs / Outputs .*

User/staff objectives will centre around the need to provide good quality patient care whilst minimising their workload. This may conflict with the objectives of the sponsor, whose primary concern is to achieve an improvement in the standard of service provided to patients – within budgeted cost levels. Central government and the project board are likely to be concerned with minimising costs, which could cause conflict with end users as this may impact upon the quality of system produced.

There is the potential for conflict between the sponsor and the project board over funding. Although a technology fund has been set up by the central government, this funding has not been easy to obtain, causing financial concerns for hospitals, medical centres and the SRHA. Some doctors have already expressed concern over resources being spent on the new system, rather than being committed directly to patient care.

The potential for conflict is further increased by central government allowing individual hospitals and medical centres to decide how they operate, rather than implementing a consistent policy.

Part (b)   *Part B is still Part of your Answer. I still Part of the memo.*

2 Project management problems

Allowing individual medical centres and hospitals to discuss individual terms of usage of the Healthweb is likely to cause problems for the project manager.

2.1 Aspects of the Healthweb utilised

Each site will have different connection preferences and needs, which could lead to a wide variety of different terms, options and patterns of usage. These options all need to be documented and implemented, which will consume project resources. Sites may wish to constantly amend their connection options, causing much time to be spent administering changes.

A consistent core approach across all sites would reduce the administration requirements of the Healthweb and allow control to be maintained more easily. A single consistent approach should also keep costs to a

BPP
PROFESSIONAL EDUCATION

minimum. Allowing individual terms is also likely to lead to a less unified approach to the overall project, as sites concentrate on their own agendas.

2.2 Timing of connection

If hospitals and medical centres are able to negotiate their own terms this will prevent the project team controlling the timing of connection of sites. The project manager and team need the freedom to plan for a gradual phasing in of the Healthweb across sites. Allowing the timing of this process to be subject to the whims of individual hospitals/centres is likely to lead to excessive demands being placed upon the project team at certain times – and under utilisation of the team at other times.

2.3 Hardware and software costs/management

— Major timing – which hospital gets on first. or medical centres.

Allowing individual terms of connection is likely to prevent hardware and software being purchased centrally, causing the loss of any discounts available for large purchases. This will add significantly to project costs and is also likely to cause delays – and require greater co-ordination and monitoring to ensure no compatibility problems occur.

As soon as max. demand is hit, the whole process slows it down.

60 Enterprise Associates 1

Top tips. This question is a good example of the level of complexity you can expect in this exam. It assumes you know *what* work breakdown structure is and *how* to do it and asks you *why* it is a good idea. *Why* questions tend to be more difficult than *how* questions, which, in turn are more difficult than *what* questions. This question illustrates the general principle that mere knowledge of facts and techniques is not enough: you must **understand** them as well.

Easy marks. Planning and control are the obvious benefits of the WBS approach. You should also have had no problem in coming up with budgeting: this is a management accounting exam, after all.

A project work breakdown structure (WBS) is an analysis of the work involved in the project. It is used to establish a comprehensive list of the tasks that must be completed if the project is to succeed.

There are four main areas of project management that benefit from the use of WBS.

(a) **Budgeting**. WBS gives a clear statement of the **work** that is involved in a project. This is valuable in itself, since it prevents any misapprehension of the extent and complexity of the project. It is also the first step towards preparing a **budgeted cost**, since it is unlikely that the same levels of cost or cost techniques can be applied to all types of activity. In the case of E's house renovation, for example, where different trade specialities are involved, the tradesmen concerned will need a clear statement of what is required from each of them.

(b) **Planning**. Even the simplest project may display complex **interactions** and **dependencies** between activities. An example of a dependency in E's building project, for example, would be that all electrical wiring work would have to be complete before plastering could commence. Clear understanding of dependencies is obviously fundamental to any project planning, especially if time is short, as here, and a critical path method is to be used.

An example of an interaction arises in the implications of damp-proofing: if any kind of waterproofing barrier is applied to the walls, it is obviously vital that its integrity is not compromised by driving nails or screws through it; this will have a significant effect on the way that subsequent work is done.

Quality is another important aspect of planning, in that there may well be quality-related choices to be made about methods and materials. These too will have implications for time and cost.

(c) **Control**. E's house renovation is a fairly simple project, but it will have to be controlled like any other. WBS can be useful in deciding the structure and application of controls. While E takes **overall responsibility**, it will be useful to divide up the **operational responsibility** for individual activities and tasks to other people as far as possible. This division can be complicated when it becomes necessary to have input from the same person on more than one occasion, as when an electrician returns to the house to fit switch and socket accessories after plastering has been done. The responsibility for such dangling tasks must not be overlooked.

The other important aspect of control facilitated by having a WBS is that small but important factors and activities are less likely to be overlooked during the implementation phase.

(d) **Risk**. An awareness of the relative riskiness of different phases and activities is an important aspect of project management; it will usually be appropriate for the project manager to **direct extra attention and resources to the areas of highest risk** in order to give the best chance of success and take appropriate action if things start to go wrong. WBS allows particularly risky elements to be identified and managed separately from less risky but connected items. In a house renovation there is always a risk of tradesmen misinterpreting instructions, so, for example, if a wall is to be demolished, it might be a good idea to be on hand to ensure that the correct wall is dealt with.

61 Enterprise Associates 2

Top tips. As usual, this question requires a mix of principles (time management techniques) and application (E's particular situation). The requirement helps you by specifically asking you to identify relevant factors in the setting as well as asking for a time management plan for E. If you think about it, you will see that this is a logical approach: by understanding the things that will make demands on E's time you are better placed to plan the best use of it.

The Examiner's suggested solution was based on three factors: the nature of the work; the nature of the individual concerned and the nature of the other people involved. This is a logical approach; we have used a simpler division into two main areas, as you will see. This is an illustration of the general principle that most questions in the Paper 5 exam can be approached in more than one way.

You will notice that we have quoted from the question scenario in our answer. This is a perfectly reasonable thing to do when you wish to make reference to a particular point; if you decide to do this, make sure that the quote is as succinct as possible. CIMA examination questions are usually quite well written, with no superfluous verbiage, so this should be easy to do.

Easy marks. The scenario provides at least two easy points to mention: E's less than ideal use of time in 'business and social transactions' and the potential distractions of business and family obligations. These easy marks underline the need to read question scenarios very carefully.

A simple analysis of the factors having a bearing on E's use of time might be to divide them into two: **internal** and **external**. The **internal** factors would be those personal matters affecting E's time management ability generally, whatever the circumstances she found herself in, while the **external** factors would be those present in the specific situation described in the setting.

As far as E herself is concerned, we are specifically told that her taste for human interaction often leads her to take 'more time than is necessary to conduct business and social transactions'. This is likely to be a significant hindrance to her. On the other hand, she seems to have been reasonably well-organised so far, having set up a company and obtained agreement from her partners to proceed with the house renovation project. Also, she is a management accountant, so it would probably be safe to assume that she is reasonably objective and organised in her daily work. However, we are not told very much about E's general management skills; she may have to develop her ability to organise other people, for example.

The situation E is taking on is complex. She has her normal work, she has her family obligations and she has the renovation. It is clear from the setting that E is, in fact, taking on the role of the **lead contractor**, as well as carrying out basic repairs and the decorating. This project management role is likely to present the most difficulties, partly because of her lack of experience and partly because it is likely to make unexpected demands upon her; she may not be able to totally compartmentalise her time and may find that urgent matters require her attention at times when she should be doing her normal work.

E should use a standard approach to time management.

First, she should identify her **objectives** and from them her **key tasks**. It is likely that continuing to do her normal job well will be an important objective, so she must establish boundaries to protect the time she needs to spend on this. Control of the telephone will be important: it will probably be necessary to deny knowledge of her work telephone number to her contractors and switch off her mobile phone when at work. She can then respond to messages at an appropriate opportunity.

She will also want to **protect her family relationships** and will have to set aside some time for this each day and at weekends.

Within both her normal job and the building project, E will find it necessary to **list**, **prioritise** and **schedule** her tasks so as to make best use of her time. We are not told what her part-time work pattern will be, but it would probably be useful if she could have a combination of whole days and part days available for the building project. When at work she will have to deal effectively with correspondence, limit the time she is prepared to give to other people for social purposes, and maintain an effective schedule for following up matters that cannot be completed in one go.

When managing the building project, the same ideas apply. In addition, a clear understanding of what is involved will be essential; a **work breakdown structure** approach will be invaluable. **Dependencies** and **interactions** must be understood so that contractors' time is not wasted and materials are available when required.

62 Enterprise Associates 3

Top tips. When answering this question, the first thing the well-prepared candidate must remember is that it is only worth 10 marks. Both of the requirements could give rise to lengthy and detailed answers; the skill here is to go into enough detail to get all the marks on offer, but no further.

At first sight, the changes in the competitive environment do not look as though they are particularly susceptible to five forces analysis. However, the model works pretty well and fits quite neatly with the marks available: two marks per force. You will have to work quite hard to get these marks, because five forces analysis is not simple to do: it is very easy to confuse the effects of the various factors.

Easy marks. The question asks for a report from a management consultant. It is worth dressing up your answer in an appropriate format, as there may be an easy half-mark for doing that, but do not spend more than a few moments on doing this.

Note the way we discuss opportunities and threats under the five forces analysis: considering them separately would lead to some repetition and unnecessary complexity.

Sharp and Keen Chartered Management Accountants

To: Chief Executive Officer, Enterprise Associates
Date: 1 July 200X

Enterprise Associates – Business environment

1   **Scope of this report**

       You asked us to prepare a report for you on the recent changes in the business environment and how they affect your company.

       Michael Porter suggests that the task environment can be analysed under five headings, which he calls the **five competitive forces**; we will use this model to assist us in our discussion.

2 **Threat of new entrants**

New businesses entering an industry in competition with established suppliers bring extra capacity. This will tend to **drive prices down** and may lead to the **loss of economies of scale** if market share is significantly eroded. In your market you have seen a significant increase in the buy-to-let property sector and we would expect this to have had the effect of depressing market rents. However, the current upward trend in interest rates is likely to create something of a barrier to entry and reduce the rate at which new suppliers emerge in the near future.

3 **Threat of substitute products**

A substitute product is a product that does the same job in a different way. In your case, the only real substitute for renting a house is to buy one. The current movement in interest rates is also significant here, since it will reduce the finance available for builders of new houses. However, the decision by the government to **release more land for building** is probably more significant in determining the potential supply of this substitute product and its effect on your competitive position.

4 **Bargaining power of customers**

Customers want more for their money of everything: volume, quality and service. They are better able to obtain this when competition between suppliers increases. This can come about when demand is low relative to supply, when products are not differentiated, when the cost to the customer of switching suppliers is low and when customers buy in bulk.

In your market, the **rise in interest rates** and consequent increase in mortgage costs is likely to reduce demand for new houses and may increase demand for rented property. At the same time, demolition of older properties to allow road construction is likely to increase demand for houses for both purchase and rent. Your products are highly differentiated, your customers have no bulk purchasing power and switching costs really only apply to repeat purchases. It seems likely, therefore, that customers' bargaining power is likely to decline in the near future.

A related factor is the apparent emergence of a **preference for new homes**. This does not really affect customers' bargaining power, however, merely their inclinations.

5 **Bargaining power of suppliers**

Suppliers want more money for what they supply. Their ability to obtain it depends on the availability of supply, the purchasers' switching costs and the importance of the individual supply to the purchaser. You should not have to worry about switching costs, but both **availability and choice of tradespeople** are likely to be affected by the current increase in general building activity caused by the release of extra land for construction.

6 **Rivalry among competitors**

The number of competitors has increased over the last four years, and this has doubtless had an effect on margins by increasing supply. Taken together with the likely future increase in the availability of new houses, this effect is unlikely to abate and may worsen.

7 **Summary**

The picture is complex, with forces pulling in opposite directions, and in the absence of hard econometric data, it is difficult to say what the overall effect is likely to be.

63 WAM Organisation 1

Part (a)

> **Top tips.** This is quite a simple question and is unusual in that there is really only one way to answer it: the WAM Organisation is making strategy in a fairly deliberate way.
>
> You will notice that we have quoted from the question scenario in our answer. This is a perfectly reasonable thing to do when you wish to make reference to a particular point; if you decide to do this, make sure that the quote is as succinct as possible. CIMA examination questions are usually quite well written, with no superfluous verbiage, so this should be easy to do.
>
> **Easy marks.** This is quite a difficult question, requiring the ability to analyse and conduct abstract thinking. Perhaps the only easy marks is the use of the *Ansoff* matrix to classify the company's policy of overseas expansion.

The WAM Organisation's strategic approach is clearly **deliberate and considered**; it displays the major characteristics of the well-known rational model of strategy. This is an iterative process, often undertaken on an annual cycle

A useful starting point for discussion is the establishment of **aims and objectives**. At the highest level of corporate strategy, this may take the form of a mission statement: this must then be interpreted into business and functional objectives so that detailed planning can take place.

Deliberate strategy is based on a thorough knowledge of the **threats and opportunities** presented by the business environment and the **strengths and weaknesses** of the organisation itself. This information is then assessed in the process of corporate appraisal. Potential strategies are generated from this process and appraised in detail. A strategy emerges and is developed into detailed **business and functional plans and budgets**. The outcomes of the activity undertaken may then be fed back to the corporate appraisal stage (and, indeed, to the mission stage) to begin the next iteration.

The WAM Organisation has undertaken this process in some detail. It is apparent that **continued growth** is a major strategic objective. After 'a careful process of internal and external analysis', the company has decided on a strategy of overseas expansion. In terms of *Ansoff's* product market vector analysis, this is a strategy of **market development**: new markets for existing products. (The company has already undertaken significant **product development** with its launch of personal finance and telecom services and has expanded the **place** component of its marketing mix with the introduction of Internet shopping.)

The chosen location for the new outlet matches a significant WAM Organisation **strength** with a clear **opportunity**. The WAM Organisation's single outlet will offer the enhanced convenience of **one-stop shopping** to customers who at present have to visit a number of small stores for their shopping. This advantage will be enhanced by the WAM Organisation's size; its **bulk purchasing power** will enable it to offer **reduced prices** that small operators cannot match, or, as an alternative, will allow it to achieve **higher margins**. It is likely that the existing small retailers will only survive if they can achieve an effective differentiation of their market offerings.

Part (b)

> **Top tips.** The setting for this question includes a lot of detail that you must deal with in your answer, so a quick audit when you think you have finished in order to check that you have covered all the salient points will be a good idea. Apart from that, this is a fairly simple question, especially if you have studied and understood *Mendelow's* stakeholder mapping concept.
>
> **Easy marks.** *Mendelow's* matrix is a sufficiently complex idea that it is probably worth a couple of marks to explain it brief. If you do this in an appropriate fashion you will find you have gone a long way to satisfying the second part of the requirement.

Stakeholders may be divided into primary and secondary groups according to whether or not they have a **contractual relationship** with the organisation in question. Internal stakeholders are dealt with under the terms of their contracts in the normal commercial fashion. Secondary stakeholders, however, have less well-defined status and their interests and influence are less clear-cut. They must be approached with care because they may, in fact, wield considerable power *via* lobbying, public campaigning or the provisions of statute law, for instance.

The absence of a contractual relationship can make the **identification** of secondary stakeholders a difficult task; it is not unusual for groups and individuals to appear from nowhere and claim the right to influence a firm's operations. It is possible to take a firm line with the more tenuously connected, but, ultimately, it is not always possible for the organisation to decide who does and who does not have a legitimate claim; public opinion and government policy are far more significant. To some extent, it is possible to achieve the status of external stakeholder simply by claiming it. It is therefore advisable for an organisation to take great care when considering claims to influence.

In the case of the WAM Organisation's new venture, several important groups of external stakeholders may be identified. These include the state and local governments, the Civic Society, local shopkeepers, local residents, the staff and governing body of the local school, potential customers, potential employees and all the interested mass communications media. No doubt these groups will have overlapping membership, with many individuals having more than one interest.

Mendelow classifies stakeholders on a matrix whose axes are **power held** and the **likelihood of showing an interest** in the organisation's activities.

Level of interest

	Low	High
Low	A	B
High	C	D

Power

This analysis could be usefully employed by the WAM Organisation when considering how to deal with its secondary stakeholders.

Key players are found in segment D: **strategy must be acceptable** to them, at least. In the worst case, the local and state governments will fall into this category, since they probably have the power to hamper operations severely and even to rescind the hard-won planning consent for the new store. In the best case, they will fall into segment C, but even then, they might be moved into segment D by vigorous protest activity. Local custom and practice in dealing with government and officialdom must be followed here and it would be a good idea to engage the services of locally based advisers and lobbyists. These would have the job of reassuring officials and politicians that the WAM Organisation was behaving in a proper manner and of presenting and emphasising the benefits to local employment and living standards that the new store would bring.

As a general principle, stakeholders in segment C must be treated with care. While often passive, they are capable of moving to segment D, as discussed above, and they should, therefore be **kept satisfied**. The mass communications media may well fall into this segment. Their power to influence both public opinion and the attitude of government is very high, but, being largely devoid of moral principles, their interest is generally restricted to obtaining a good story. They can be managed by retaining the services of good PR agents, who would also emphasise the positive aspects of the project.

Stakeholders in segment B do not have great ability to influence strategy, but their views can be important in **influencing more powerful stakeholders**, perhaps by lobbying. Most of the remaining groups identified earlier will probably fall into this segment. An important part of dealing with these groups is to keep them informed, since a great deal of their interest may well be based on inaccurate or even deliberately distorted information. There should be a two-way communication process so that stakeholders have proper information and the organisation can make a careful assessment of specific problems.

Minimal effort is expended on segment A, but those identified as falling into it should be monitored in case they move into another segment for any reason.

In dealing with all aspects of its foreign venture, the WAM Organisation should be prepared to adjust its plans in the light of changing circumstances, including the activities of the groups opposed to the building of the new store. In order to do this it must have a clear view of its overall aims and of what is essential to them; and what is negotiable.

64 WAM Organisation 2

Part (a)

> **Top tips.** Why does this question call for your answer to be in the form of a report to a major investment bank? The question would have been just as valid had it started 'Explain the resource-based approach ...'. We can only conclude that using some kind of formal heading features in the marking scheme, though surely it cannot be worth more than one mark. However, make sure you get that mark!
>
> Also be sure that you understand the difference between resource-based strategy and the transaction cost approach to the firm. They both have implications for outsourcing, but approach it from very different directions.
>
> **Easy marks.** As is so often the case in this paper, the easy marks are available for explaining the basic theory: here you are specifically asked for an explanation of resource-based strategy, so there will be a substantial number of marks available for doing so: perhaps as many as half of the total.

To: The Directors, A Major Investment Bank plc
Date: 1 July 200X

The WAM Organisation and resource-based strategy

1   Resource based strategy

Much strategic thinking is based upon adapting the organisation's characteristics to match the demands of its environment; that is, to the exploitation of opportunities and the avoidance of threats. The resourced-based approach shifts the emphasis towards the organisation's strengths and weaknesses and proceeds on the basis that competitive advantage comes from the possession of **scarce resources** and the exploitation of **unique competences**.

This approach is therefore equally applicable to organisations that have **favoured access** to material resources such as, for instance, vital raw materials; those that possess a specific but intangible protected **intellectual property** such as a patent on a drug; and those whose advantage consists of the **experience and expertise of its staff and the capabilities of its systems**. The advantage of firms in the last category is based on what are now known as **core competences**. A good example is the way *Enron* exploited deregulation and created a new field of business activity when it established itself as a specialist broker in energy resources.

Johnson and Scholes define core competences as those that both **outperform competitors** and are **difficult to imitate**. Organisations must achieve an acceptable or **threshold** level of competence in all of their activities, but it is core competences that give a lasting competitive edge. Indeed, the exploitation of such core competences is potentially a more durable source of competitive advantage than more specific assets such as raw materials and intellectual property. Raw material sites become exhausted and patents expire, but good management can maintain a technical lead almost indefinitely, by paying proper attention to innovation and the nurturing of what the firm does well.

2   The WAM Organisation: resources and core competences

We do not have a great deal of information on the WAM Organisation other than that it is a very successful supermarket chain with the largest share of its domestic market. We know that it is customer focused;

provides value for money; is operationally efficient; and uses the latest technology. It is also innovative and has launched successful personal finance, telecom and Internet shopping services.

We might, if we were pushed, make some tentative suggestions about the firm's resources and core competences based on this rather sketchy account.

2.1 Costs

The WAM Organisation's size should give it extensive purchasing power and enable it to achieve significant **economies of scale**. This, taken together with its operational efficiency should make a policy of cost leadership attainable.

2.2 Customer focus

Customer focus is valuable in any business, but it is essential in a retailer; the example of *Marks & Spencer* illustrates what happens when a previously successful retailer loses touch with its customers. If the WAM Organisation has really achieved more extensive customer focus than its rivals it should show in such areas as continuing successful new product development, a high degree of customer satisfaction and differentiated product offerings in geographical areas that vary in socio-demographic makeup.

2.3 Technology

The WAM Organisation uses the latest technology. This does not just have the potential to cut costs, as in *Wal-Mart's* introduction of radio frequency identification tags; it has the potential to achieve important improvements in customer focus through the use of **loyalty cards**. Effective use of this technology is very difficult, simply because of the volume of data involved, but *Tesco* has used it with great success in such areas as targeted price cuts, response to emerging preferences and effective promotions.

2.4 Innovation

The WAM Organisation's customer focus has no doubt helped it in its introduction of new products that challenge traditional notions of what the grocery business is about. Introduction of more new products and new product categories is an obvious route to continued turnover growth. We may assess the ability to make regular and successful product launches to be a core competence of the organisation and one that it should sustain and exploit.

Part (b)

> **Top tips.** This question really requires a discussion of culture at two levels: overall national culture and the more specific idea of corporate or management culture. *Hofstede's* model is obviously an essential component of the material to be covered.
>
> As we have been given no details of the prevailing cultural norms in either the WAM Organisation's home country or in country Y, it will not be possible to give any real illustrations of how cultural interactions might affect the new venture.
>
> **Easy marks.** A perfectly acceptable answer to this question can be prepared with minimal reference to the scenario: it revolves around theory. We discuss both *Ouchi's* model and Hofstede's for completeness: you could probably score up to five marks for explaining either.

Culture is an important determinant of behaviour. It is about beliefs, values, attitudes, customs, rituals and artefacts. The nature of culture varies between countries and, indeed, within them. Typically, different regions, social classes, religious denominations, industries and professions will all have their own variations on the generally prevailing cultural norms.

There can be wide cultural differences between neighbouring countries that are part of the same basic society; if country Y's national culture is significantly different from that of the WAM Organisation, it is likely that there will be problems. This is particularly so as customs and taboos associated with food are particularly strong. These problems will be exacerbated by the current tendency to decry 'globalisation' as an evil and to denounce cultural insensitivity and even cultural imperialism whenever there is the slightest excuse.

A factor which has an impact on the culture of transnational organisations, or organisations competing in global markets, is **management culture**. This consists of the views about managing held by managers, their shared educational experiences, and the 'way business is done'. Obviously, this reflects wider cultural differences between countries, but national cultures can sometimes be subordinated to the corporate culture of the organisation.

Ouchi identified important differences between a typically US management approach and a typically Japanese one. This work was done at a time when Japanese methods appeared to be far more successful than Western ones and there was great concern to adopt them. This process is now largely complete, and the failure of the Japanese economy in recent years has tempered any further move towards Japanese methods. It is perhaps mostly in the field of organisation culture that the Japanese approach has had least influence.

Theory Z. Ouchi called the US approach **Theory A** and the Japanese approach **Theory J**. He then proposed that US firms should adopt a compromise between the two, which he called **Theory Z**.

Feature	Theory A	Theory J
Attitude to work people	Performance centred, layoffs common	Concern for worker's whole life, jobs for life
Careers	Very specialised, rapid promotion the ideal	Very general, with rotation through departments and slow promotion
Decisions and responsibility	Individual managers accept clearly defined responsibility and make their own decisions	Group decision making and collective responsibility
Control	Very explicit systems	Informal. Heavy reliance on trust and harmony

The Hofstede model

The **Hofstede model** was developed in 1980 by Professor Geert Hofstede in order to explain national differences by identifying **key dimensions** in the value systems of all countries. Each country is represented on a scale for each dimension so as to explain and understand values, attitudes and behaviour. Global businesses have to be sensitive to these issues.

In particular, Hofstede pointed out that countries differ on the following dimensions.

Power distance. This dimension measures how far superiors are expected to exercise power. In a high power-distance culture, the boss decides and people do not question.

Uncertainty avoidance. Some cultures prefer clarity and order, whereas others are prepared to accept novelty. This affects the willingness of people to change rules, rather than simply obey them.

Individualism-collectivism. In some countries individual achievement is what matters. In a collectivist culture people are supported and controlled by their in-group and put the interests of the group first.

'Masculinity'. In 'masculine' cultures assertiveness and acquisitiveness are valued. 'Masculine' cultures place greater emphasis on possessions, status, and display as opposed to quality of life and caring for others.

Hofstede grouped countries into eight clusters using these dimensions. Here are some examples.

Countries in the **Anglo** group (the UK, the USA)

- Low to medium power-distance
- Low to medium uncertainty avoidance

- High individualism
- High 'masculinity'

Countries in the **Nordic** group (Scandinavia and also The Netherlands)

- Low power distance
- Low to medium uncertainty avoidance
- Medium individualism
- Low 'masculinity'

Countries in the **more developed Asian** group (ie Japan)

- Medium power distance
- High uncertainty avoidance
- Medium individualism
- High 'masculinity'

Clearly, there is potential for misunderstanding and conflict between managers and their subordinates when their native societies make different assumptions on these matters. The WAM Organisation's managers must be alert to any potential problems.

65 WAM organisation 3

Part (a)

> **Top tips.** 'Identify' is a low-level instruction, corresponding to 'comprehension' in the CIMA table of learning objectives, so it should not be too difficult to satisfy the requirements of this question. A simple list would seem to provide an appropriate answer. Even giving a detailed description of each risk would not be too challenging. However, the question is worth 15 marks, which seems quite a lot for such a simple task. We thus have a problem of interpretation.
>
> Unfortunately, it is not unusual for the Examiner to present such dilemmas. If you come across a problem like this, it is better to err on the side of overkill than to take the question requirement too literally. You must provide an answer that is worth the marks on offer rather than one that is restricted to the minimum requirement implied by the wording of the question. In this question, for example, you might choose to proceed as though the requirement said 'Discuss the nature of …' rather than 'Identify …', 'discuss' being a higher level requirement corresponding to 'analysis.'
>
> However, do not be tempted to waffle! Merely increasing the length of your answer will not increase its value.
>
> The Examiner's own suggested solution bears out the value of our suggestion above: it discusses success criteria in order to be able identify risks as things that might prejudice such criteria; goes on to mention the categorisation of risks according to their potential impact and where control of them should lie; and mentions some of the ideas associated with risk management.
>
> **Easy marks.** The easy marks come from the process of identification mentioned above.

The WAM Organisation has chosen to enter its new market in a risky way. It has decided to create a completely new supermarket operation from nothing. This will require the commitment of **considerable funds** and **extensive management time and effort**. We may assume the organisation took this path because it wanted to install its own business model complete, wholly owned and controlled by itself. Compare this with *Wal-Mart's* entry into Europe and Japan, where it has bought controlling interests in existing supermarket chains and is gradually remodelling to conform more closely to its own ideas. The WAM Organisation has total control and risks total failure; Wal-Mart's control is less extensive, but its worst outcome is a poorly performing local chain that could be sold if necessary. Generally, **increased control requires an increase in the resources committed**, which in turn brings **increased risk**.

Analysis of risk requires the identification of potential threats to success. This, in turn, requires a **clear definition of success**; a narrow definition might preclude the recognition of factors that would be relevant to a wider one. For example, if the WAM Organisation defined success for its project as opening a properly completed and stocked store by a certain date without including any mention of a turnover targets, the possibility of an organised customer boycott would not be recognised as a risk factor.

If we work on the assumption that success is defined in terms of **achieving commercial viability in a reasonable time**, then we might identify a number of risks. It is, however, unlikely that the limited amount of detail we have would allow us to progress to the next stage and assess them for **likelihood** and **potential impact**.

A wide range of threats might be relevant to the building project. These would include all the usual **technical risks** such as misdelivery of supplies; poor quality of work and materials; accidents; design inadequacies; and co-ordination failures. Some of these problems might be exacerbated by local conditions; after all, this is the WAM Organisation's first foreign venture and it is not expert in the way things are done in country Y. Indeed, there may be completely new threats that arise from this unfamiliarity, particularly in matters affected by local law, custom and practice. For example, activity duration estimates may be compromised by the extent of public holidays, local working practices and working time regulations.

A further category of threats exists in the general area of **business risk**. This is very wide ranging and includes factors in the immediate task environment and in the wider PEST environment as well. Obvious simple examples include the possibility of a change in national economic conditions leading to a reduction in potential demand; the appearance of a competitor from another country; difficulty in recruiting or training local staff; and, if some element of local finance is being used (as would be sound financial management), a rise in the cost of capital.

More specific risk factors revolve around the strong body of opinion that is opposed to the WAM Organisation's plans. It is not impossible that this opposition might achieve some success, perhaps constraining the new store's opening hours, for example, even if it did not succeed in having the construction permit revoked.

Once risks have been identified and assessed, a proper **programme of risk reduction** may be undertaken. The technical and cultural risks associated with the building programme might be reduced by engaging the services of local architects and building project managers who should be familiar with local conditions and can advise accordingly. A similar approach might be used with the business risk category, making use of the services of local consultants. Certainly local lobbying and PR specialists should be employed to manage the threat from the campaign of opposition to the new venture.

Part (b)

> **Top tips.** Your ability to answer this question really depends on your knowledge of the way negotiations are carried on: you have very little opportunity to apply principle to the scenario here, other than by couching your remarks in terms of what the WAM Organisation should and should not do.
>
> **Easy marks.** An outline of a basic negotiation process and its implications for the negotiators should provide up to five marks here.

A **negotiation** is a conference between parties who have different views on how an issue should be resolved.

Negotiation has its **conventions**; they are valuable because they help the parties to reach a conclusion.

(a)   Both parties actually wish to reach a settlement and accept that some compromise may be necessary.

(b)   Civilised behaviour is desirable, but hard words and loss of temper are sometimes used as tactics to emphasise determination. Outbursts should not be allowed to undermine commitment to the process.

(c)   Some discussion may take place off the record.

(d)   Firm offers and concessions should not be withdrawn.

(e)   A final agreement should be implemented without amendment or further manoeuvring.

An important aspect of negotiation is that the parties reach agreement feeling that their needs have been respected, even if they have not achieved everything they wished for. It may be wise, therefore, for the stronger party to be generous.

If the parties are realistic, they will have established in their own minds not only their **ideal** outcomes, but also a minimum **acceptable outcome**. This is actually quite difficult to do and requires careful thought. If the acceptable outcomes overlap, it should be relatively easy to reach a **mutually acceptable** result. If they do not, the task becomes much harder. It is clearly very useful for a negotiator to have a good idea of what the other side's minimum position really is, and, equally, to conceal his or her own.

In the case of obtaining permission for the WAM Organisation's new supermarket, there would probably be **much common ground**, in that a successful venture would have the potential to increase the local level of economic activity, providing increased employment opportunities and greater consumer utility. However, differences of emphasis would arise: the WAM Organisation would be more concerned about its costs and commercial prospects, while the government would be more concerned about local amenity and environmental effects and the way established local retailers would be affected. However, it should be possible to reach an agreement that is **acceptable to both sides**.

At the start of the negotiation, the WAM Organisation should state its **opening position** clearly and realistically. The opposing position should be **challenged on its merits**; it is important to leave the opponent with room for manoeuvre. It is desirable to say as little as possible at this stage and to concentrate on assessing the other side's strengths and weaknesses. A bargaining phase may then ensue.

The bargaining phase is a process of argument and persuasion. There are some important tactics.

(a) The WAM Organisation should not allow elements of the dispute to be settled **piecemeal**. This limits room for subsequent manoeuvre.

(b) Any concession should be **matched** by a concession from the other side.

(c) To avoid one-sided concessions, the WAM Organisation should make proposals that are conditional on the other side moving too: 'If you do this I will agree to that'.

Closing a negotiation is similar to closing a sale; it means attempting to bring the process to a conclusion. There are several techniques The WAM Organisation could use.

(d) Offer to trade a concession for an agreement to settle.

(e) When there is a single outstanding issue, offer to split the difference.

(f) Offer a choice between two courses of action.

(g) Summarise the arguments, emphasise the concessions that have been made and state a final position. However, a bluff runs the risk of being called.

66 Pilot paper

66.1 B   This is a definition.

66.2 C   This is a definition.

66.3 C   Flatter structure implies wider span of control and thence the acceptance of greater responsibility by work people.

66.4 B   This is a reference to *Belbin's* work on the roles played by team members. Note, in relation to option D, that while more than one role may be played by a single member of the group, it is not necessary for group effectiveness for all the roles to be played by a few people.

66.5 B   Organisation structure is an aspect of strategic implementation and should support the strategic objectives and general strategic approach.

Network diagram for questions 1.6 and 1.7

The critical path is A – B – C – E – F – G – J – K

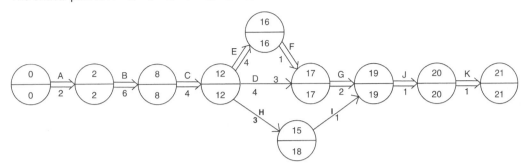

66.6   C   21 weeks

66.7   B   Activity A is complete. Annie Li is commencing activity B, which is scheduled to last 6 weeks. Activities C to K will take 13 weeks. Annie must thus reduce the duration of activity B to no more than 3 weeks in order to achieve a delivery date 16 weeks from now.

66.8   AAA
        Blake plc
        AGAI

67 May 2005 examination

67.1   C   The name *Mintzberg* should immediately remind you of the idea of emergent strategies. This was part of his well-known attack on the rational model of strategy. Logical incrementalism is, purely on the face of it, an attractive answer to this question, but, of course, it is an idea based, like the rational model, on careful analysis. The term 'positioning' is used to contrast strategies that seek to fit the organisation to its environment with those that are based on the possession of some unique or valuable resource.

67.2   A   B and D are incorrect because they include the term *decision*. It is more useful to think of reaching agreement, since the point of negotiation is that neither side is in a position to take and enforce a final decision. C is wrong because it includes both bargaining and negotiation as distinct phases: negotiation is the name of the overall process. Also, C makes no mention of *opening*, the phase in which detailed initial positions are established and without which bargaining is not possible.

67.3   D   This is a low-level question concerning basic knowledge. It could actually be the topic of endless debate over real world examples, so do not look too deeply into it.

67.4   B   A statement of client needs would form an important input into the project charter (project brief, initiation document). The specification of resources required and the sequence of activities would form part of the overall project plan

        Unless you were exempt from the Certificate stage, you should have been able to answer this question with knowledge brought forward from Paper C4, Economics for Business. Barriers to entry are of great practical importance in all industries and include those listed below.

        Scale economies (perhaps the most important of all)

        Capital requirements

        Strong brands

        Legal protection, such as patents

        Switching costs

Technical expertise

Access to distribution channels

Access to input

67.6   The answers are a: *initiating*; b: *controlling*; c: *closing*. The Examiner noted that acceptable alternatives included *defining* for a; *monitoring* or *reviewing* for b; and *completion* for c.

67.7   It is important to realise that in this question, the Examiner did not intend to imply that feasibility studies could be carried on in three distinct ways, which is what you might have understood by his use of the word 'type'. He was actually asking you to list three *topics* that might be the subject of feasibility studies. The list of such topics is quite long and includes those below. The three most important ones are listed first.

Technology

Finance

Environment and sustainability

Social

Politics

Marketing

67.8   This is a very basic piece of knowledge. It is difficult to see why it was worth three marks, especially as the Examiner's answer did not include the numbered scales on the axes. Presumably there was one mark for each of the axes and one for positioning the team management style correctly.

Blake & Mouton's grid

Mock Exams

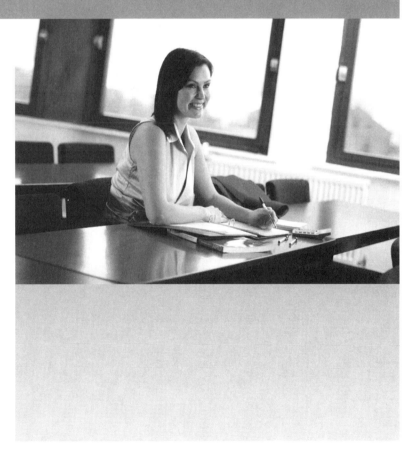

CIMA
Paper P5 (Managerial)
Integrated Management

Mock Exam 1

Question Paper	
Time allowed	**3 hours**
This paper is divided into three sections	
Section A	**Answer ALL questions in this section**
Section B	**Answer ALL THREE questions in this section**
Section C	**TWO questions ONLY to be attempted**

DO NOT OPEN THIS PAPER UNTIL YOU ARE READY TO START UNDER EXAMINATION CONDITIONS

SECTION A – 20 marks

Answer ALL EIGHT sub-questions in this section: two to four marks each

Each of the sub-questions numbered from 1.1 to 1.8 inclusive, given below, has only one right answer.

1.1 Which researcher is associated with work on the roles necessary for an effective team?

    A   *Tuckman*
    B   *Belbin*
    C   *Sherif*
    D   *Likert*   **(2 marks)**

1.2 *Mintzberg* identifies several political games played within organizations. Which of the following is not one of the games he described?

    A   Games to defeat rivals
    B   Games to resist authority
    C   Games to confuse stakeholders
    D   Games to build power bases   **(2 marks)**

1.3 Company J is considering an adjustment to its strategy based on a newly patented technology to which it has exclusive rights. Should this strategy be evaluated in terms of

    A   Suitability
    B   Feasibility
    C   Both of the above
    D   Neither of the above   **(2 marks)**

1.4 Projects are subject to major constraints that must be satisfied if they are to be considered successful. Which of the following is not such a constraint?

    A   Cost
    B   Time
    C   Risk
    D   Quality   **(2 marks)**

1.5 *Harrison* identified four organisational types, each with its own culture. Which of the following is not one of those types?

    A   Role
    B   Machine
    C   Power
    D   Task   **(2 marks)**

The following data is to be used to answer questions 1.6, 1.7 and 1.8

FOODAID is a UK-based charity that delivers food to communities in need because of war or natural disaster. Its overall management is in the hands of the Director-General, Sally Porter, who reports to the Board of Trustees. This Board sets overall priorities for aid distribution in line with the charity's constitution. FOODAID currently operates in Africa, Asia and the Americas. Sally Porter is assisted by three Directors: Sam Mbube, Director of Transport and Distribution, Jack Staff, Director of Fundraising and Isobel Brammer, Director of Administration. The Directors are supported by their departmental staffs.

As well as raising liquid funds, FOODAID also runs regular campaigns in which it collects, stores and distributes tinned foodstuffs donated by individuals in the UK. To do this the charity has entered into a leasing arrangement with Whiteknuckle Airlines to use a transport aircraft for 200 hours each year. The movement of foodstuffs from the UK to its destination is planned in detail by Sam Mbube's planning cell, headed by Alex Boyle, a very experienced transport operations manager.

Jack Staff, Director of Fundraising, has recently authorised a press advertising campaign at a cost of £500,000. His media buyer, Lucy Chen, has advised him that rising costs mean that this campaign is unlikely to be as effective as that mounted one year previously.

1.6 Identify the words from the list below needed to complete this passage.

FOODAID is organised into .... departments with a Director ....
for the activities of each department. Within the Transport and Distribution department, Alex Boyle exercises
both .... and .... power.

accountable	legitimate
delegated	authority
functional	matrix
mechanistic	organic
expert	hierarchy

(4 marks)

1.7 Using the terminology of Porter's value chain, identify the value activity most closely associated Lucy Chen and Alex Boyle

Give the name of the person most closely associated with 'human resource management'.

(3 marks)

1.8 Identify two primary stakeholders (other than trustees and staff) and one secondary stakeholder mentioned in the narrative. **(3 marks)**

(Total = 20 marks)

SECTION B – 30 marks

Answer ALL THREE questions – 10 marks each

Note to candidates:

The scenario for the three questions in this section is divided into two parts. Read Part 1 to answer questions two and three and then read Part 2 before answering question four.

Spiral of decline – Part 1

Because of its failure to serve a sufficient number of clients and/or to provide a service of the required quality, Company J, a state-owned business has had its funding cut for three consecutive years. This is putting pressure on people throughout the organisation. Departments and individuals have been set more demanding targets and large-scale redundancies have recently been announced. This has resulted in considerable conflict. The service professionals are convinced that the marketing and sales department is responsible for the troubles of the organisation. This view is not shared by the marketing and sales people. They believe that the poor quality of service offered is the real reason for the decline in demand for services and for the resulting cuts in government funding. The effect of these differences between departments is one of declining co-operation between the direct service providers and the personnel in marketing and sales.

Of the more immediate concern to senior management, however, is the threat of industrial action by the trades unions determined to protect their members' jobs. Even individuals like the management accountant are finding themselves in conflict with departmental managers with whom they have previously enjoyed good relations. Requests for information on the costs of providing services are being met with hostility and the management accountant's job becomes more difficult by the day.

Question 2

Required

Discuss the potential consequences arising from the conflict between the various departments and groups within SOB. **(10 marks)**

Question 3

Required

Describe how senior management can best manage the conflicts between the various parties. **(10 marks)**

Spiral of decline – Part 2

Two years later, Company J has overcome its immediate problems but is still not working efficiently. The Board have decided that a new information system is required and have entered discussions with contractors. The management accountant has been appointed project manager. She is concerned about several problems that she can foresee arising during the lifetime of the project.

First, she is worried about the CEO's habit of vagueness and lack of precision in speech and writing. She fears that her responsibilities will be confused and the aims of the project unclear. She is also concerned about her personal working relationships, in that neither the Finance Director nor the Operations Director appears to be taking much interest in the project. She is not sure who she should report to, with what frequency and about what. Finally, she worries that proper control over the external contractors will not be exercised since she has had no contact with them: all discussions have been at Board level.

Question 4

Required

Explain how the PRINCE2 system of project management could help the management accountant solve these specific problems. **(10 marks)**

SECTION C – 50 marks

Read the following scenario and answer TWO questions ONLY – 25 marks each

Gensup plc has been formed from the acquisition by a major distributor – Universal Sales plc (Unisal) – of three manufacturing businesses – A, B and C. This occurred following discussions among the shareholders of A Ltd, B Ltd and C Ltd regarding the problems and opportunities facing their companies. An approach was made to Unisal, as a result of which it has acquired all three businesses.

As part of the reorganisation which followed the acquisition, Gensup has established a joint research and development centre for the manufacturing units. Corporate planning, management services, finance functions and group purchasing of common raw materials have been centralised at the Head Office of Gensup.

Universal Sales plc (Unisal)

This was an internationally-established distribution company specialising in the worldwide distribution of products and components to the engineering industry. Its customers included those of A Ltd, B Ltd and C Ltd.

Unisal had a number of distribution centres in countries where demand was strong. The distribution managers liaised directly with contract customers. The distribution centres were also a base for the sales force. Sales persons focused on particular types of customer, such as manufacturers of cars or power plant, to which they sold a wide range of products. Marketing was co-ordinated at Head Office.

The shares of Universal Sales plc were traded on various stock exchanges. The acquisition leaves the former owners of A Ltd, B Ltd and C Ltd as minority shareholders in the quoted company, Gensup plc.

Manufacturing

A Ltd, B Ltd and C Ltd were all private limited companies. A Ltd manufactured aluminium rods and wire. B Ltd manufactured copper rods and wire. C Ltd manufactured plastic rods and thread.

The manufacturers all produced their products using continuous processes with a relatively small number of production workers, most of whom were unskilled. These continuous processes required large, expensive manufacturing plants. Packaging of the output, and distribution were on a batch basis. Their main raw materials were ores, raw chemicals, water and electric power. These raw materials represented a large part of the finished product cost. Many new sources of ore and chemicals have become available from Eastern Europe.

Maintenance, purchasing, quality control and research and development were important functions, with skilled and professional staff. These functions were managed by directors who were not shareholders.

The market

There were numerous competing companies in the industry, operating either in a similar way or as part of larger groups. The market of A Ltd, B Ltd and C Ltd was exclusively in the United Kingdom. It consisted of a large number of engineering companies which used the products in their own conversion processes.

During the last few years, amalgamations and takeovers have reduced the number of customers, but changing economic conditions have also opened considerable export potential for A Ltd, B Ltd and C Ltd. Unfortunately, the companies did not have the staff or expertise to take advantage of the opportunities.

Total quality control policies among the customers have meant that quality specifications and ordering procedures have become much more sophisticated, requiring substantial expenditure to meet customers' demands.

Question 5

Required

(a)   Identify and explain the structural forms that might be appropriate for Gensup.   **(7 marks)**

(b)   Explain, with reference to the information provided in the scenario, the advantages and disadvantages of each structural form identified.   **(18 marks)**

(Total = 25 marks)

Question 6

Required

(a)   Suggest a mission statement which might be applicable for Gensup. Explain the significance of **each** component of this mission statement.   **(10 marks)**

(b)   Suggest suitable **operational goals** for **four** primary tasks of Gensup.   **(11 marks)**

(c)   Explain which generic strategy is currently being used by Gensup.   **(4 marks)**

(Total = 25 marks)

Question 7

Required

(a)   Contrast the task environments of the manufacturing plants and of Gensup.   **(7 marks)**
(b)   Describe **four** sectors of the task environment of the manufacturing plants.   **(8 marks)**
(c)   Contrast the task environment of Gensup with that of the original manufacturers.   **(10 marks)**

(Total = 25 marks)

Answers

DO NOT TURN THIS PAGE UNTIL YOU HAVE
COMPLETED THE MOCK EXAM

A plan of attack

Most of us panic at least a little when we open an exam paper, so having a reasonable idea of what you are going to do is likely to help.

Section A

It is probably best to tackle Section A right at the beginning, since it is compulsory and you should be able to get off to a good start by picking up some easy marks. Be very strict with the time you allot to Section A. It is worth 20 marks so you must not spend more than 36 minutes on it initially. If you are baffled by one of the questions, press on, finish Section A that much faster and return to it at the end of the exam if you still have time.

Section B

You know that there are going to be three compulsory questions in Section B, worth ten marks each. You have no choices to make here and it is a good idea to plunge straight into this section first. However, you must allocate your time carefully. Section B is worth 30% of the marks, so you should give it 30% of your time. And within that 54 minutes, you should aim to spend 18 minutes on each question. This is a good approach because the ten marks available for each question are not all equally difficult to get. The first five marks in most questions are easy. The last five marks are difficult. You must get all the easy marks on each question! The best way to do this is to be very disciplined about time, and not linger on a question you think you know lots about and ignore one you don't like.

However, be prepared to think on the spot. If there is a compulsory question, or part of a question which baffles you, it would be foolish to sit looking at it for the prescribed 1.8 minutes per mark. Similarly, if you see a question that fills you with joy and you just know you can score heavily, then don't stop writing on it if you are sure you are still making valid, relevant points. But be careful! Misapplication of this aspect of examination technique claims more victims than any other.

Section C

In Section C you have to make a choice. One good approach is to take a quick overview and form some sort of idea of which questions you are going to tackle. This should only take a few minutes since you do not need to read all the scenarios in detail. You can make a first estimate by looking at the question requirements only. Once you have done this, look in more detail at your likely questions and ask yourself what the Examiner is after and whether you can supply it. Only then look at the other two, if you cannot confirm your first impression.

An alternative approach is to read all three questions in detail and make a firm decision.

In any case, you may find it helpful to do the question you are most confident about first. The danger here is the temptation to overrun your time.

Checking

80% of the marks in this exam are for answers in written form and the great majority for answers in the form of essays. One of the most important rules for written work is to leave sufficient time at the end of each question to read your answer through. You will pick up spelling mistakes, errors of grammar and instances of poor expression. You will also find you have missed out things you intended to put in and possibly put in things that shouldn't be there. Candidates find this checking process very difficult to start, but it can be invaluable.

Handwriting

Handwriting is a thorn in the side for markers. If they cannot read you work, they cannot give you marks. Unless you are actually proud of your handwriting, think about writing double-spaced at all times. You don't have to pay for the extra paper you will use.

Sudden inspiration

The human brain works in strange ways. It is very common, halfway through an exam, to suddenly think of something relevant to a question that you thought you had finished. If you leave a few lines blank after the end of each answer you will be able to handle this if it happens to you.

Spare time at the end of the exam?

This should not happen if you have allocated your time carefully. However, if you run out of inspiration on your last question, start to go over your whole script from the beginning, thinking hard about how to improve it. You can relax when the invigilator says 'Stop!'

SECTION A

Question 1

1.1 B   *Belbin* described the effective team's roles. *Tuckman* is known for his work on the development of team cohesion and effectiveness. *Sherif* and *Likert* worked in other areas of management research.

1.2 C   Attempts to spread confusion might be part of several of the games *Mintzberg* describes, but he does not describe a game in these specific terms.

1.3 C   A new strategy based on proprietary technology is **suitable** since it exploits a distinctive competence and **feasible** to the extent that the company has access to the technology in question.

1.4 C   Risk is a factor that must be managed if the three main constraints of time, cost and quality are to be satisfied.

1.5 B   The fourth of *Harrison's* types was labelled 'people'.

1.6   FOODAID is organised into **functional** departments with a Director **accountable** for the activities of each department. Within the transport and distribution department, Alex Boyle exercises both **expert** and **legitimate** power.

Note: the words **expert** and **legitimate** are interchangeable in the second sentence.

1.7

Lucy Chen	**Marketing and sales**
Alex Boyle	**Outbound logistics**
Human resource management	**Isobel Brammer**

1.8   Primary: Whiteknuckle Airlines and the publications used in the advertising campaign.
Secondary: the donors of tinned food.

SECTION B

Question 2

> **Top tips.** Clearly, this question is not based on any simple or well-known model: a satisfactory answer requires you to think around the topic of conflict. You will not be able to produce a pass mark by misapplying a model such as one of the many change management processes. However, you may be able to use one or more simple models to assist your thought processes. The value chain is often very useful for this sort of exercise and here would prompt you to think about consequences involving suppliers and customers.
>
> **Easy marks.** Many problems in management revolve around human behaviour: in this question there are fairly easy implications on such topics as communication, morale, staff attitudes and culture.

Consequences of conflict   *of arising from Conflict.*

There is clearly a vicious circle in operation within the organisation. Its **funding** has been cut because of poor service; this must make it even more difficult to improve its service. Also, as **morale** has fallen, **conflict** has arisen and the consequent **deterioration of communication and co-operation** must inevitably further erode **performance standards**. The process is likely to continue, with undesirable consequences.

Within the organisation, **conflict will increase and morale will continue to fall**. This will produce its own undesirable symptoms such as **increased staff turnover**, **absenteeism** and **trade union hostility**. These problems in turn bring their own costs.

Service to customers is likely to decline even further, with **loss of goodwill and orders** where substitutes are available. Competitors will exploit the business's weakness where they can and attempt to poach the best staff.

As the business declines, **suppliers will also lose business**.

As the business is state owned, the Government will take a close interest in developments and are likely to impose further **sanctions, restrictions and conditions**. These will inevitably hamper progress. If there is an independent regulatory office, it will make its own unwelcome inputs.

The business's problems will attract **extensive media coverage** and much adverse publicity is likely to be generated. This will further hamper attempts at recovery, **deterring potential customers and recruits**.

Eventually, if nothing is done, management will expend all its efforts dealing with crises and **overall direction will disappear**. This tendency will be exacerbated by the declining timeliness and quality of management information.

Question 3

> **Top tips.** Company J's status as a state-owned business is important since any plan must be politically acceptable. It is not necessary to make extensive assumptions about government policy in order to make this point.
>
> **Easy marks.** You should be able to score a few marks very easily with appropriate references to mechanisms for consultation, communication and negotiation, since these are obvious requirements for sensible management of conflict.

Managing the conflict

The organisation clearly has a **major problem separate from the present disruptive conflicts**: its continuing failure to provide a satisfactory level and quality of service to its customers. Any attempt to improve matters must start by **diagnosing the reasons for this failure** and **deciding what is to be done about it**. Another over-arching consideration is that **leadership of a very high quality will be required** from top management throughout the process of recovery.

It may be that **interdisciplinary working parties** could contribute to the process of diagnosis. The establishment of such groups would also be a good first step to reducing conflict, since members could air their grievances and would be forced to work together.

When a **coherent and convincing plan for recovery** has been drafted, government must be approached with the aim of obtaining the **necessary finance**. A particularly important aspect will be the negotiated settlement of the trades unions' concerns. Improving future operations may, in fact, require redundancy or it may require increased numbers, but **manpower planning** must start from a consideration of ends rather than means. Simply cutting numbers to save cost may be entirely **inappropriate** if it prejudices the company's ability to achieve its mission.

Assuming that the plan is accepted by government, it will then be top management's role to put it into effect. This will require a combination of techniques. The plan is effectively a **programme of change** and ideas of **change management** may help.

Enhanced, continuing and effective communication of goals, plans and progress to all staff will be required. There should be scope for upwards communication of individuals' concerns and these should be dealt with as sympathetically as possible. The aim should be to convince all staff that there is a rational programme underway to tackle the organisation's problems and remove the causes of friction. This should help to create a **culture of co-operation in a common cause**.

Resistance to change may be weakened by a changed system of rewards; the cost implications of this must be built into the plan.

At the same time, **top management must be prepared to dominate** the organisation and impose its will if necessary. It may impose **super-ordinate goals** on the various departments. These are goals which can only be reached through effective co-operation. Foot-dragging and adversarial behaviour must not be tolerated.

Question 4

> **Top tips.** We are told that the Examiner regards PRINCE2 as *de facto* standard for project management , so it is important that you understand how the system works. In particular, you must be able to explain the system's emphasis on outputs rather than processes. This principle is carried forward into the analysis of project scope in terms of what is to be achieved rather than what is to be done.
>
> **Easy marks.** There are no easy marks here unless you are familiar with PRINCE 2.

PRINCE2 is a widely accepted, standard method of project management. It offers clear management structures and planning and control methods and is noteworthy for its focus on **outputs** rather than processes.

The methodology is built up mainly from eight **components** and eight **processes**. Three of the components and two of the processes are likely to be of particular interest to the management accountant.

Business case

A business case is not something that is confined to commercial organisations; the term may be understood as meaning a reasoned account of what is to be achieved and why it will be of benefit. It is fundamental to the PRINCE2 system that a project is driven by its business case. The business case may require updating as the project progresses. The need to agree a clear and comprehensive business case may assist the management accountant in her dealings with the CEO.

Organisation

Management implies a structure of authority and accountability. PRINCE2 recognises four layers of managemen responsibility, though levels may be combined or eliminated if appropriate. Company J's project has been init at Board level; it may be appropriate for the Board to appoint one of its number to guide policy on the proj management accountant's concerns about her reporting responsibilities would be solved by the appointment of a **project board** to provide overall guidance and represent the business interests of the organisation.

Two other constituencies would also be represented.

(a)   The **senior user** represents the interests of those who are affected by the introduction of the new system and is accountable for the quality of the specification. This role would seem appropriate for the Director of Operations.

(b)   The **senior supplier/senior technical** person represents those charged with implementing the project. This role could be filled by the senior representative of the external prime contractor.

In PRINCE2, the project manager reports to the project board.

Configuration management

A **configuration** is a technical description, a complete specification of everything that is needed to bring a project to a successful conclusion. With complex projects, it is likely that frequent technical changes will be made: all of these changes must be approved and documented. Configuration management controls the processes by which projects develop.

A proper system of configuration management would assist the management accountant in dealing with any confusion that might arise over just what the new system was supposed to do

Controlling a stage

Controlling a stage is the process undertaken by the project manager to ensure that any given stage of the project remains on course. A project might consist of just one stage, of course.

PRINCE2 project control includes a comprehensive structure of reports and meetings that will give structure to the management accountant's discharge of her responsibilities.

A **project initiation** meeting agrees the scope and objectives of the project and gives approval for it to start.

The completion of each project stage is marked by an **end stage assessment**, which includes reports from the project manager and the project assurance team. The next stage does not commence until its plans have been reviewed and approved.

Highlight reports are submitted regularly to the project board by the project manager. These reports are the main overall routine control mechanism and their frequency (often monthly) is agreed at project initiation. They are essentially progress reports and should include brief summaries of project schedule and budget status.

Managing product delivery

Managing product delivery is the process that controls work done by specialist teams by agreeing what work is to be done and ensuring that it is carried out to the proper standard. The management accountant would use this process to define and implement her relationship with the external contractors.

SECTION C

···n 5

plicit requirement to relate ideas about structure to the nature of Gensup as an organisation. ill not be adequate. For example, we do not mention the matrix since it does not seem up's activities. There is plenty of evidence of how Gensup might choose to develop its iven in the scenario. In a question like part (a), worth only seven marks but with plenty be reasonably brief. Do not try to exhaustive.

In part (b) the marking scheme might be expected to be based on the handful of possible structural forms, with up to five marks available for the discussion of each, to the stated overall maximum of eighteen marks.

Easy marks. As is often the case, a little theoretical knowledge will earn you the easy marks in this question.

(a) **Classical approaches to organisation structure**

(i) **Functional structure**. The organisation hierarchy is drawn up according to the type of work that people do. Marketing staff are managed in one department; finance staff are managed in another and so on. Functional departments existed within A Ltd, B Ltd and C Ltd. In Gensup as a whole, **purchasing** is an example of a central business function.

(ii) **Geographical structure**. **Unisal** appears to have been organised on a geographical basis, as it was a distribution and logistics firm.

(iii) **Product organisation**. Gensup seems to have adopted this approach for A Ltd, B Ltd and C Ltd. All the activities involved in producing and selling a product are brought under one roof.

(iv) **Customer/market**. The organisation structure reflects the customer base. Unisal had aspects of this, with specialised sales forces for different industries.

In practice, Unisal has a hybrid structure, combining these approaches.

(i) Some activities as we have seen are run on a functional basis

(ii) A, B, and C are to a degree run as product divisions

(b) **Advantages and disadvantages of each structural form**

(i) **Functional departments**

Advantages

(1) They enable **specialist expertise to be concentrated** in one place, and a more **effective division of labour** within the function. For Gensup, this is seen in the centralised R & D function, which can probably do better as one than if it remained split into three.

(2) Functional organisation is **simple and logical**. Gensup has exploited this to obtain **economies of scale** – the larger purchasing function should be able to achieve bulk discounts on orders, and hopefully reduced administration costs.

Disadvantages

(1) **Functions** reflect the way the business works internally, but not **products or markets it makes and serves**.

(2) It is **hard to identify profits/losses on individual products**, unless something like activity based costing is used.

(3) They **inhibit organisational learning**, in that systems thinking (seeing the wood for the trees) and multi-disciplinary teams are not encouraged.

(4) **Horizontal communication is limited** so decisions related to more than one department are only taken at the highest levels.

(ii) As for **geographical organisation**, there is an obvious logic for Unisal's distribution operations, especially dealing with export markets over a wide area.

(1) **Better decision-making** at the point of contact with the customer.

(2) The **goods are closer to the customer**, so delivery is quick and cheap – important in just-in-time applications.

(3) There is potentially a **duplication of management effort**.

In such a set-up, **each warehouse needs to operate as an independent** unit, with its own local customers. Whereas the output of each warehouse is locally managed, the **inputs are manag** the central purchasing department.

(1)   To work, the centralised purchasing operation must be in **regular and close contact with the warehouses** to see they have the right supplies in stock; the firm needs **excellent internal communications**.

(2)   Gensup will have to work hard to ensure **consistency of performance** in all its export markets, especially if it sells to multinational firms.

(iii)   **Product divisions. Gensup is effectively in two businesses now**: manufacturing and distribution.

Advantages of a product division structure

(1)   It **enhances accountability for a product range**. Gensup's reorganisation has in fact clouded this issue, as purchases for the manufacturing firms and the old Unisal have been combined.

(2)   **Gensup must decide how far A B and C remain independent of the distribution centres**. Unisal was not a manufacturer, and the scenario does not make clear how A, B and C's products are to be distributed. If A, B and C retain their own sales forces, or deal with the old Unisal distribution centre at an arm's length basis, function as divisions. But none of this is particularly clear from the data.

The **disadvantage** of **product division** is the **increased complexity** of the firm. A B and C could be integrated into one production organisation. This would enhance the transfer of manufacturing know-how (eg TQM techniques) and personnel between them. They produce similar products for similar markets. Retaining them as separate divisions would seem to undermine some potential; economies of scale that a unified functional management structure would bring them.

(iv)   As for customer or market segment, this form of departmentation has not been adopted, other than at a fairly low level for the sales force. Marketing is to be a central function of the business.

Gensup's **hybrid structure** seems sensible the light of its diverse activities but it is not perfect. The **manufacturing divisions are imperfectly integrated** into the structure as a whole: no indication is given of the precise nature of the relationship with the distribution centres, who have traditionally purchased from a range of suppliers. We do not know if the purchasing function will treat A, B and C at an arms length, thus injecting market control into the process.

To summarise, the current hybrid structure proposed has not gone far enough in addressing some of the important structural issues raised by the acquisition.

Top tips. Alternative answer to part (b) based on Mintzberg's structural configurations model

The **pros and cons of each structural configuration**

(i)   Simple structure. This is not appropriate for Gensup. Gensup is too big and complex. Whilst Gensup must innovate, much of its production output is standardised. Individual departments, however, might be arranged in a fairly informal manner (eg R & D).

(ii)   **Machine bureaucracy**. Such bureaucracies exist to perform standardised work according to a set routine, and are **appropriate in stable simple environments**. At the moment, there appears to be **environmental instability**, with the consolidation of the customer base into larger firms, new markets and sources of supply opening up. The firm is positioned on a fairly long value chain, **so a machine bureaucracy is not** ~~~~**~~hle if flexibility is required**. The manufacturing plants require standardisation, however, to ~~~~nt quality, and some sort of functional specialisation is, therefore, inevitable.

Given that the manufacturing firms and the distribution firm are very different, some degree ~~~~will be necessary although some synergies (eg central R&D and purchasing) can be ~~~~ight therefore contain:

~~~~vision, formerly Unisal, to service customers;

~~~~division, featuring A, B and C Ltd.

The **two divisions should be kept at arms length**, to ensure the customer still benefits from Unisal's purchasing expertise. Unisal may be able to obtain some products cheaper from the manufacturing division. However the existence of many common functions means that full divisionalisation will not be practised.

(iv)   Unisal has some of the features of a **professional bureaucracy**, in that **sales staff are 'experts'** on particular types of customer, and that the firm was essentially involved in services. This is still appropriate for the **distribution operation**, but not suitable for the whole of Gensup.

(v)   There may be some scope for developing features of an **operating or administrative adhocracy**. This will depend on the degree to which the firm can mobilise the expertise of its various personnel in: sales, research and development and purchasing.

The **shared expertise** gives the firm the opportunity to innovate more. As the **'operating core' of the manufacturing plants has effectively been automated**, a configuration encouraging project teams across the firm may be the best way of ensuring competitive advantage and customer benefits. Sales staff can communicate customer requirements to staff in R & D.

Question 6

Top tips. Fairly obviously, part (a) is best answered with a fairly lengthly mission statement perhaps based on the common four part model.

- Purpose
- Strategy
- Policies and standards
- Values

A snappy one-liner, such as Komatsu's 'Beat Caterpillar', will not give you much to write about.

(a)   **Mission statement for Gensup**

Mission statements range from brief sentences to long paragraphs.

'Gensup is a materials manufacturing and components sourcing and distribution group, which services selected niches in the engineering market on a global basis.

Our continuing central aim is the continuing optimisation of shareholders' investment through earnings per share and increase in capital value. Our activities are in raw materials manufacture and the provision of specialist expertise to our dealings with customers.

To this end we seek to:

- operate in markets where we have comprehensive expertise and knowledge;

- continually ensure that we identify and anticipate our customers' needs;

- develop new materials and processes through the application of technological development programmes.

We aim to be the best in our chosen fields, and thereby to increase the wealth of our shareholders and enhance the prosperity and well-being of our customers, employees and the communities of which we are a part.'

Importance of the different components of the mission statement

(i)   The statement **defines what business the firm is in**, and the customers it serves. This **communicates basic facts** about the company to an outsider. In the materials business, th suggests extension into other materials markets.

(ii)   Shareholders are addressed in the statement's **'central aim'**. Unisal was quoted on several stockmarkets world-wide, so the overall commitment to enhance **shareholder value** would seem appropriate.

(iii)   The firm **competes** in a number of different ways, but it seems to be highlighting quality of service and manufacturing innovation.

(iv)   Connected stakeholders are mentioned: the mission refers to the well-being of **customers, employees and the community**. The statement is perhaps deficient in that it does not state how this is to be achieved. Interestingly, it **excludes suppliers**, which are resource rich countries, but which may be poor in terms of economic development.

(v)   There is no mention of **social responsibility**, other than vague waffle about the community. Gensup does not trumpet its desire to be a 'good corporate citizen' nor is any mention made of the **environment**, even though many firms in extractive industries make such a point. Given Gensup's manufacturing capability, some mention of these issues could have been expected.

(b)   **Operational goals**

Top tips. The word 'primary' should prompt you to think of the value chain model. Identifying four of the primary value activities should be worth at least two marks, and possibly four if you provided a brief explanation of each.

Easy marks. Further easy marks are going to be difficult to find. Making sensible suggestions about goals and critical success factors is difficult to do without good experience of the industry in question. The best most candidates will be able to do will be to pick reasonably obvious ideas such as speed of delivery. Ask yourself what you appreciate when you buy a good or service and what disappoints you.

An operational or operative goal is a goal that can be expressed in a **quantifiable or measurable form as an objective**.

Operational goals can cover a wide variety of organisational activities, including overall performance measurement, production, maintenance, boundary-spanning (eg purchasing, marketing) and so forth. The examples offered below are activities selected from Porter's value chain analysis. (In this model, primary activities are those directly related with production, sales, marketing, delivery and services.)

(i)   **Inbound logistics** deal with receiving, handling and storing inputs to the production system. They cover warehousing, transport, stock control and so forth. Operational goals could include the following.

(1)   Lead times from suppliers
(2)   Incidence of stock-outs
(3)   Quality of purchased inputs (eg through quality assurance)
(4)   Warehousing costs

The goal would be to make **efficient use of warehouse to support the production function** at lower cost. A related 'support activity' (procurement) would be concerned with issues such as price per unit purchased and supplies.

Operations convert resource inputs into a final product. In a manufacturing firm, this is relatively ~~identify~~ as the factory. In a service company, operations include those activities which make ~~ic~~ service. Operations include the entire management of the production function. With ~~trategy~~ of customer service, and the customers' espousal of TQM, something such as BS 17 certification may be required. Goals can include those below.

~~targets~~
~~ut~~ speed
~~reducing~~ waste

(iii) **Outbound logistics** relate to storing the product and its distribution to customers. They include packaging, warehousing, testing and so forth. Goals will include the following.

    (1)   Speed of processing

    (2)   Response times

    (3)   Error-free deliveries

(iv) **Marketing and sales** are those activities that relate to informing customers about the product, persuading them to buy it, and enabling them to do so. This includes advertising, promotion and so forth. Some performance measures can include the following.

    (1)   Raising customers' awareness (measured by survey) of the firm

    (2)   The incidence of repeat business

    (3)   Market share

(v) **After sales service**. For many companies, there are activities such as installing products, repairing them, upgrading them, providing spare parts and so forth. This is at the **heart of Unisal's business**. Suitable goals could include the use of aftersales service visits as a means of generating new orders or finding more about the customer.

In short, the firm will be driven by goals relating both to product quality and service quality. Suppliers who are on contractual relationships are perhaps less worried about price, in the short term at least, than about reliability.

(c) **Generic strategies**

Top tips. Remember Porter's conclusion that both cost leadership and differentiation are expensive strategies and that most businesses will have to settle for some kind of focus strategy.

Easy marks. At managerial level there may well be some credit available for a brief summary of relevant theory such as we provide. However, it could not be worth more than two marks.

(i) **Cost leadership**: be the lowest cost producer in the industry as a whole.

(ii) **Differentiation**: offer a unique product or service to the market as a whole.

(iii) **Focus**: restrict activities to only part of the market (a segment).

    (1)   Provide goods and/or services at lower cost to that segment (cost-focus).

    (2)   Provide a differentiated product/service for that segment (differentiation-focus).

What strategy is Gensup pursuing?

(i) **Unisal probably pursued a differentiation-focus strategy** in that it concentrated on servicing the needs of customers in identified market segments.

(ii) On the other hand, the **manufacturing plants produced commodity items**. In such a case, especially where raw materials are an important part of cost, cost leadership is important. As there are so many suppliers, these firms **probably pursued a cost-focus strategy**, based on the UK market.

(iii) The new developments offer new opportunities and so **Gensup's strategy of differentiation-focus in the global market will probably predominate** especially if the manufacturing plants are to be exploited to extend Gensup's product range.

Question 7

> **Top tips.** Make sure you read all the requirements carefully and plan what you are going to put into the answer to each part. It would be very easy to produce a poor answer by making good points in the wrong place.
>
> **Easy marks.** All three parts of this question revolve around task environment, so spend a few moments making sure you are aware of all the factors that go into the various task environments discussed. This will take you a long way towards a pass mark, though you will have to provide some discussion to reach it.

(a)   The environment is 'all elements that exist outside the boundary of the organisation' which have the potential to affect all or part of the organisation.

The task environment of the **manufacturing plants** is fairly restricted.

(i)   **Investors**. All the firms were privately owned, without the need to communicate with a large number of investors or potential investors on a stock exchange.

(ii)   **Resources**. Each of the manufacturing firms depends on raw materials. In this respect, the firms might be vulnerable to:

(1)   interruptions in supply, as metals, in particular, are not found everywhere. Aluminium and copper, or ores at least, have to be imported;

(2)   changes in price levels from their major suppliers. As far as plastics are concerned, the main supply would appear to be the oil and chemicals industries. There is a developed international market.

(iii)   Other common inputs are **water** and **electric power** in the UK. Normally, there should be no problem (but beware droughts!)

(iv)   The firms are **not affected by social trends or changes in consumer tastes**.

(v)   **Technology** is a crucial area to keep costs down and to attain, through innovation, a significant advantage.

Gensup's task environment is much wider. Effectively, Unisal has engaged in a degree of **backwards vertical integration**.

Gensup is vulnerable to the same international trade and political issues relating to acquiring its resources as the former manufacturing companies. Furthermore, it is able to take advantage of export opportunities more effectively, so its chosen domain has shifted towards an **international** orientation, and it will therefore be **more exposed to international political influences** than the three firms before.

Gensup's **value chain** is more extensive than that of the manufacturing firms or indeed of Unisal. The firm combines both a manufacturing and distribution capacity, so the domain in which it operates is large.

(b)   **Sectors of the task environment**

> **Top tips.** We have described more than four sections, as you had a choice.

Some sectors of the task environment of manufacturing plants

(i)   **Financial resources**. Management of cash and other **working capital** items is an essential part of the day to day management of any business; a firm which runs out of cash goes under. Obviously, **long-term finance** is less of a day to day issue. Purchasing raw materials exposes the firm to exchange risk: they might operate on the futures market.

(ii)   **Human resources**. Even in times of unemployment, many companies complain of 'skills shortages' implying that they cannot obtain the right staff. This is obviously affected by demography and government policy on education and training policies.

(1)   No problem with recruiting unskilled production workers.

(2)   Skilled staff are needed in R&D and maintenance.

(iii)   **Market**. The 'market' is a firm's current and potential customers. The manufacturing firm's markets were fairly small. Unisal's markets are extensive.

   (1)   **Customer needs change over time**: the marketing department should identify these needs, and to suggest how they can be met most effectively.

   (2)   The market is changing to one where size is important and where the customer base is becoming concentrated. See (iv) below. Unisal is taking over marketing activities.

(iv)   **Industry and competition.**

   Unisal and the manufacturing plants merged because of the **evident concentration among the customer base** and the potential increase in customer bargaining power (Porter).

(v)   **Raw materials**. The manufacturing plants need raw materials (and energy) to make their products. Is there competition for raw materials, effectively bidding up the price? Are they easily obtainable, or is there a restricted supply? Are prices volatile?

   (1)   New supplies in eastern Europe should reduce the dependency on one source.

   (2)   Unisal is a sourcing and distribution firm, so some expertise already exists. Gensup will perhaps be able to take advantage of bulk discounts.

(c)   **Contrasts between the task environment of Gensup and that of the original manufacturers**

(i)   **Financial resources**. Gensup is a plc. In theory, long-term financial resources should be easier to obtain, but that the **share price will determine the cost of capital** and the **returns** expected. In this, Gensup differs from the original manufacturing firms, which were not quoted companies (although Unisal was quoted).

(ii)   **Human resources**. Gensup results from a merger of manufacturers and a distribution firm.

   (1)   Unisal had developed a large sales force, who will now have to liaise directly with the plants. Whereas **the plants** dealt with external customers or the market directly, **they will now do so through the former Unisal's sales force**.

   (2)   There might have to be **changes in corporate culture** to accommodate the specialists now working in corporate R & D.

   (3)   Gensup probably has a **larger pool from which to recruit** than A, B and C Ltd, as it is an international firm.

(iii)   **Market**. This relates to (ii) (human resources) above. From dealing with customers directly, the **manufacturing plants will become internal suppliers** of a sales force already used to dealing with a large number of suppliers. **For the manufacturing plants, their environment will be simpler**.

(iv)   **Industry**. The **plants will be more secure** as part of a larger firm, dealing with customers whose **increasing size** effectively increases their bargaining power and competitive ability.

(v)   **Raw materials**. This situation has not changed significantly, other than in east Europe. Gensup might be able to force price decreases in electricity or even water. The firm's total demand for ores and chemicals is not increased by virtue of the merger alone. Increased activity levels might lead to more purchases. However, centralisation of some purchasing functions should enable greater expertise in purchasing to be developed.

(vi)   **International**. The firm is now dealing in a global market, which offers more threats but more opportunities.

(vii) **Complexity**

Gensup's task environment is inevitably more complex than the environment of its predecessor companies, because the **value chain of a vertically integrated conglomerate is longer and more complex** than that of a firm focused on one area.

(1) The **variety of influences**. The greater the number of markets the organisation operates in, the greater the number of influences to which it is subject.

Gensup faces an increased variety of influences, as it tackles new markets. The complexity is probably at a medium level. Although Gensup is effectively a new company, Unisal, its predecessor, was a plc already listed on a number of stock exchanges.

(2) The amount of **knowledge** necessary. Some environments, to be handled successfully, require knowledge. Gensup needs some specialist knowledge in a fairly restricted area. However, this required knowledge and expertise is likely to increase, as customers require more sophisticated materials.

(3) The **interconnectedness** of environmental influences. Importing and exporting companies are sensitive to exchange rates, which in turn are sensitive to interest rates. Interest rates then influence a company's borrowing costs.

Many of the **environmental factors are interconnected. Commodity prices are perhaps very susceptible to changes in exchange rates**. These might be volatility in raw materials prices.

CIMA
Paper P5 (Managerial)
Integrated Management

Mock Exam 2 (November 2005)

Question Paper	
Time allowed	**3 hours**
This paper is divided into three sections	
Section A	**Answer ALL questions in this section**
Section B	**Answer ALL THREE questions in this section**
Section C	**TWO questions ONLY to be attempted**

DO NOT OPEN THIS PAPER UNTIL YOU ARE READY TO START UNDER EXAMINATION CONDITIONS

SECTION A – 20 marks

Answer ALL EIGHT sub-questions in this section: two to four marks each

Each of the sub-questions numbered from 1.1 to 1.8 inclusive, given below, has only one right answer.

Instructions for answering Section A:

Question 1

1.1 Identify which ONE of the following strategies should be used to deal with stakeholders who have high power but low interest:

A   Keep informed

B   Minimal effort

C   Keep satisfied

D   Key player   **(2 marks)**

1.2 The cultural dimension that describes a cultural value where individuals are expected to take care of themselves is referred to by Hofstede as:

A   Individualism

B   Collectivism

C   Power distance

D   Masculinity   **(2 marks)**

1.3 According to transaction cost theory, the mechanisms that organisations have to choose between to control their resources and carry out their operations are:

A   Markets or structures

B   Hierarchies or markets

C   Structures or culture

D   Hierarchies or culture   **(2 marks)**

1.4 Which ONE of the following is a part of the 'identification of need' phase of the project life cycle:

A   The Completion Report

B   The Milestone Review

C   Project scheduling

D   The project initiation document   **(2 marks)**

1.5 List **three** benefits of mentoring.   **(3 marks)**

1.6 Identify the missing words needed to complete the rational model of strategic management. Record your answers by making reference to the corresponding letters **A**, **B**, **C** and **D**. (4 marks)

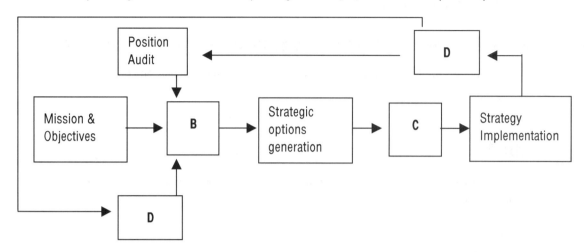

(4 marks)

1.7 Complete the gaps to determine the four stages in the project lifecycle.

(1) Identification of a need; (2)_____(3) Implementation; (4)_____. (2 marks)

1.8 Briefly explain the interests of a 'project owner'. (3 marks)

(Total for Section A = 20 marks)

SECTION B – 30 marks

Answer ALL THREE questions – 10 marks each

Question 2

N Airline operates in the short haul flight industry. Unlike many of its competitors who are constantly seeking to reduce costs, often at the expense of customer service, the foundation of N's business strategy is based on providing a superior quality of service. Its mission is to be market leader, providing unrivalled customer service, in flight comfort and reliability in the short haul airline industry. N Airlines views its customers as central to strategic developments, and values its staff in building success.

Required

(a)   Distinguish between the concepts of mission and objectives.   **(4 marks)**

(b)   Using examples, illustrate how the mission for N Airline could be translated into strategic objectives.
                                                                                                                                    (6 marks)

                                                                                                                    (Total = 10 marks)

Question 3

R Company, a manufacturer and retailer of fashion clothes, has invested in a new technology system to improve the logistics of the movement of clothes between its warehouses and chain of 250 retail outlets. Ensuring that the outlets have the right supply of clothes is a critical success factor for the company. However, the warehousing stock control and logistics project set up to develop and deliver the new system has experienced numerous problems. The project ended up being well over budget and was also late in delivering the system. Now, only three months after the new system has been installed, it is apparent that the project has not delivered its objective. Instead, the company is facing a crisis with many store managers complaining that they are not receiving the

correct stock. Even worse, some stores are out of stock of key ranges, whereas the warehouses are full of clothing.

A meeting between the project team and project sponsor has ended up with everyone blaming each other, saying it was not their responsibility. It is clear that they did not use a project management methodology and did not have adequate project control systems in place so that the problems that have now transpired could have been identified and rectified earlier in the project lifecycle.

Required

Recommend to R Company a project management methodology/approach, explaining how it could have helped to prevent the failures of the warehousing, stock control and logistics project.

                                                                                                                    (Total = 10 marks)

Project Mgt Methodology/approach

Question 4

S has recently been appointed as the Finance Department Manager in Z Company. During the first month in her new role she has observed that one member of staff, C, is underperforming. C is frequently arriving late to work with no explanation and he is taking extended lunch breaks without permission. He is also making errors and refuses to do certain tasks which are part of his role. One of his colleagues has spoken to S confidentially, saying that C's poor performance in his work is having an adverse impact on the rest of the team. It is apparent that the problems have been going on for some time but the previous manager had preferred to ignore them. S has decided that she must now take action on what appears to be a disciplinary case, but is unclear on how to deal with the situation.

Required

Explain to S the stages involved in taking disciplinary action against C.

(Total = 10 marks)

(Total for Section B = 30 marks)

SECTION C – 50 marks

Answer any TWO questions from this section – 25 marks each

Question 5

X Company is a global consultancy company specialising in organisational change and restructuring. The service offered to clients usually involves the formation of teams to carry out change projects in companies. The teams are drawn from different areas of X Company, based around different specialisms.

T, the HR Director, is concerned that the methods of recruitment and selection for new consultants has emphasised the skills associated with particular specialisms, for example marketing expertise, technology or financial technical skills. He feels that insufficient attention has been given to the skills of the project manager which are essential to the success of the company's project based work.

As a result, he has recently introduced a new recruitment and selection system, which includes a specification of the skills the company should be looking for in future project managers. One of the selection tests he has devised will involve candidates in delivering a presentation which explains why they may need to use different styles of leadership during a project and provides examples of the other key skills that they feel a project manager should possess.

Y recently applied for a job in X Company, specialising in finance, and whilst confident that he has the financial expertise required, he is less certain about the project manager skills he might

need. He is pleased that he has been short listed for interview and is researching what he might include in his presentation. As part of this he has asked you to help him to understand the key skills of an effective project manager.

Required

(a)   Explain to Y how an understanding of leadership style theories could help him to be more effective as a project manager. **(10 marks)**

(b)   Describe the other project manager skills, besides leadership skills, that Y should include in his presentation, explaining why they are important. **(15 marks)**

(Total = 25 marks)

Question 6

F Company is a medium sized business that manufactures electrical kitchen appliances including food processors, toasters, juicers and coffee makers. In the last twelve months the company has lost market share to its competitors and has underperformed on most of its key performance indicators. Its future survival is threatened as new entrants are stealing market share and the customers are demanding new product and design features.

G, the company's management accountant, suggests that F Company's difficulties are because it has been too complacent, not responding to changing environmental conditions and not having undertaken any formal strategic planning. He is also concerned that different areas of the company appear to be pursuing conflicting objectives.

To help the company develop a sustainable competitive advantage, G proposes that a more formal top down approach to developing business strategy should be adopted. He is also of the view that greater emphasis should be placed on understanding the external environment.

However, at a recent meeting where G outlined the benefits that a more formal approach to planning would bring, he was surprised that P, the HR director, disagreed. P argued that the dynamic environment that F Company operates in means that the formal approach is a waste of management time. She suggested that the company should assess how sustainable competitive advantage can be achieved through using its unique combination of resources, skills and capabilities.

Required

(a)   Explain the benefits and drawbacks associated with F Company adopting a top down approach to the formulation of business strategy.   **(12 marks)**

(b)   Compare and contrast the different views held by G and P on how F Company can gain competitive advantage.   **(13 marks)**

(Total = 25 marks)

Question 7

T has just returned to his job in the Finance Department of Z Company, having spent the last six months as a member of a project team working on the development of an Educational Visitors Centre for the company.

Reflecting on his experiences whilst working on the project, he feels that most of his time was spent in meetings that did not achieve anything, but rather wasted his time. He also feels that the final stages of the project were not dealt with effectively, with the project members going back to their functional jobs without any discussion or feedback on the project performance and outcomes.

He has now been asked to take on the role of project manager for a new project and is determined that he will improve the experience for his project team.

Required

(a)   Discuss the problems that may be associated with project meetings. Make recommendations on the methods T could use to ensure the meetings he arranges as project manager, are effective.   **(15 marks)**

(b)   Evaluate the contribution of the various activities that should be carried out as part of project closure, the post completion review and audit of the project.   **(10 marks)**

(Total = 25 marks)

(Total for Section C = 50 marks)

Answers

DO NOT TURN THIS PAGE UNTIL YOU HAVE
COMPLETED THE MOCK EXAM

A plan of attack

Most of us panic at least a little when we open an exam paper, so having a reasonable idea of what you are going to do is likely to help.

Section A

It is probably best to tackle Section A right at the beginning, since it is compulsory and you should be able to get off to a good start by picking up some easy marks. Be very strict with the time you allot to Section A. It is worth 20 marks so you must not spend more than 36 minutes on it initially. If you are baffled by one of the questions, press on, finish Section A that much faster and return to it at the end of the exam if you still have time.

Section B

You know that there are going to be three compulsory questions in Section B, worth ten marks each. You have no choices to make here and it is a good idea to plunge straight into this section first. However, you must allocate your time carefully. Section B is worth 30% of the marks, so you should give it 30% of your time. And within that 54 minutes, you should aim to spend 18 minutes on each question. This is a good approach because the ten marks available for each question are not all equally difficult to get. The first five marks in most questions are easy. The last five marks are difficult. You must get all the easy marks on each question! The best way to do this is to be very disciplined about time, and not linger on a question you think you know lots about and ignore one you don't like.

However, be prepared to think on the spot. If there is a compulsory question, or part of a question which baffles you, it would be foolish to sit looking at it for the prescribed 1.8 minutes per mark. Similarly, if you see a question that fills you with joy and you just know you can score heavily, then don't stop writing on it if you are sure you are still making valid, relevant points. But be careful! Misapplication of this aspect of examination technique claims more victims than any other.

Section C

In Section C you have to make a choice. One good approach is to take a quick overview and form some sort of idea of which questions you are going to tackle. This should only take a few minutes since you do not need to read all the scenarios in detail. You can make a first estimate by looking at the question requirements only. Once you have done this, look in more detail at your likely questions and ask yourself what the Examiner is after and whether you can supply it. Only then look at the other two, if you cannot confirm your first impression.

An alternative approach is to read all three questions in detail and make a firm decision.

In any case, you may find it helpful to do the question you are most confident about first. The danger here is the temptation to overrun your time.

Checking

80% of the marks in this exam are for answers in written form and the great majority for answers in the form of essays. One of the most important rules for written work is to leave sufficient time at the end of each question to read your answer through. You will pick up spelling mistakes, errors of grammar and instances of poor expression. You will also find you have missed out things you intended to put in and possibly put in things that shouldn't be there. Candidates find this checking process very difficult to start, but it can be invaluable.

Handwriting

Handwriting is a thorn in the side for markers. If they cannot read you work, they cannot give you marks. Unless you are actually proud of your handwriting, think about writing double-spaced at all times. You don't have to pay for the extra paper you will use.

Sudden inspiration

The human brain works in strange ways. It is very common, halfway through an exam, to suddenly think of something relevant to a question that you thought you had finished. If you leave a few lines blank after the end of each answer you will be able to handle this if it happens to you.

Spare time at the end of the exam?

This should not happen if you have allocated your time carefully. However, if you run out of inspiration on your last question, start to go over your whole script from the beginning, thinking hard about how to improve it. You can relax when the invigilator says 'Stop!'

Question 1

1.1 C This question is based on *Mendelow's* stakeholder model. By coincidence, the letter C is also used by Mendelow for the quadrant occupied by these stakeholders. Such stakeholders must be treated with care: while often passive, they are capable of developing a higher degree of interest and starting to use their power.

1.2 A High regard for individual self-sufficiency and achievement contrasts with a more supportive and controlling approach: these two attitudes form the extremes of the individualism–collectivism dimension of *Hofstede's* cultural analysis.

1.3 B The phrase 'markets or hierarchies' was originated by *Williamson* who suggested that in the longer term and with increasing complexity, the organisation of production through a network of contracts would become unsatisfactory. Larger, hierarchically structured organisations would have to be developed.

1.4 D This is a reference to one particular model of the project life cycle: the project initiation document would effectively conclude the first phase, known in this model, as 'identification of need'.

1.5 The benefits of mentoring are said to include improved staff motivation; lower staff turnover; faster career progress; and fewer and more quickly resolved disputes. To these we might add improved work performance and increased job satisfaction for both mentor and protegé.

1.6 A Environmental analysis

B Corporate appraisal

C Evaluation and choice of options

D Strategic control

1.7 (2) Development of a solution

(4) Completion

This question is based on the same model as that used for question 1.4, which seems like overkill. *Maylor's* model would use 'Design the project' and 'Develop the process' for stages two and four of the project life cycle, while the US project Management Institute Body of Knowledge would use 'planning' and 'controlling' for the equivalent stages.

1.8 'Project owner' is one of a number of terms used to designate the head of the department or organisation that will benefit from the project output. Other terms used for this person are 'business owner', 'customer' and, under PRINCE2, 'senior user'. The difference between the project sponsor and the project owner is that the owner does not usually provide the resources needed, though, of course, these roles are often combined. The specific interests of this stakeholder are therefore concerned with the timely delivery of a satisfactory project outcome; this will satisfy the design requirements for functionality and will achieve everything defined by the scope of the project.

Question 2

Top tips. This is a simple question on a very basic topic in strategic management and should be easy for you to answer well.

Part (a)

Top tips. The terminology used here is widely standardised, so there should be no confusion in your mind.

> **Easy marks.** A question like this revolves around definitions: you do not have to quote *Mintzberg* verbatim, as we do, so long as you can produce a clear and succinct version of your own

Mintzberg says that **mission** 'defines the organisation's basic function in society, in terms of the products and services it produces for its clients'. A wider definition of mission would include reference to four elements.

- **Purpose** would differ among types of organisations, but would define why the organisation was created.

- **Strategy** would define the nature of the organisation's activities and would therefore cover Mintzberg's definition quoted above.

- **Policis and performance standards** as overall imperatives can be included in mission to emphasise their importance.

- **Values** are the pervasive beliefs and attitudes that underpin the organisation's culture.

Mission is therefore the overall definition of what the organisation exists to do.

Objectives are specific, well, defined targets whose attainment will support progress towards achieving the mission. They translate the generalised aspirations of mission into more specific, measurable and concrete terms that can be used to organise the organisation's work and provide specific targets to measure its success against. They therefore flow from and support mission.

While an organisation generally has only one mission, it is likely to have many objectives. These will be arranged in a hierarchy, with a relatively small number of high level objectives directly derived from and supporting the mission, and each of these being broken down into a cascade of supporting departmental, functional and even individual supporting objectives.

Part (b)

> **Top tips.** This question is unusual in its use of the instruction verb 'illustrate'. 'Illustrate' means 'use an example to describe or explain something'. The Examiner reminds you to use examples, so there is really no excuse for failing to link your answer to the setting in very concrete terms.
>
> Notice also the phrase 'strategic objectives'. Try to focus on objectives that are truly strategic; that is, objectives that directly support N Airline's mission. A good test of a possible objective would be to ask if it could be part of something with a wider scope. For example, 'minimise check-in delays' might be part of a wider objective to 'provide the best ground-based customer service'.
>
> This part of the question is worth six marks. The scenario is very short. You should therefore be aiming to find three, or possibly four, strategic objectives.
>
> Finally, do not forget the **SMART** mnemonic.
>
> **Easy marks.** The setting uses the word 'service' three times, which is an indication of a major priority for N Airline.

It is commonly considered that objectives should be specific, measurable, attainable, realistic and time bounded. The last quality is probably inappropriate for many strategic objectives, since they will have continuing applicability.

A **high level of customer service** is clearly a major part of N Airline's strategic vision and is intended to constitute its chief point of differentiation from its competitors. This might give rise to an objective such as the one below.

'To provide the highest level of customer service on the ground and in the air as measured by customer survey, unsolicited feedback and competitor benchmarking.'

The quality of customer service achieved will depend largely on **the people who deliver it**. HRM objectives might therefore be regarded as subordinate to the overall customer service objective. However, N Airline may wish to elevate its HRM objective to the strategic level in order to underscore its commitment to and dependence on its staff.

'To optimise recruitment, selection, training, development and remuneration practices so that all staff have the ability and motivation to deliver the highest level of customer service.'

N Airline's business model will inevitably involve a level of costs higher than those incurred by its rivals. This must imply higher revenues from higher ticket prices, which, in turn, will limit its market. **Careful management of costs and revenues** will be required if the company is to avoid cash flow crises. This is quantifiable in terms of gross and net margin, but the problem will be to set targets that are both adequate and attainable. An objective might be defined in terms such as those below.

'To manage the company's costs and revenues so as to facilitate the attainment of its objectives for customers and staff while generating a gross margin of X% and a net margin of Y%.'

Question 3

> **Top tips**. A number of bodies have designed project management methodologies, with perhaps the best known being the US Project Management Institute's Project Management Body of Knowledge and, in the UK, the PRINCE2 system. We have chosen to use PRINCE2 as the basis for our answer, but there is no reason why other approaches should not be used.
>
> We have a single requirement worth ten marks here: treat it in the same way you would a part of a Section C question.
>
> **Easy marks**. Perhaps the aspect of PRINCE2 that is most relevant to the scenario is its **focus on results** rather than processes: this is clearly of great relevance to this question scenario.

R Company would have benefited from the employment of the PRINCE2 project management method, which is now the *de facto* UK standard. PRINCE2 has three important design features that would have been particularly relevant to preventing the current problems.

(a)   The system **focuses on delivering results** (called 'products') rather than on the technical processes of project management. This alone would have produced a bias towards the required outcomes.

(b)   The system ensures that a project is driven by its **business case**: the continuing viability of the project is checked at regular intervals.

(c)   A **clear management structure** of roles and responsibilities is defined.

Planning

One aspect PRINCE2's focus on outputs rather than processes is the planning system it uses. Normal work breakdown structure is not used: instead, a **product breakdown structure** approach is used, thus providing an automatic focus on results. Products are initially divided into three groups.

(a)   **Technical products** are the things the project has been set up to provide: in the case of R Company, these are the artefacts of a comprehensive logistic system.

(b)   **Quality products** define both project quality standards and quality controls.

(c)   **Management products** are the systems used to manage the project.

The second and third groups of products mentioned above were obviously largely missing from R Company's project.

Business case

R Company's project appears to have drifted along in an unorganised manner, with all concerned pursuing their own ideas of what it was about. Clear statement of the business case for the project would have helped to produce an equally clear statement of the **scope** of the project.

Organisation

R Company's project sounds as though it included both IT and physical system elements, which would have complicated the project aims, activities and priorities. Under such circumstances, an effective **management structure** is particularly necessary.

Under PRINCE2, the top level of management for an individual project is the **project board**. In the case of R Company's project, this would be chaired by a senior manager whose role would be to provide overall guidance and represent the business interests of the organisation. Two other constituencies would also be represented.

(a)   The **senior user** represents the interests of those whom are affected by the introduction of the new system and is accountable for the quality of the specification. It would have been this person's job to ensure that the technical requirements of R Company's new system were clear and understood.

(b)   The **senior supplier/technical person** represents those charged with implementing the project and would point out any unrealistic or excessively costly aspects of the specification as the work developed.

This is a comprehensive approach: regular meetings of this board would have gone a long way to prevent the un-co-ordinated work that has obviously taken place.

Question 4

> **Top tips**. You need a good knowledge of the appropriate area of employment law to answer this question: there is an unspoken assumption that a proper answer will reflect modern attitudes to the relationship between employer and employee.
>
> Our answer is based on UK law and procedure, which can be taken as representative of the situation in the EU generally. You could use another legal system as a basis for an answer if you were more familiar with it.
>
> **Easy marks**. Employment law is complex and it would not be appropriate to approach this question looking for easy marks.

Disciplinary action is undertaken to improve future behaviour. It has considerable potential for creating serious disputes, so managers should always act consistently and in accordance with their organisation's established procedures. All disciplinary incidents should be **thoroughly investigated** and a written record kept by the manager concerned.

Many minor cases of poor performance or misconduct are best dealt with by informal advice, coaching or counselling. S should certainly start by taking this course of action, using the medium of an **informal interview**. C should be informed that his behaviour has caused concern and be asked to account for it. This should focus his mind and reveal if there are any extenuating circumstances, such as illness or a family crisis. In the absence of such circumstances, C should be informed firmly that an improvement is required. A record should be made of the interview.

Should there be no improvement, it may be necessary to deal with C through more formal disciplinary procedures. In the UK, such procedures are governed by the **ACAS code of practice**, which among other things, provides for full investigation, a right to be accompanied at any disciplinary proceeding and a right of appeal against sanctions. S, as a newly appointed manager should take advice from HRM professionals within Z Company.

The next stage would be the issue of a warning. This could be oral or written.

(a)   An **oral warning** should include the reason for issuing it; notice that it constitutes the first stage of the disciplinary procedure; and details of the right of appeal. A note of the warning should be kept on file but disregarded after a specified period, such as six months.

(b)   A **first written warning** is appropriate in more serious cases. It should inform the employee of the improvement required and state that a **final written warning** may be considered if there is no satisfactory improvement. A copy of a first written warning should be kept on file but disregarded after a specified period, such as twelve months.

(c)   A first written warning may also be appropriate if there has not been satisfactory improvement after an oral warning.

In the case of C, an oral warning is probably appropriate, as the disciplinary offences are fairly minor.

If the first warning is still current and there is no improvement, S may have to consider disciplinary sanction. Any sanction must be preceded by a **final written warning**.

The ultimate disciplinary sanction is dismissal. This is only appropriate for the most serious breaches of discipline. Demotion and suspension without pay are lesS drastic alternatives, but they must be provided for in the contract of employment.

In the UK, any imposition of disciplinary sanction must be in accordance with the statutory procedure introduced on 1 October 2004. This has three steps.

Step 1   S writes to C stating why disciplinary action is being taken and inviting him to meeting to discuss the matter. C has the right to be accompanied by an advisor at the meeting.

Step 2   At the meeting, S must explain the problem and allow C to respond. C must decide what is to be done and, after the meeting, explain her decision and inform C that he has the right to appeal to a different and preferably senior manager.

Step 3   C may appeal and has the right to be accompanied by an adviser at the appeal meeting.

Question 5

> **Top tips**. It is important to read both requirements of this question before starting to answer part (a) so as not to confuse the two answers: part (a) is about leadership, while part (b) is about everything else.

Part (a)

> **Top tips**. This is quite a cunning question since it demands knowledge of both leadership style theory and the nature of project management. The key to answering it is to understand that, in practice, managers rarely confine themselves to a single style in all circumstances: a contingent approach is more usual. This will tend to be especially true of project managers, who are likely to be faced with a greater variety of problems than normally occur in routine operations. You could base your answer on any of the well-known spectrum models, but you will need to include some kind of explanation of how contingencies will affect effectiveness.
>
> **Easy marks**. The easy marks in this question are for explaining the variable nature of leadership style. Explaining why this is relevant to managing projects will be the more difficult task.

The phrase 'leadership style' is commonly taken to mean the manager's beliefs and practices in relation to such things as degree of concern for the welfare and motivation of staff; degree of concern for achieving the task in hand; and extent of participation by subordinates in decision-making. Several models based on a **spectrum** running from autocracy to a *laissez-faire* approach have been suggested, as have more complex two dimensional descriptions and **contingency** models that have incorporated consideration of the work situation. It is these contingency models that may be useful to Y in becoming more effective as a project manager, since it seems unlikely that a single style of management is appropriate to all circumstances.

Likert found that the most productive departments in an insurance company were managed in a participative or democratic style, while *Hertzberg* found strong evidence that motivation in professionals depended largely on such things as achievement, challenge and recognition. These ideas are highly relevant to an organisation such as X Company that must inevitably employ **intelligent and well-qualified staff**. An autocratic style would be unlikely to get the best out of such staff. The basic model for Y to adopt, therefore, would be towards the **participative-democratic end of the spectrum**.

However, this would not be appropriate for all occasions. A good manager will be able to make use of a variety of styles and will choose a style that is **appropriate to the prevailing circumstances**. Thus, it may be appropriate for a manager of a department to involve competent and experienced staff in the consideration of plans for a rearrangement of workflows, but equally appropriate for the same manager to issue unequivocal instructions on a matter of safety practice.

It is in the nature of projects and project management that circumstances change, things go wrong and crises occur. It is also likely that normal variation of professional opinion will become more pronounced on such occasions. A project manager must be prepared to deal **rapidly and firmly** with such untoward occurrences, imposing his or her will in order to restore the situation. Democratic and participative ideals become less attractive when this happens and a more autocratic style is appropriate.

The need for leadership style to reflect the various contingencies present in the work situation has been explored by *Fiedler* and by *Hersey and Blanchard*. Their models are quite complex and tend to be most appropriate for understanding a range of fairly stable work situations. *Adair's* functional or action-centred approach is perhaps more useful for understanding the more dynamic project management problem.

Adair suggests that the roles the leader or manager has to play fall into three main groups focussed respectively on the needs of the **individual**, the needs of the **work group** and the needs presented by the **task**. Leaders shift the focus of their attention among these three sets of needs according to their assessment of circumstances.

This approach would be particularly appropriate for the management of projects. Project managers often have a significant team-building role to discharge, since many project teams are newly assembled to deal with a given project. The team members are likely to be well-qualified and experienced staff with their own firm views about what should be done, but they must be brought together to work in harmony if the project is to achieve its aims. Any project manager must, in effect, apply Adair's theory, balancing the attention paid to task, individual and group needs.

Part (b)

> **Top tips**. There is a small trap waiting for the unwary candidate in this question: it would be very easy to confuse the Project Manager's **skills** with the **functions** of the Project Manager role, especially since words like *teambuilding*, *communication* and *problem solving* occur in both lists.
>
> Notice that there are fifteen marks available for this part of the question. This is not unreasonable as we have to cover the whole range of project manager skills other than those relating to management style.
>
> You will often find that the mark allocation for a question breaks down into roughly equal parts; this is not the case here. We discuss project management skills under six headings, but the topics are not of equal size or complexity.
>
> **Easy marks**. The requirement for project managers to be able to use project management tools, to solve problems and to be flexible are reasonably obvious.

The project manager (PM) must deploy a wide range of skills and personal qualities in addition to those associated with leadership and team building.

Organisational skills

By 'organisational skills' we denote the **tools and practices** that are specific to project management. These include the maintenance of appropriate **project documentation**, so that planning, progress and problems can be properly understood and dealt with; and the use of **project management tools** such as network analysis and Gantt charts.

Communication

The PM must be able to **speak, write and listen effectively**, deploying these skills when dealing with both members of the project team and with more senior managers. Effective presentation of progress reports at project review meetings will be particularly important, as will issuing clear instructions to direct project activity. **Negotiation**, particularly over proposed changes and to obtain resources, will be important.

Technical skills

Here we refer to skills that relate to the nature of the project work. It is not necessary that managers of IT projects, for example, should be skilled IT engineers, but they must know enough about the subject to understand what the experts are saying and to form broad opinions on technical issues.

Personal qualities

Some personal qualities are particularly desirable in the PM.

- **Flexibility** and **creativity** are needed to deal with changes in the project's aims, the plan and the resources available.
- **Persistence** is essential to deal with a succession of major problems.
- Patience enables the PM to be wary of quick fixes and seek sound solutions, even in the face of tight deadlines.

Problem solving

Uncertainty and **risk** are an inherent part of project work and problems can arise rapidly and without warning. The PM must be capable of **fast and effective reaction**. Solving significant problems will require the co-ordinated efforts of the whole project team. The PM should encourage team members to solve their own problems if they can, but to maintain good reporting in any case so that solutions to potentially major problems can be sought collectively, in a process led by the PM.

Change control and management

In this context, we are concerned with managing changes **to the project** rather than the wider problems of change management. Changes can arise from a range of sources and have the potential to cause severe disruption of progress. A particular problem is changes to the project's objectives and desired outcomes. Changes must be properly authorised, planned and resourced, and records must be kept of their source, impact and authorisation if the project is not to become unmanageable.

Question 6

Top tips. This question is rather puzzlingly worded. The requirements of either part (a) or part (b), if taken in isolation, are clear enough. However, when they are combined it is difficult to see where one ends and the other begins: part (a) asks, effectively for the benefits and drawbacks of the policy suggested by G, while part (b) asks for a comparison of the views of G and P. The problem would appear to be avoiding in the answer to part (b) repetition of much that was said in the answer to part (a).

We think the best way to resolve this conundrum is to note carefully the last sentence of paragraph three of the scenario and to build an answer to part (b) around a comparison between the positioning and resource-based approaches to strategy. We can then relegate the formal, top-down model to a minor role as just one approach to a positioning-based strategy.

You may care to note the way we have made reference to theorists in our answer: this sort of thing adds authority, but you have to get the names right!

Easy marks. Candidates who have a basic knowledge of the rational model should find part (a) fairly easy to score a pass mark in.

Part (a)

The most comprehensive kind of formal, top down strategic planning is described by the **rational model**, summarised by the diagram below.

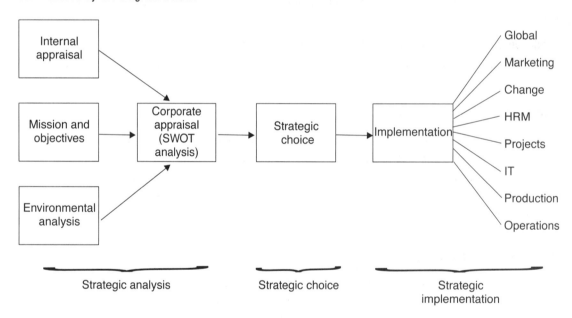

The rational model of strategic management is a logical and comprehensive approach. It attempts to consider all relevant information and options. It is iterative; there is a planning cycle (usually annual) in which the results of one cycle become an input into the next.

Advantages of planning for F Company

F Company seems to be particularly concerned about **developments in its immediate market environment**, having lost market share and to new entrants and failed to respond to customer demand for new products. Proper, continuing **environmental analysis** should be one of the most important features, therefore, of any system of planning introduced by the company. This would be a fundamental aspect of the rational model, as indicated in the diagram.

The rational model could bring other advantages to F Company.

(a) It helps the organisation to take a **long view** and avoid short-termism while at the same time providing a sensible approach to the uncertainty of the future.

(b) It guides the **allocation of resources**.

(c) It **co-ordinates the activities** of the various parts of the organisation, ensuring the integration of operational management decisions into the higher strategy, the wider organisational context and longer term goals. This is another particular concern G has about F Company

(d) It sets a standard by which the actual performance of the organisation is **measured and controlled**.

(e) It comforts providers of finance in particular and encourages **suppliers and employees** to think in terms of a long-term relationship.

(f) The process of forming strategy requires wide and complex input so it can have a beneficial effect on managers' **personal development** and awareness and can assist with management succession planning.

Drawbacks of formal planning methods

The concept of formal processes for strategy generation and their limited success in practice has led to criticisms of both the rational model and the very idea of strategic planning as a separate business activity.

(a) The formal approach encourages a sense of **omniscience and control** among planners: this is dangerous because of the **inherent unpredictability of the business environment**, which F Company has already had experience of. In practice, strategic thinking tends to be iterative and even muddled, with the various processes and stages being undertaken on an *ad hoc* basis. Moreover, many developments of strategic significance, or information about them, occur at **operational** level. Environmental uncertainty also tends to lead managers to adopt an approach of **bounded rationality**, satisfying themselves with solutions that are acceptable rather than ideal.

(b) There is an associated problem of **detachment**: planners' tendency to assume that strategy can be divorced from operations is inappropriate. Planners rarely have to implement the strategies they devise and feedback occurs too late or is badly filtered. Similarly, more junior managers, not directly involved in the planning process may misunderstand or resist the plans they are required to implement.

(c) The idea of the **learning organisation** has been applied to strategy on the basis that an organisation's strengths and weaknesses can be in constant flux and strategy should reflect current developments as a kind of learning process itself.

(d) The formal approach is usually couched in terms of a **planning cycle**: this may extend for up to five years; even a one year cycle is not responsive enough to changing circumstances.

(e) The **expense and complexity** of the formal approach are inappropriate for smaller businesses. Cost control is important for any organization and F Company, as an under-performing medium-sized business, must be particularly wary about spending on functions that do not have an immediate impact on the bottom line

(f) There has been much comment on the place of **strategic objectives**. A sociological perspective, such as that of *Cyert and March*, views the emergence of strategic objectives as the result of a **political** or **bargaining process** involving a variety of priorities and interest groups. Here we may remark that today the capitalist, free market philosophy seems more strongly established than ever and most Western business organisations acknowledge the creation of shareholder value as their primary objective.

(g) There is a view that great strategies should not really be rational at all, but should emerge from **inspiration and entrepreneurial talent**. *Brunsson* argues for the selection of a reasonable course of action from among a small number of choices, while *Ohmae* finds that good strategy is made by practical people who 'have an intuitive grasp of the basic elements of strategy'. The criticisms are directed less at planning in principle, than at the assumption that **planning can create strategies** as opposed to supporting strategic decisions, co-ordinating them and mobilising resources.

Part (b)

The views of G and P represent opposite sides in a current debate about the best way to approach strategy. The rational model is only the most formal of several approaches to a strategic method that is based the process of **adapting the organisation to its environment**. This adaptive or **positioning-based strategy** approach, which pays great attention to markets, consumers and competitors, may be contrasted with the **resource-based approach**.

(a)   In many modern industries, the **rate of environmental change is too great** for effective positioning strategies to be developed. F Company's experience seems to bear this out.The rate of economic and social change brought about by globalisation; shorter product lifecycles; rapid technological innovation; and changing consumer taste all make a measured response out of date before it can take effect.

(b)   **Positioning advantages cannot be sustained in the long term**. Advantageous product market positions are **too easy to copy** to last long and more rapid product lifecycles erode initial advantage. F Company is suffering from the efforts of agile new entrants to its industry.

(c)   It is more difficult to **adapt the organisation** than to **adopt a new environment**. The positioning approach may require significant change within the firm, which is difficult to achieve. It may be easier to move to a market environment that suits existing arrangements, skills, culture and capabilities.

The resource based approach to strategy emphasises the **possession of scarce resources** and **core competences** by the organisation. Strategy, it is suggested, consists of exploiting such resources and core competences in order to gain competitive advantage. This approach lies behind the growing practice of **outsourcing**: the organisation concentrates its efforts on those parts of its operations that no other organisation can perform for it.

Resources may be obvious things such as favoured access to a particular **raw material** or a piece of legally protected **intellectual property**; they may also take less tangible forms, such as a well- known **brand**. F Company may be able to utilize these ideas by emphasizing **quality** or **innovation** in its future operations.

It is important to realise that it is possible to acquire or develop new competences, but this takes time. The possession of a particular advantage thus constitutes a competitive advantage but its validity may decline if other firms develop equivalent capabilities.

Competences must therefore be developed and kept up to date on a continuing basis. *Johnson and Scholes* define core competences as those that both **outperform competitors** and are **difficult to imitate**.

The resource-based approach is not without its difficulties.

(a)   Core competences are **difficult to identify and assess**: a wrong appraisal could lead to the loss of wider competence or source of advantage by misdirected outsourcing.

(b)   Attempts to apply core competences (or other resources) widely across a range of markets and operations may make the firm **vulnerable to more focused, single market operations**.

(c)   The emphasis on unique resources is reminiscent of the 'product orientation' decried by marketing experts: competitors who are more in touch with **market requirements** may be more successful. On the other hand, a strategy based on a sequence of unique products, as in the pharmaceutical industry, can be successful.

(d)   **Investors** may or may not be convinced by the resource based view. Where there is a clear, identifiable and credible strategy, they may well maintain their support. However, a strategy based on exploiting existing markets may be more intuitively acceptable.

(e)   The competence approach seems to support ideas such as cross-functional, activity based management, team working and the use of network structures both within the organization and in its relations with suppliers and customers. However, the need to safeguard core competence capability against erosion by staff turnover and direct sharing of know-how may lead to a **perceived need for close control of activities** and narrow limits on outsourcing.

Question 7

Part (a)

Top tips. This question is more about meetings than it is about project management, because, while project meetings may deal with matters peculiar to a given project, organising, chairing and participating in them is not different from doing the same things in some other kind of meeting.

Easy marks. You either have an idea of how to run meetings, or you don't. If you do, this is easy stuff.

The effectiveness of every hour the individual spends in a meeting has to be considered in terms of **opportunity cost**. A problem with meetings is that they can so easily grow. Meetings seem to have an inbuilt dynamic which spurs their expansion. T needs to ensure that he gets value for money. The first question about any proposed meeting should be whether or not it should be held at all. If the meeting will purely be a forum for disseminating information, a memo may be a more efficient means of communication.

Meetings should be planned

T should decide the **objectives of the meeting**. Unclear objectives will lead to irrelevancies being discussed. It is also necessary to decide who should attend the meeting. Only those people with a genuine need to be at a meeting should be invited. Project problem-solving meetings should have guidance on their decision-making authority.

When involving a number of people, particularly when they do not work at the same location, **coordinating diaries** to establish a convenient time can be an extremely challenging operation. T must remember to allow plenty of time: this increases the chance of people being free. If one or two people are unable to attend, T should ask if they can send deputies.

T should send a **formal notification** of the meeting with either an **agenda** or a request for any further items for the agenda should be supplied. It is worth reminding people about a meeting a few days beforehand, if the meeting was arranged a long time in advance. Paperwork sent out before the meeting should include the agenda, location maps if it is being held away from the normal place of work and any relevant background papers.

The agenda

T will find that a **detailed agenda** can contribute heavily to the success of a meeting. It gives attendees time to prepare themselves properly.

(a) The agenda should be in a logical order.

(b) The agenda should give details about the purpose of each item.

(c) The agenda should show the start and finish times of the meeting, and also roughly how much time will be allocated to each item.

(d) Any other business should be used (if at all) for minor matters. Anything significant should be on the main agenda.

Conduct of the meeting

T should try to motivate people to arrive on time to his meetings and be thoroughly prepared. IT should be aware of the responsibilities involved in chairing meetings and should have appropriate communication and leadership skills.

(a) All items on the agenda should be thoroughly considered.

(b) Future action should be agreed and minuted. Action points from previous meetings should be followed up.

(c)   Everyone should have an opportunity to contribute to the discussion and decision-making. Hostility between delegates must be minimized by the use of negotiation; physical separation during the meeting may be required.

(d)   Time must not be wasted by sidetracking or leaving the agenda.

(e)   Everyone must understand agreed action.

(f)   Future meetings should be arranged as necessary.

(g)   The chair should summarise the discussion at suitable intervals during the meeting.

(h)   If agreement cannot be reached on any point, the chair should attempt to lead a negotiation. If this does not work, an action point is required, so that further work can be done and a compromise sought.

Poor chairing can have several adverse consequences. It can mean that too much time is spent on unimportant matters and not enough on significant matters. It can also mean that the meeting is hijacked by a few participants, whilst others do not have the chance to contribute properly. These problems may have contributed to T's dissatisfaction with the earlier project meetings he attended.

Minutes

All meetings should be minuted. After the meeting the person responsible for taking minutes needs to check with the chair that minutes and action points are a fair reflection of events. Action points should specify the action to be taken, by whom the action should be taken, and by when. There should be follow up and progress check on those with responsibilities before the next meeting.

Part (b)

> **Top tips**. The Examiner uses the word 'contribution'. It is clear that she is not using it to mean revenue minus variable costs, but she does not tell us to what purpose she envisages this contribution being made. We must assume she means something like the contribution proper project closure makes to the organisation generally, rather than to the process of project management itself, which would be a rather smaller target.
>
> **Easy marks**. The final D of *Maylor's* 4D model answers this question succinctly and accurately.

T is quite right to be concerned about failure to finish off a project properly. Because project management is episodic in nature, it is **difficult to improve**. The lack of continuous operation means that the skills and experience developed during a project are likely to fragment and atrophy after it is complete. This is especially true of organisations that do not have many projects or manage them on an *ad hoc* basis. Managers move around, projects are sponsored in different departments from time to time and the pressure of normal work inhibits organisational learning. Even in project-based organisations, there can be a reluctance to devote resources to improving the corporate body of project management knowledge. The completion and review phase involves a number of important but often neglected activities that T should ensure are carried out at the conclusion of his new project.

(a)   **Completion** itself is often neglected. All project deliverables must be, in fact, delivered and all activities properly and promptly finished; care must be taken that contractors do not either leave small things undone or, if paid by time, spin things out for as long as possible.

(b)   **Documentation** must be completed. This is important on any project but it is vital if there are quality certification issues or it is necessary to provide the user with operating documentation. Indeed, these two types of documentation should be specified as deliverables at the outset. Contracts, letters, accounting records and so on must be filed properly.

(c)   **Project systems** must be closed down, but in a proper fashion. In particular, the project accounts and any special accounting systems must remain in operation and under control until all costs have been posted but must then be closed down to avoid improper posting.

(d)   **Handover** must take place where the project has been managed for a client under contract. At some point the client must formally accept that the contract is complete and take responsibility for any future action that may be required, such as the operation and maintenance of a system.

(e)   **Immediate review** is required to provide staff with immediate feedback on performance and to identify short-term needs such as staff training or remedial action for procedure failures.

The review process

A thorough review is the organisation's opportunity to make significant **improvements in how it manages its projects**. T should ensure that his review clear **terms of reference** and covers all aspects of the project, possibly organised on a functional basis. This cannot be done on the cheap: appropriate quantities of management time and attention must be allocated to the review process and to the assimilation of its results and recommendations.

Longer-term review
Longer-term review is useful for the consideration of **lifetime costs**; which should be the eventual criterion for project success. It also allows individuals time to reflect on their experiences and to learn more thoroughly from them.

Review Form & Free Prize Draw - Paper P5 Integrated management (1/06)

All original review forms from the entire BPP range, completed with genuine comments, will be entered into one of two draws on 31 July 2006 and 31 January 2007. The names on the first four forms picked out on each occasion will be sent a cheque for £50.

Name: _____   Address: _____
_____
_____

How have you used this Kit?
(Tick one box only)

☐ Home study (book only)
☐ On a course: college _____
☐ With 'correspondence' package
☐ Other _____

Why did you decide to purchase this Kit?
(Tick one box only)

☐ Have used the complementary Study text
☐ Have used other BPP products in the past
☐ Recommendation by friend/colleague
☐ Recommendation by a lecturer at college
☐ Saw advertising
☐ Other _____

During the past six months do you recall seeing/receiving any of the following?
(Tick as many boxes as are relevant)

☐ Our advertisement in *Financial Management*
☐ Our advertisement in *Pass*
☐ Our advertisement in *PQ*
☐ Our brochure with a letter through the post
☐ Our website www.bpp.com

Which (if any) aspects of our advertising do you find useful?
(Tick as many boxes as are relevant)

☐ Prices and publication dates of new editions
☐ Information on product content
☐ Facility to order books off-the-page
☐ None of the above

Which BPP products have you used?

Text	☐	Success CD	☐	Learn Online	☐
Kit	☑	i-Learn	☐	Home Study Package	☐
Passcard	☐	i-Pass	☐	Home Study PLUS	☐

Your ratings, comments and suggestions would be appreciated on the following areas.

	Very useful	Useful	Not useful
Effective revision and revision plan	☐	☐	☐
Exam guidance	☐	☐	☐
Questions	☐	☐	☐
Top Tips etc in answers	☐	☐	☐
Content and structure of answers	☐	☐	☐
'Plan of attack' in mock exams	☐	☐	☐
Mock exam answers	☐	☐	☐
	☐	☐	☐

Overall opinion of this Kit   Excellent ☐   Good ☐   Adequate ☐   Poor ☐

Do you intend to continue using BPP products?   Yes ☐   No ☐

The BPP author of this edition can be e-mailed at: marymaclean@bpp.com

Please return this form to: Nick Weller, CIMA Publishing Manager, BPP Professional Education, FREEPOST, London, W12 8BR

Review Form & Free Prize Draw (continued)

TELL US WHAT YOU THINK

BPP has provided enhanced guidance accompanying certain questions and answers. Please can you let us have your comments/ suggestions on the help we have given.

Please note any further comments and suggestions/errors below.

Free Prize Draw Rules

1   Closing date for 31 July 2006 draw is 30 June 2006. Closing date for 31 January 2007 draw is 31 December 2006.

2   Restricted to entries with UK and Eire addresses only. BPP employees, their families and business associates are excluded.

3   No purchase necessary. Entry forms are available upon request from BPP Professional Education. No more than one entry per title, per person. Draw restricted to persons aged 16 and over.

4   Winners will be notified by post and receive their cheques not later than 6 weeks after the relevant draw date.

5   The decision of the promoter in all matters is final and binding. No correspondence will be entered into.